CW00373710

A Parliamentary Miscellany

A Parliamentary Miscellany: Papers on the History of the House of Lords, Published 1964–1991

By

J.C. Sainty

Wiley Blackwell

for

The Parliamentary History Yearbook Trust

This edition first published 2015

© 2015 Parliamentary History Yearbook Trust

Registered Office

John Wiley & Sons Ltd, The Atrium, Southern Gate, Chichester, West Sussex, PO19 8SQ, UK

Editorial Offices

350 Main Street, Malden, MA 02148-5020, USA

9600 Garsington Road, Oxford, OX4 2DQ, UK

The Atrium, Southern Gate, Chichester, West Sussex, PO19 8SQ, UK

For details of our global editorial offices, for customer services, and for information about how to apply for permission to reuse the copyright material in this book please see our website at www.wiley.com/wiley-blackwell.

The right of J.C. Sainty to be identified as the author of this work has been asserted in accordance with the UK Copyright, Designs and Patents Act 1988.

Library of Congress Cataloging-in-Publication Data

Sainty, John Christopher, author.

[Essays. Selections]

A parliamentary miscellany : papers on the history of the House of Lords, published 1964-1991 / by J.C. Sainty.

pages cm

Originally published as individual papers by the House of Lords Records Office between the years 1964 and 1991.

Includes bibliographical references.

ISBN 978-1-119-13035-2 (alk. paper)

1. Great Britain. Parliament. House of Lords–History.   I. Parliamentary History Yearbook Trust, issuing body.   II. Title.

JN621.S253 2015

328.41′071–dc23

2015017671

A catalogue record for this book is available from the British Library.

Set in size 10/12pt Bembo

Printed in Singapore

1   2015

CONTENTS

ABBREVIATIONS

Al. Cantab.	*Alumni Cantabrigienses to 1751*, comp. J. and J.A. Venn (4 vols, Cambridge, 1922–7)
Al. Oxon 1500–1714	*Alumni Oxonienses 1500–1714*, comp. J. Foster (4 vols, Oxford, 1891)
Al. Oxon 1715–1886	*Alumni Oxonienses 1715–1886*, comp. J. Foster (4 vols, Oxford, 1886)
BL	British Library, London
Bond, 'Clerks of Parliaments'	M.F. Bond, 'Clerks of the Parliaments, 1509–1953', *EHR*, lxiii (1958), 78–85
CCR	*Court and City Register*
CJ	*Commons Journals*
cr.	created
CSPD	*Calendar of State Papers Domestic*
CTB	*Calendar of Treasury Books* (32 vols, 1904–69)
CTBP	*Calendar of Treasury Books and Papers* (5 vols, 1897–1903)
CTG	*Collectanea Topographica et Genealogica* (8 vols, 1834–43)
D.	duke
D'Ewes	*A Complete Journal of the Votes, Speeches and Debates, both of the House of Lords and House of Commons throughout the whole Reign of Queen Elizabeth*, collected by Sir Simonds D'Ewes (2nd edn, 1963)
diss.	dissolution (of parliament)
DNB	*Dictionary of National Biography*, ed. L. Stephen and S. Lee (66 vols, 1885–1901)
E.	earl
(E)	peerage of England
EHR	*English Historical Review*
(GB)	peerage of Great Britain
GM	*Gentleman's Magazine*
History of Surrey	O. Manning and W. Bray, *The History and Antiquities of the County of Surrey* (3 vols, 1804–14)
HMC	Historical Manuscripts Commission
I	Irish peerage
L.	lord
LJ	*Lords Journals*
M.	marquess
Memorials of St Margaret's	*Memorials of St Margaret's Church, Westminster*, ed. A.M. Burke (1914)
MGH	*Miscellanea Genealogica et Heraldica*, 4th ser. (5 vols, 1906–14)
MI	monumental inscription

Old Westminsters	*Record of Old Westminsters*, comp. G.F.R. Barker and A.H. Stenning (3 vols, 1928)
PA	Parliamentary Archives
RAMT	*Register of Admissions to the Middle Temple*, comp. H.A.C. Sturgess (3 vols, 1949)
rest.	restored (to the peerage)
RK	*Royal Kalendar*
RO	Record Office
S	Scottish peerage
Soc.	Society
SR	a Scottish representative peer
succ.	succeeded
summ.	summoned
TNA	The National Archives, Kew
(UK)	United Kingdom peerage
V.	viscount
VCH	Victoria County History
WAR	*Westminster Abbey Registers* (Harleian Soc., x, 1875)

FOREWORD

Sir John Sainty, sometime clerk of the parliaments, is also a historian of the house of lords, concentrating on procedural development and the identification of the staff of the upper House.[1] These publications are exceedingly useful for the more general researcher, providing information which is difficult and time consuming to extract both from the parliamentary and the state records at the Public Record Office (now The National Archives). Thus John was providing a body of work which in many cases formed the foundations upon which other historians built their work, saving them much detailed research. A good deal of this work was published in the obscure memoranda of what was then the House of Lords Record Office (now The Parliamentary Archives). These memoranda were available to consult in the Record Office and in some academic libraries, and occasional researchers in the archives of parliament acquired their own treasured copies from the staff. Many historians, particularly those not specialising in parliamentary history, may not know about these publications which could provide them with useful information, for example providing the identification and details of the life and career of a person named in a source who may have proved elusive in more well-known reference works. Even a visit to the Parliamentary Archives will not necessarily provide the answer, or to one's university library as in the latter case these publications may be difficult to locate, sometimes having proved too tempting to acquisitive fingers. Publication of these memoranda stopped in the 1990s and the stock of copies at the Parliamentary Archives has long since been dispersed to grateful historians. Thus, to mark the 80th birthday of John Sainty, on the last day of 2014, and John's status as godfather to *Parliamentary History*,[2] the grateful trustees and staff of the journal have decided to republish the texts of all John's memoranda (together with three other House of Lords Record Office publications) as one of the journal's Texts & Studies series.

Clyve Jones
Editor, *Parliamentary History* Texts & Studies series

---

[1] See the bibliography of his publications in his *festschrift*, *Institutional Practices and Memory: Parliamentary People, Records and Histories. Essays in Honour of Sir John Sainty*, ed. Clyve Jones (Oxford, 2013), 2–7. This publication is also part 1 of volume xxxii of the journal *Parliamentary History*.

[2] See *Institutional Practices and Memory*, 1, where further words of admiration may be found.

Chapter 1. Leaders and Whips in the House of Lords 1783–1960

1. *Leaders in the House of Lords*

The Position of Leader of the House of Lords

The emergence of Leaders in the two Houses of Parliament is closely associated with the development of Cabinet government. The essential fact about such Leaders is that their responsibilities should not be confined to the particular departments of which they happen to be heads, but that they should be entrusted with the presentation and defence of the government's policy as a whole. A precise definition of the powers and duties of a Parliamentary Leader over the last 200 years is impossible to give, since it has inevitably varied with the changing character of Cabinet government.

The Prime Minister has always been the Leader of the House in which he sits. It has for the last quarter of a century been the invariable practice for a separate Leader to be appointed in the House of Commons charged with the detailed conduct of government business. This fact, however, in no way alters the Prime Minister's ultimate responsibility in the matter. In the later 18th century there was a consistent pattern in the distribution of offices between the two Houses. If the Prime Minister was in the House of Commons he also held the position of Chancellor of the Exchequer and both Secretaries of State were in the House of Lords. If he was in the Lords, the post of Chancellor of the Exchequer was held by a member of the Commons. One Secretary of State was in the Commons; the other in the Lords.

In the later eighteenth century, if the Prime Minister was in the Commons, it was part of the duties of one of the Secretaries of State to be responsible for the conduct of government business in the Lords. There appears to have been a tradition that this task should be undertaken by the Home Secretary but it was not always adhered to, and Lord Grenville led the Lords from 1791 to 1801 as Foreign Secretary. During the nineteenth century, however, the position of Leader of the House of Lords ceased to be associated with the Secretaryships of State. Increasingly it was coupled with the honorific offices of Lord President or Lord Privy Seal. He is always a member of the Cabinet.

The Prime Minister, if a Peer, is always Leader of the House of Lords. The only exception to this rule was the occasion when Lord Hawkesbury led the Lords in the brief ministry of which the Duke of Portland was the nominal head (1807–9). If the Prime Minister is in the Commons he has the right of appointment of the Leader of the Lords. Since the rise of the party system, however, it has been the practice for the Prime Minister to appoint the Leader of his Party in the Lords to the position. If a Prime Minister is raised to the Peerage during his tenure of office he automatically becomes Leader of the Lords (as in the case of Lord Beaconsfield in 1876). If a Peer other than the existing Leader of the Lords becomes Prime Minister, he automatically displaces the existing Leader. Thus in 1865 Lord Russell, on succeeding Lord Palmerston, displaced Lord Granville as Leader, and in 1894 Lord Rosebery, on succeeding Mr Gladstone, displaced Lord Kimberley, the then Leader.

Since the leadership of the House of Lords is not in itself an office, no formal appointment is made in connection with it. Although the position was clearly understood as early as the second administration of the younger Pitt, it is only since 1940 that the designation of the Leader has been regularly included in the list of ministerial appointments issued by the Prime Minister's Office. A note has been made below of the relevant issues of *The Times* for changes contained in these announcements. Authorities have been given for changes in the leadership down to 1807. After this date details may be found in the *Dictionary of National Biography* or in the standard biographies of the peers in question. The accompanying list of Party Leaders in the Lords should also be consulted in this connection.

Leaders of the House

TEMPLE, 3rd Earl   1783 Dec.
     As Secretary of State for Home and Foreign Affairs in Administration of Mr Pitt. Resigned before taking up duties (Aspinall, *Later Correspondence of George III*, 1, 6, note 2).

SYDNEY, 1st Lord   1783 Dec.–1789 June
     As Secretary of State for Home Affairs in Administration of Mr Pitt, (Olson, *Radical Duke*, 217).

LEEDS, 5th Duke of   1789 June–1790 Nov.
     As Secretary of State for Foreign Affairs in Administration of Mr Pitt (Olson, *Radical Duke*, 214–19).

GRENVILLE, 1st Lord   1790 Nov.–1801 Feb.
     As Secretary of State for Home Affairs (1790 Nov.–1791 June) and Secretary of State for Foreign Affairs (1791 June–1801 Feb.) in Administration of Mr Pitt (Olson, *Radical Duke*, 214–19 for appointment). He was still acting as Government spokesman in the Debate on the Address, 22 Jan. 1801 (*Parl. Debs*, Vol. xxxv, cols 866–7).

PELHAM, Lord   1801 July–1803 Aug.
     As Secretary of State for Home Affairs in Administration of Mr Addington. His position as Leader is not clear. He acted as Government spokesman in the Debate on the Address 16 Nov. 1802 (*Parl. Debs*, Vol. xxxvi, cols 935–6). It is not certain who acted as Leader between Feb. and July 1801. Portland and Hobart were both Secretaries of State in the House of Lords at this time.

HAWKESBURY, Lord   1803 Nov.–1806 Feb.
     As Secretary of State for Foreign Affairs (1803 Nov.–1804 May) and Secretary of State for Home Affairs (1804 May–1806 Feb.) in Administrations of Mr

Addington and Mr Pitt. For his position as Leader see Yonge, *Life of Liverpool*, i, 145, 184, 189, 193, 228–9; Petrie, *Lord Liverpool*, 83, 96, 112, 117, 123, 128, 143.

GRENVILLE, 1st Lord   1806 Feb.–1807 Mar.
    As First Lord of Treasury (Prime Minister).

HAWKESBURY, Lord (succ. as 2nd Earl of LIVERPOOL
    17 Dec. 1808)   1807 Mar.–1827 Apr.
    As Secretary of State for Home Affairs (1807 Mar.–1809 Oct.) and Secretary for War and Colonies (1809 Oct.–1812 June) in Administrations of the Duke of Portland and Mr Perceval; and First Lord of Treasury (Prime Minister) (1812 June–1827 Apr.).

GODERICH, lst Viscount   1827 Apr.–1828 Jan.
    As Secretary for War and Colonies (1827 Apr.–1827 Sep.) in Administration of Mr Canning; and First Lord of Treasury (Prime Minister) (1827 Sep.–1828 Jan.).

WELLINGTON, 1st Duke of   1828 Jan.–1830 Nov.
    As First Lord of Treasury (Prime Minister).

GREY, 2nd Earl   1830 Nov.–1834 July
    As First Lord of Treasury (Prime Minister).

MELBOURNE, 2nd Viscount (I)
    (MELBOURNE, 2nd Lord (UK))   1834 July–1834 Nov.
    As First Lord of Treasury (Prime Minister).

WELLINGTON, 1st Duke of (Conservative)   1834 Nov.–1835 Apr.
    As First Lord of Treasury (Prime Minister) (1834 Nov.–Dec.) and Secretary of State for Foreign Affairs (1834 Dec.–1835 Apr.) in Administration of Sir Robert Peel.

MELBOURNE, 2nd Viscount (I)
    (MELBOURNE, 2nd Lord (UK)) (Liberal)   1835 Apr.–1841 Sept.
    As First Lord of Treasury (Prime Minister).

WELLINGTON, 1st Duke of (Conservative)   1841 Sept.–1846 July
    As Minister without office in Administration of Sir Robert Peel.

LANSDOWNE, 3rd Marquess of (Liberal)   1846 July–1852 Feb.
    As Lord President of Council in Administration of Lord John Russell.

DERBY, 14th Earl of (Conservative)   1852 Feb.–1852 Dec.
    As First Lord of Treasury (Prime Minister).

ABERDEEN, 4th Earl of (S)
    (GORDON, 1st Viscount (UK)) (Peelite)   1852 Dec.–1855 Feb.
    As First Lord of Treasury (Prime Minister).

GRANVILLE, 2nd Earl (Liberal)   1855 Feb.–1858 Feb.
    As Lord President of Council in Administration of Viscount Palmerston.

DERBY, 14th Earl of (Conservative)   1858 Feb.–1859 June
    As First Lord of Treasury (Prime Minister).

GRANVILLE, 2nd Earl (Liberal)   1859 June–1865 Nov.
  As Lord President of Council in Administration of Viscount Palmerston.

RUSSELL, 1st Earl (Liberal)   1865 Nov.–1866 June
  As First Lord of Treasury (Prime Minister).

DERBY, 14th Earl of (Conservative)   1866 July–1868 Feb.
  As First Lord of Treasury (Prime Minister).

MALMESBURY, 3rd Earl of (Conservative)   1868 Feb.–1868 Dec.
  As Lord Privy Seal in Administration of Mr Disraeli.

GRANVILLE, 2nd Earl (Liberal)   1868 Dec.–1874 Feb.
  As Secretary of State for Colonies (1868 Dec.–1870 July) and Secretary of State
for Foreign Affairs (1870 July–1874 Feb.) in Administration of Mr Gladstone.

RICHMOND, 6th Duke of (Conservative)   1874 Feb.–1876 Aug.
  As Lord President of Council in Administration of Mr Disraeli.

BEACONSFIELD, 1st Earl of (Conservative)   1876 Aug.–1880 Apr.
  As First Lord of Treasury (Prime Minister).

GRANVILLE, 2nd Earl (Liberal)   1880 Apr.–1885 June
  As Secretary of State for Foreign Affairs in Administration of Mr Gladstone.

SALISBURY, 3rd Marquess of (Conservative)   1885 June–1886 Feb.
  As Secretary of State for Foreign Affairs (Prime Minister).

GRANVILLE, 2nd Earl (Liberal)   1886 Feb.–1886 Aug.
  As Secretary of State for Colonies in Administration of Mr Gladstone.

SALISBURY, 3rd Marquess of (Conservative)   1886 Aug.–1892 Aug.
  As First Lord of Treasury (1886 Aug.–1887 Mar.) and Secretary of State for
Foreign Affairs (1887 Mar.–1892 Aug.) (Prime Minister).

KIMBERLEY, 1st Earl of (Liberal)   1892 Aug.–1894 Mar.
  As Lord President of Council in Administration of Mr Gladstone.

ROSEBERY, 5th Earl of (S)
  (ROSEBERY, 2nd Lord (UK))   1894 Mar.–1895 June
  As Lord President of Council and First Lord of Treasury (Prime Minister).

SALISBURY, 3rd Marquess of (Conservative)   1895 June–1902 July
  As Secretary of State for Foreign Affairs (1895 June–1900 Nov.) and Lord Privy
Seal (1900 Nov.–1902 July) (Prime Minister).

DEVONSHIRE, 8th Duke of (Liberal Unionist)   1902 July–1903 Oct.
  As Lord President of Council in Administration of Mr Balfour.

LANSDOWNE, 5th Marquess of (Conservative)   1903 Oct.–1905 Dec.
  As Secretary of State for Foreign Affairs in Administration of Mr Balfour.

RIPON, 1st Marquess of (Liberal)   1905 Dec.–1908 Apr.
  As Lord Privy Seal in Administration of Sir Henry Campbell-Bannerman.

CREWE, 1st Earl of (cr. Marquess of CREWE 1911)
  3 July (Liberal)   1908 Apr.–1916 Dec.
  As Secretary of State for Colonies (1908 Apr.–1910 Nov.), Lord Privy Seal
(1908 Oct.–1911 Oct.; 1912 Feb.–1915 May), Secretary of State for India (1910
Nov.–1911 Mar.; 1911 May–1915 May) and Lord President of Council (1915
May–1916 Dec.) in Administrations (Liberal and Coalition) of Mr Asquith.

CURZON OF KEDLESTON, 1st Earl (cr. Marquess CURZON
  OF KEDLESTON 1921 28 June) (Conservative)   1916 Dec.–1924 Jan.
  As Lord President of Council (1916 Dec.–1919 Oct.) and Secretary of State for
Foreign Affairs (1919 Oct.–1924 Jan.) in Administration (Coalition) of Mr Lloyd
George and in Administrations (Conservative) of Mr Bonar Law and Mr Baldwin.

HALDANE, 1st Viscount (Labour)   1924 Jan.–1924 Nov.
  As Lord Chancellor in Administration of Mr Macdonald.

CURZON OF KEDLESTON, 1st Marquess
  (Conservative)   1924 Nov.–1925 Mar.
  As Lord President of Council in Administration of Mr Baldwin.

SALISBURY, 4th Marquess of (Conservative)   1925 Mar.–1929 June
  As Lord Privy Seal in Administration of Mr Baldwin.

PARMOOR, 1st Lord (Labour)   1929 June–1931 Aug.
  As Lord President of Council in Administration of Mr Macdonald
                                        (Parmoor, *A Retrospect*, 297).

READING, 1st Marquess of (Liberal)   1931 Aug.–1931 Nov.
  As Secretary of State for Foreign Affairs in Administration (National) of Mr
Macdonald.

HAILSHAM, 1st Viscount (Conservative)   1931 Nov.–1935 June
  As Secretary of State for War in Administration (National) of Mr Macdonald.

LONDONDERRY, 7th Marquess of (I)
  (VANE, 3rd Earl (UK))   1935 June–1935 Nov.
  As Lord Privy Seal in Administration (National) of Mr Baldwin.

HALIFAX, 5th Viscount (Conservative)   1935 Nov.–1938 Feb.
  As Lord Privy Seal (1935 Nov.–1937 May) and Lord President of Council (1937
May–1938 Feb.) in Administrations (National) of Mr Baldwin and Mr Chamberlain.

STANHOPE, 7th Earl (Conservative)   1938 Mar.–1940 May
  As President of Board of Education (1938 Mar.–1938 Oct.), First Lord of
Admiralty (1938 Oct.–1939 Sept.) and Lord President of Council (1939 Sept.–1940
May) in Administration (National) of Mr Chamberlain.

CALDECOTE, 1st Viscount (Conservative)   1940 May–1940 Oct.
  As Secretary of State for Dominion Affairs in Administration (Coalition) of Mr
Churchill (*The Times*, 16 May 1940).

HALIFAX, 5th Viscount (Conservative)   1940 Oct.–1940 Dec.
As Secretary of State for Foreign Affairs in Administration (Coalition) of Mr Churchill (*The Times*, 4 Oct. 1940).

LLOYD, 1st Lord (Conservative)   1941 Jan.–1941 Feb.
As Secretary of State for Colonies in Administration (Coalition) of Mr Churchill (*The Times*, 11 Jan. 1941).

MOYNE, 1st Lord (Conservative)   1941 Feb.–1942 Feb.
As Secretary of State for Colonies in Administration (Coalition) of Mr Churchill (*The Times*, 10 Feb. 1941).

CRANBORNE, Viscount (summ. as CECIL, Lord)
(Conservative)   1942 Feb.–1945 July
As Secretary of State for Colonies (1942 Feb.–Nov.), Lord Privy Seal (1942 Nov.–1943 Sept.) and Secretary of State for Dominion Affairs (1943 Sept.–1945 July) in Administrations (Coalition and Conservative) of Mr Churchill (*The Times*, 23 Feb. 1942).

ADDISON, 1st Viscount (Labour)   1945 Aug.–1951 Oct.
As Secretary of State for Dominion (Commonwealth) Affairs (1945 Aug.–1947 Oct.), Lord Privy Seal (1947 Oct.–1951 Mar.) and Lord President of Council (1951 Mar.–Oct.) in Administration of Mr Attlee (*The Times*, 4 Aug. 1945).

SALISBURY, 5th Marquess of (Conservative)   1951 Oct.–1957 Mar.
As Lord Privy Seal (1951 Oct.–1952 May), Secretary of State for Commonwealth Relations (1952 May–Nov.) and Lord President of Council (1952 Nov.–1957 Mar.) in Administrations of Mr Churchill, Sir Anthony Eden and Mr Macmillan (*The Times*, 29 Oct. 1951).

HOME, 14th Earl of (S) (DOUGLAS, 4th Lord (UK))   1957 Mar.–1960 July
As Secretary of State for Commonwealth Relations (1957 Mar.–1960 July) and Lord President of Council (1957 Mar.–Sept.; 1959 Oct.–1960 July) in Administration of Mr Macmillan (*The Times*, 30 Mar. 1957).

HAILSHAM, 2nd Viscount (Conservative)   1960 July–1963 Oct.
As Lord President of Council in Administration of Mr Macmillan (*The Times*, 28 July 1960).

CARRINGTON, 6th Lord (Conservative)   1963 Oct.–
As Minister without Portfolio in Administration of Sir Alec Douglas-Home (*The Times*, 21 Oct. 1963).

Deputy Leaders of the House

Before 1940 it was not the practice for Deputy Leaders of the House of Lords to be appointed. On the formation of the Coalition Government in May 1940 Lord Snell the former Leader of the Labour Party accepted office and was made Deputy Leader. Since 1940 it has been usual for there to be a Deputy Leader, and since the Conservative Party were returned to power in October 1951 this has been the invariable practice. In 1960 the position of Assistant Deputy Leader came into being.

SNELL, 1st Lord (Labour)   1940 May–1944 Apr.
    As Captain of Gentlemen-at-Arms in Administration (Coalition) of Mr Churchill (*The Times*, 1 June 1940).

LISTOWEL, 5th Earl of (HARE, 3rd Lord (UK)) (Labour)   1944 Oct.–1945 May
    As Parliamentary Under Secretary of State for India and Burma in Administration (Coalition) of Mr Churchill.

HALL, 1st Viscount (Labour)   1947–1951 May
    As First Lord of Admiralty in Administration of Mr Attlee.

SWINTON, 1st Viscount (Conservative)   1951 Oct.–1955 Apr.
    As Chancellor of Duchy of Lancaster (1951 Oct.–1952 Nov.) and Secretary of State for Commonwealth Relations (1952 Nov.–1955 Apr.) in Administration of Mr Churchill (*The Times*, 1 Nov. 1951).

WOOLTON, 1st Viscount (Conservative)   1955 Apr.–1955 Dec.
    As Chancellor of Duchy of Lancaster in Administration of Sir Anthony Eden.

HOME, 14th Earl of (S) (DOUGLAS, 4th Lord (UK))
   (Conservative)   1956 Jan.–1957 Mar.
    As Secretary of State for Commonwealth Relations in Administration of Sir Anthony Eden and Mr Macmillan (*The Times*, 20 Jan. 1956, 30 Mar. 1957).

HAILSHAM, 2nd Viscount (Conservative)   1957 Mar.–1960 July
    As Minister of Education (1957 Mar.–1957 Sept.), Lord President (1957 Sept.–1959 Oct.) and Lord Privy Seal and Minister for Science (1959 Oct.–1960 July) in Administration of Mr Macmillan (*The Times*, 30 Mar. 1957, 28 July 1960).

MILLS, 1st Lord (Conservative)   1960 Oct.–1962 July
    As Paymaster General (1960 Oct.–1961 Oct.) and Minister without Portfolio in Administration of Mr Macmillan (*The Times*, 5 Nov. 1960).

DUNDEE, 11th Earl of (S) (GLASSARY, 1st Lord
   (UK)) (Conservative)   1962 July–1963 Oct.
    As Minister of State, Foreign Office, in Administration of Mr Macmillan (*The Times*, 21 July 1962).

BLAKENHAM, 1st Viscount (Conservative)   1963 Oct.–
    As Chancellor of Duchy of Lancaster in Administration of Sir Alec Douglas-Home.

Leaders of the Conservative Party

During the nineteenth century certain practices grew up in connection with the appointment of the Leader of the Conservative Party in the House of Lords. The appointment always lay with the Prime Minister if the party was in power. If a vacancy occurred when the party was in opposition, the Conservative peers elected their Leader even if the Leader of the Commons was, as a result of having been Prime Minister, Leader of the whole party. This was made clear by Disraeli's attitude when a vacancy occurred in the leadership in the Lords on the resignation of Lord Malmesbury in 1869. The practice seems now to be obsolete, however, because on the only occasion since 1881 when a vacancy has occurred while the party was in opposition, the appointment of Lord Hailsham in 1931 as the Leader in the Lords was made by Mr Baldwin, the Leader of the party, apparently without the participation of the Conservative peers.

It has not been considered profitable to pursue this study of Tory (Conservative) Leaders beyond the Duke of Wellington since this would involve an investigation into the difficult subject of the meaning of 'party' before 1830. Between 1800 and 1830 the bulk of the Tory peers would have regarded the Government Leader as their Leader except for the brief Whig intervention 1806–7, when they would have given their allegiance to Lord Hawkesbury.

WELLINGTON, 1st Duke of   1828 Jan.–1846 July
    LEADER OF HOUSE: 1. 1828 Jan.–1830 Nov. as Prime Minister.
                    2. 1834 Nov.–1835 Apr. as Prime Minister and in
                       Administration of Sir Robert Peel.
                    3. 1841 Sept.–1846 July in Administration of Sir
                       Robert Peel.

Although it would be anachronistic to speak of Wellington as Leader of the Conservative Party in the House of Lords in 1828, he could clearly be regarded as such long before his retirement in 1846. He remained in Peel's Cabinet until its fall in July 1846 although in disagreement with its policies. As early as 19 Feb. 1846 he had indicated to Stanley that he wished him to take over the leadership (Malmesbury, *Memoirs of an Ex-Minister*, i, 166).

STANLEY, Lord (succ. as 14th Earl of DERBY
  30 June 1851)   1846 Mar.–1868 Feb.
    LEADER OF HOUSE: 1. 1852 Feb.–1852 Dec. as Prime Minister.
                    2. 1858 Feb.–1859 June as Prime Minister.
                    3. 1866 July–1868 Feb. as Prime Minister.

Chosen Leader of Protectionist Party 9 Mar. 1846 (Malmesbury, *Memoirs of an Ex-Minister*, i, 169). Gradually acquired the position of Leader of the Conservative Party in the House after resignation of Wellington. Resigned Feb. 1868.

MALMESBURY, 3rd Earl of   1868 Feb.–1869 Feb.
    LEADER OF HOUSE: 1868 Feb.–1868 Dec. in Administration of Mr Disraeli.

Appointed Leader 25 Feb. 1868 by Disraeli (Buckle, *Disraeli*, iv, 596–7; Malmesbury, *Memoirs of an Ex-Minister*, ii, 378). Resigned 15 Feb. 1869; Malmesbury, *Memoirs of an Ex-Minister*, ii, 390.

CAIRNS, 1st Lord   1869 Feb.–1870 Feb.
    Elected Leader 15 Feb. 1869 (Malmesbury, *Memoirs of an Ex-Minister*, ii, 390).
Resigned 19 Feb. 1870 (*The Times*, 21 Feb. 1870).

DERBY, 15th Earl of
    Elected Leader 19 Feb. 1870 (*The Times*, 21 Feb. 1870). Declined to serve
(Letter to Lord Colville, *The Times*, 22 Feb. 1870).

RICHMOND, 6th Duke of   1870 Feb.–1876 Aug.
    LEADER OF HOUSE: 1874 Feb.–1876 Aug. in Administration of Mr Disraeli.

Elected Leader 26 Feb. 1870 (*The Times*, 28 Feb. 1870). Left position on Disraeli's elevation to Peerage in Aug. 1876.

BEACONSFIELD, 1st Earl of   1876 Aug.–1881 Apr.
    LEADER OF HOUSE: 1876 Aug.–1880 Apr. as Prime Minister.

Became Leader Aug. 1876 on elevation, as Prime Minister, to the Peerage. Died 19 Apr. 1881.

SALISBURY, 3rd Marquess of   1881 May–1902 July
    LEADER OF HOUSE: 1. 1885 June–1886 Jan. as Prime Minister.
                         2. 1886 Aug.–1892 Aug. as Prime Minister.
                         3. 1895 June–1902 July as Prime Minister.

Elected Leader 9 May 1881 (*The Times*, 10 May 1881). Resigned July 1902.

DEVONSHIRE, 8th Duke of (Unionist)   1902 July–1903 Oct.
    LEADER OF HOUSE: 1902 July–1903 Oct. in Administration of Mr Balfour.

Appointed Leader July 1902 by Balfour. He was a Liberal Unionist. Resigned Oct. 1903.

LANSDOWNE, 5th Marquess of   1903 Oct.–1916 Dec.
    LEADER OF HOUSE: 1903 Oct.–1905 Dec. in Administration of Mr Balfour.

Appointed Leader Oct. 1903 by Balfour. Minister without Portfolio 1915 May–1916 Dec. in Administration (Coalition) of Asquith. Resigned Dec. 1916.

CURZON OF KEDLESTON, 1st Earl
  (cr. Marquess 28 June 1921)   1916 Dec.–1925 Mar.
    LEADER OF HOUSE: 1. 1916 Dec.–1924 Jan. in Administration (Coalition)
                           of Mr Lloyd George and Administrations
                           (Conservative) of Mr Bonar Law and Mr Baldwin.
                    2. 1924 Nov.–1925 Mar. in Administration of Mr
                       Baldwin.

Appointed Leader of House Dec. 1916 by Lloyd George (*The Times*, 11 Dec. 1916). Died 20 Mar. 1925.

SALISBURY, 4th Marquess of   1925 Mar.–1931 June
    LEADER OF HOUSE: 1925 Mar.–1929 June in Administration of Mr Baldwin.

Appointed Mar. 1925 by Baldwin (*The Times*, 23 Mar. 1925). Resigned June 1931 (*The Times*, 17 June 1931).

HAILSHAM, 1st Viscount   1931 June–1935 June
    LEADER OF HOUSE: 1931 Oct.–1935 June in Administration (National) of Mr Macdonald.

Took over the post of Leader June 1931 'at the request of Mr Baldwin' (*The Times*, 17 June 1931). Left position June 1935.

LONDONDERRY, 7th Marquess of (I)
    (VANE, 5th Earl (UK))   1935 June–1935 Nov.
      LEADER OF HOUSE: 1935 June–1935 Nov. in Administration (National) of Mr Baldwin.

Appointed June 1935 by Baldwin (*The Times*, 8 June 1935). Resigned Nov. 1935.

HALIFAX, 5th Viscount   1935 Nov.–1938 Feb.
      LEADER OF HOUSE: 1. 1935 Nov.–1938 Feb. in Administrations (National) of Mr Baldwin and Mr Chamberlain.

Appointed Nov. 1935 by Baldwin (*The Times*, 23 Nov. 1935). Left position Feb. 1938.

STANHOPE, 7th Earl   1938 Mar.–1940 May
      LEADER OF HOUSE: 1938 Mar.–1940 May in Administration (National) of Mr Chamberlain.

Appointed Mar. 1938 by Chamberlain. Resigned May 1940.

CALDECOTE, 1st Viscount   1940 May–1940 Oct.
      LEADER OF HOUSE: 1940 May–1940 Oct. in Administration (Coalition) of Mr Churchill.

Appointed May 1940 by Churchill (*The Times*, 16 May 1940). Left position Oct. 1940.

HALIFAX, 5th Viscount   1940 Oct.–1940 Dec.
      LEADER OF HOUSE: 2. 1940 Oct.–1940 Dec. in Administration (Coalition) of Mr Churchill.

Appointed Oct. 1940 by Churchill (*The Times*, 4 Oct. 1940). Left position Dec. 1940.

LLOYD, 1st Lord   1941 Jan.–1941 Feb.
      LEADER OF HOUSE: 1941 Jan.–1941 Feb. in Administration (Coalition) of Mr Churchill.

Appointed Jan. 1941 by Churchill (*The Times*, 11 Jan. 1941). Died 4 Feb. 1941.

MOYNE, 1st Lord   1941 Feb.–1942 Feb.
      LEADER OF HOUSE: 1941 Feb.–1942 Feb. in Administration (Coalition) of Mr Churchill.

Appointed Feb. 1941 by Churchill (*The Times*, 10 Feb. 1941). Left position Feb. 1942.

CRANBORNE, Viscount (summoned as CECIL, Lord;
  succ. as 5th Marquess of SALISBURY 4 Apr. 1947)   1942 Feb.–1957 Mar.
    LEADER OF HOUSE: 1. 1942 Feb.–1945 July in Administrations (Coalition
                          and National) of Mr Churchill.
                      2. 1951 Oct.–1957 Mar. in Administrations of Mr
                        Churchill, Sir Anthony Eden and Mr Macmillan.

Appointed Feb. 1942 by Churchill (*The Times*, 23 Feb. 1942). Resigned Mar. 1957 (*The Times*, 30 Mar. 1957).

HOME, 14th Earl of (S) (DOUGLAS, 4th Lord (UK))   1957 Mar.–1960 July
    LEADER OF HOUSE: 1957 Mar.–1960 July in Administration of Mr Macmillan.

Appointed Mar. 1957 by Macmillan (*The Times*, 30 Mar. 1957). Left position July 1960 (*The Times*, 28 July 1960).

HAILSHAM, 2nd Viscount   1960 July–1963 Oct.
    LEADER OF HOUSE: 1960 July–1963 Oct. in Administration of Mr Macmillan.

Appointed July 1960 by Macmillan (*The Times*, 28 July 1960). Left position Oct. 1963 (*The Times*, 23 Oct. 1963).

CARRINGTON, 6th Lord   1963 Oct.–
    LEADER OF HOUSE: 1963 Oct. in Administration of Sir Alec Douglas-Home.

Appointed Oct. 1963 by Home (*The Times*, 23 Oct. 1963).

Deputy Leaders of the Conservative Party

Before 1951 it was not the practice for a Deputy Leader of the Conservative Party in the House of Lords to be appointed. Since then it has been invariable. They are not listed separately as to date they have been identical with those occupying the position of Deputy Leader of the House, an account of which has already been given.

Leaders of the Whig (Liberal) Party

Although it would be misleading to convey the impression that there was in any precise sense a Leader of the Whig Party in the House of Lords before 1830, information about the position may be obtained from the attitudes of certain peers after 1801. From this date Lords Grenville, Grey and Lansdowne considered themselves at various times the Leaders of the Whig Party and were so considered by the Government Leaders when they were in opposition. The debates on the King's Speech provide useful indications in this connection. Unfortunately, parliamentary reporting at this period is of varying accuracy and fullness. However it may be worth recording those occasions when the report of the debate makes the position quite clear. Lord Grenville spoke as Leader in 1805, 1806 (in office), 1807, 1808, 1809, 1810 (twice), 1812, 1813, 1814; Lord Lansdowne in 1816, 1818, 1819; 1822, 1823, 1824, 1826, 1829, 1830; and Lord Grey in 1817 and 1821. After 1830 with the rapid development of the party system the position becomes much clearer.

    Since 1830 the same practice appears to have governed the selection of Liberal Leaders in the Lords as obtained amongst the Conservative peers. The Liberals have, however, adhered consistently to the elective principle when in opposition.

GREY, 2nd Earl   1830 Nov.–1834 July
   LEADER OF HOUSE: 1830 Nov.–1834 July as Prime Minister.

Became Leader on his appointment as Prime Minister. Resigned July 1834.

MELBOURNE, 2nd Viscount (I) (MELBOURNE,
   2nd Lord (UK))   1834 July–1842 Oct.
   LEADER OF HOUSE: 1. 1834 July–1834 Nov. as Prime Minister.
                    2. 1835 Apr.–1841 Sept. as Prime Minister.

Became Leader July 1834 on appointment as Prime Minister. Left Leadership to
Lansdowne Oct. 1842 (*DNB*, xxxi, 437).

LANSDOWNE, 3rd Marquess of   1842 Oct.–1855 Feb.
   LEADER OF HOUSE: 1846 July–1852 Feb. in Administration of Lord John
Russell.

Took over leadership Oct. 1842 on resignation of Melbourne (*DNB*, xxxi, 437). Held
office until formation of administration by Palmerston in Feb. 1855 (Fitzmaurice, *Life of
Granville*, i, 95).

GRANVILLE, 2nd Earl   1855 Feb.–1865 Oct.
   LEADER OF HOUSE: 1. 1855 Feb.–1858 Feb. in Administration of Viscount
                       Palmerston.
                    2. 1859 June–1865 Oct. in Administration of Viscount
                       Palmerston.

Appointed Leader Feb. 1855 by Palmerston (Fitzmaurice, *Life of Granville*, i, 95–6). Left
office on Russell's appointment as Prime Minister, Oct. 1865.

RUSSELL, 1st Earl   1865 Oct.–1868 Dec.
   LEADER OF HOUSE: 1865 Oct.–1866 June as Prime Minister.

Became Leader on appointment as Prime Minister Oct. 1865. Apparently held office as
Leader in Lords until formation of administration by Gladstone Dec. 1868. A certain
amount of confusion existed as to his precise position after his resignation as Prime
Minister (Fitzmaurice, *Life of Granville*, i, 517, 531–3).

GRANVILLE, 2nd Earl   1868 Dec.–1891 Mar.
   LEADER OF HOUSE: 3. 1868 Dec.–1874 Feb. in Administration of Mr
                       Gladstone.
                    4. 1880 Apr.–1885 June in Administration of Mr
                       Gladstone.
                    5. 1886 Feb.–1886 Aug. in Administration of Mr
                       Gladstone.

Reappointed Leader Dec. 1868 by Gladstone (*The Times*, 7 Dec. 1868). Died 31
Mar. 1891.

KIMBERLEY, lst Earl of   1891 Apr.–1894 Mar.
   LEADER OF HOUSE: 1892 Aug.–1894 Mar. in Administration of Mr Gladstone.

At a meeting on 14 Apr. 1891 the Liberal peers decided that Kimberley should act for the time being as Leader but no formal election took place. Kimberley did not become Leader in the fullest sense until his appointment as Leader of House by Gladstone in Aug. 1892. Ceased to hold position on appointment of Rosebery as Prime Minister.

ROSEBERY, 5th Earl of (S) (ROSEBERY,
   2nd Lord (UK))   1894 Mar.–1896 Nov.
      LEADER OF HOUSE: 1894 Mar.–1895 June as Prime Minister.

Became Leader Mar. 1894 on appointment as Prime Minister. Resigned leadership of Liberal Party in House of Lords 'towards the end of November' 1896 (Wolf, *Life of Ripon*, ii, 249).

KIMBERLEY, 1st Earl of   1897 Jan.–1902 Apr.
      Elected Leader 18 Jan. 1897 (*The Times*, 19 Jan. 1897). Died 8 Apr. 1902.

SPENCER, 5th Earl   1902 Apr.–1905 Dec.
      Elected Leader 29 Apr. 1902 (*The Times*, 30 Apr. 1902). Held position until formation of Administration by Campbell-Bannerman in Dec. 1905.

RIPON, 1st Marquess of   1905 Dec.–1908 Apr.
      LEADER OF HOUSE: 1905 Dec.–1908 Apr. in Administration of Sir Henry Campbell-Bannerman.

Appointed Dec. 1905 by Campbell-Bannerman. Left position Apr. 1908.

CREWE, 1st Earl of (cr. Marquess of CREWE
   3 July 1911)   1908 Apr.–1922 Nov.
      LEADER OF HOUSE: 1908 Apr.–1916 Dec. in Administrations (Liberal and Coalition) of Mr Asquith.

Appointed Leader Apr. 1908 by Asquith (*The Times*, 14 Apr. 1908). Resigned as Leader of House Dec. 1916 on resignation of Asquith. Established Independent Liberal Opposition to Coalition Government Jan. 1919 (Pope-Hennessy, *Life of Crewe*, 152–3). Resigned leadership of Liberal Party in House of Lords Nov. 1922 on appointment as Ambassador in Paris (*The Times*, 20 Nov. 1922).

GREY OF FALLODEN, 1st Viscount   1923 Jan.–1924 Aug.
      Elected Leader 31 Jan. 1923 (*The Times*, 1 Feb. 1923). Resigned Aug. 1924 (*The Times*, 20 Aug. 1924).

BEAUCHAMP, 7th Earl   1924 Sept.–1931
      Elected Leader 30 Sept. 1924 (*The Times*, 1 Oct. 1924). Still Leader 22 Apr. 1931 (5 *Lords Debates*, lxxx, col. 994).

READING, 1st Marquess of   1931–1935 Dec.
      LEADER OF HOUSE: 1931 Aug.–1931 Nov. in Administration (National) of
                     Mr Macdonald.

Became Leader 1931. Died 30 Dec. 1935.

CREWE, 1st Marquess of   1936 Mar.–1944 Dec.
    Elected Leader 5 Mar. 1936 (*The Times*, 6 Mar. 1936). Resigned Dec. 1944
(*The Times*, 7 Dec. 1944).

SAMUEL, 1st Viscount   1944 Dec.–1955 June
    Elected Leader 6 Dec. 1944 (*The Times*, 7 Dec. 1944). Resigned June 1955
(*The Times*, 9 June 1955).

REA, 2nd Lord   1955 June–
    Elected Leader 13 June 1955 (*The Times*, 14 June 1955).

Deputy Leaders of the Liberal Party

Deputy Leaders are from time to time appointed by the Leader. The following have
held the position:

SAMUEL, 1st Viscount   1941 Apr.–1944 Dec.
    Accepted position at request of M. Crewe (*The Times*, 4 Apr. 1941); ceased to
hold it 6 Dec. 1944 on election as Leader.

PERTH, 17th Earl of (SR)   1946 Oct.–1951 Dec.
    Appointed Oct. 1946 (*The Times*, 16 Oct. 1946); died 15 Dec. 1951.

LAYTON, 1st Lord   1952 Feb.–1955
    Appointed by V. Samuel Feb. 1952 (*The Times*, 29 Feb. 1952); left position
1955 (*Debrett*).

Leaders of the Labour Party

Before the formation of Mr Macdonald's first Administration in January 1924, the
Labour party was unrepresented in the House of Lords. Since this time the party has
adopted a system of selecting Leaders in the Lords which is slightly different from that
of the other parties. When the party is in power the Prime Minister appoints the Leader
but when it is in opposition the Leader, together with certain other officers such as the
Chief Whip, is elected on a sessional basis by the Labour peers.

HALDANE, 1st Viscount   1924 Jan.–1928 Aug.
    LEADER OF HOUSE: 1924 Jan.–1924 Nov. in Administration of Mr
Macdonald.

Appointed Leader Jan. 1924 by Macdonald (Haldane, *Autobiography*, 319–42). Died 19
Aug. 1928.

PARMOOR, 1st Lord   1928 Oct.–1931 Sept.
    LEADER OF HOUSE: 1929 June–1931 Aug. in Administration of Mr
Macdonald.

Elected Leader Oct. 1928 (*The Times*, 27 Oct. 1928). Last speech as Leader 30 Sept.
1931 (Parmoor, *A Retrospect*, 320).

PONSONBY OF SHULBREDE, 1st Lord   1931–1935 Sept.
    Had become Leader by 10 Nov. 1931 (5 *Lords Debates*, lxxxiii, col. 15).
Resigned Sept. 1935 (Letter to *The Times*, 15 Sept. 1935).

SNELL, 1st Lord   1935 Oct.–1940 June
    Elected Leader 21 Oct. 1935 (*The Times*, 22 Oct. 1935). Resigned June 1940
on joining Coalition Government (*The Times*, 1 and 6 June 1940).

ADDISON, 1st Lord (cr. Viscount ADDISON
    6 July 1945)   1940 June–1951 Dec.
    LEADER OF HOUSE: 1945 Aug.–1951 Oct. in Administration of Mr Attlee.

Elected Leader 5 June 1940 (*The Times*, 6 June 1940). Died 11 Dec. 1951.

JOWITT, 1st Earl   1952 Feb.–1955 Dec.
    Elected Leader Feb. 1952 (*The Times*, 18 Feb. 1952). Notice of intention to
resign at end of 1955 given 8 Nov. 1955 (*The Times*, 9 Nov. and 14 Dec. 1955).

ALEXANDER OF HILLSBOROUGH, 1st Viscount
    (cr. Earl ALEXANDER OF HILLSBOROUGH 30 Jan. 1963)   1955 Dec.–
    Elected Leader Nov. 1955 to take office on resignation of E. Jowitt (*The Times*,
12 Nov. and 8 Dec. 1955).

Deputy Leaders of the Labour Party

No Deputy Leaders of the Labour party in the House of Lords appear to have been
appointed before 1947. When the party is in opposition the Deputy Leader, like other
officials of the party in the Lords, is elected by the Labour peers.

HALL, 1st Viscount   1947–1952
    DEPUTY LEADER OF HOUSE: 1947–1951 May as First Lord of Admiralty
in Administration of Mr Attlee.

Re-elected Deputy Leader Feb. 1952 (*The Times*, 18 Feb. 1952).

ALEXANDER OF HILLSBOROUGH, 1st Viscount   –1955 Dec.
    Ceased to hold position on becoming Leader Dec. 1955 (*The Times*), 12, 16, 24
Nov. 1955).

SILKIN, 1st Lord   1955 Dec.–
    Elected Nov. 1955 (*The Times*, 26 Nov. 1955) to take up position on Lord
Alexander becoming Leader.

2. *Whips in the House of Lords*

The Position of Chief Whip in the House of Lords

The following lists of Chief Whips are of a provisional character, particularly for the
nineteenth century. They are based almost exclusively on secondary sources. Very little

work has been done on the subject although Mr D. Large in an article entitled 'The Decline of "The Party of the Crown" and the Rise of Parties in the House of Lords, 1783–1837' (*EHR*, lxxviii (1963), 669–95) has thrown useful light on the origins of Whips in the House of Lords before 1840 and Professor H.J. Hanham (*Elections and Party Management in the Age of Disraeli and Gladstone*) has an interesting chapter on their activities in the 1870s and 1880s. Professor Hanham has kindly supplied additional material for these lists.

The 'unofficial' character of Whips has inevitably meant that little information concerning them has found its way into publications. *Dod's Parliamentary Companion* first includes Whips in its 1896 Edition. While giving a straightforward list of Commons Whips the editor appears unreasonably tentative in his account of the corresponding figures in the Lords. The editions from 1906 to 1912 simply contain the statement that 'There is scarcely any formal allotment of the office of 'whip' in the House of Lords'. From 1913 onwards, however, there is a full list of Lords Whips. While providing invaluable information Dod's lists are demonstrably inaccurate on occasion. Liberal Whips are omitted altogether from 1932 to 1936 and the lists are confused for the period 1940 to 1945. *Whitaker's Almanack* first included Government Whips in the Lords in the edition for 1948 and other Lords Whips in that for 1949. Apart from these publications other annual directories also provide helpful material. *Burke's Peerage, Debrett's Peerage, Dod* (Biographical section), *Who's Who* and *Who Was Who* have been consulted. After 1900 *The Times* began to report information about Lords Whips with a fair degree of regularity and these reports together with Obituary notices have been used extensively.

Since 1848 it has been the practice for the Government Chief Whip in the House of Lords to be given an office. The only exception to this was Lord Ribblesdale's tenure of the position from 1905 to 1907 without office. The office given to Chief Whips has always been a Household one except for the very brief tenure of the position of Joint Government Chief Whip by the Duke of Devonshire as Civil Lord of the Admiralty 1915 to 1916. The position of Chief Whip was not originally attached to any particular office, being held most usually in the nineteenth century by the Master of the Buckhounds or the Captain of the Yeomen of the Guard or, more rarely, by the Chief Equerry, the Lord Steward or a Lord in Waiting. Since 1900, however, a strong predilection has been shown for the office of Captain of the Gentlemen at Arms. Since 1945 the association has been invariable and was given implied statutory sanction by section 3 of the Ministers of the Crown (Parliamentary Secretaries) Act, 1960 which gave the Captain of the Gentlemen at Arms an increase of salary, the assumption at the time being that he would be Chief Government Whip in the House of Lords.

Government Chief Whips

BESSBOROUGH, 5th Earl of (I) (PONSONBY,
    5th Lord (GB)) (Liberal)   1848 May–1852 Feb.
        As Master of Buckhounds.

COLVILLE, l0th Lord (SR) (Conservative)   1852 Feb.–1852 Dec.
        As Chief Equerry and Clerk Marshal.

BESSBOROUGH, 5th Earl of (I) (PONSONBY, 5th Lord
(GB)) (Liberal)   1852 Dec.–1858 Feb.
As Master of Buckhounds.

COLVILLE, 10th Lord (SR) (Conservative)   1858 Feb.–1859 June
As Chief Equerry and Clerk Marshal.

BESSBOROUGH, 5th Earl of (I) (PONSONBY,
5th Lord (GB)) (Liberal)   1859 June–1866 June
As Master of Buckhounds (1859 June–1866 Jan.) and Lord Steward
(1866 Jan.–1866 June).

COLVILLE, 10th Lord (SR) (Conservative)   1866 June–1868 Dec.
As Master of Buckhounds.

BESSBOROUGH, 5th Earl of (I) (PONSONBY,
5th Lord (GB)) (Liberal)   1868 Dec.–1874 Feb.
As Lord Steward.

SKELMERSDALE, 2nd Lord (Conservative)   1874 Feb.–1880 Apr.
As Captain of Yeomen of Guard.

MONSON, 7th Lord (Liberal)   1880 Apr.–1885 June
As Captain of Yeomen of Guard.

KINTORE, 9th Earl of (S) (KINTORE, 3rd Lord (UK))
(Conservative)   1885 June–1886 Jan.
As Lord in Waiting.

MONSON, 7th Lord (Liberal)   1886 Jan.–1886 July
As Captain of Yeomen of Guard.

KINTORE, 9th Earl of (S) (KINTORE, 3rd Lord (UK))
(Conservative)   1886 July–1889 Jan.
As Captain of Yeomen of Guard.

LIMERICK, 3rd Earl of (I) (FOXFORD, 3rd Lord (UK))
(Conservative)   1889 Jan.–1892 Aug.
As Captain of Yeomen of Guard.

KENSINGTON, 4th Lord (I) (KENSINGTON,
1st Lord (UK)) (Liberal)   1892 Aug.–1895 June
As Captain of Yeomen of Guard.

LIMERICK, 3rd Earl of (I) (FOXFORD, 3rd Lord (UK))
(Conservative)   1895 June–1896 Aug.
As Captain of Yeomen of Guard.

WALDEGRAVE, 9th Earl (Conservative)   1896 Aug.–1905 Dec.
As Captain of Yeomen of Guard.

RIBBLESDALE, 4th Lord (Liberal)   1905 Dec.–1907
Without office.

DENMAN, 3rd Lord (Liberal)   1907 May–1911 Mar.
    As Lord in Waiting (1907 May–1907 July) and Captain of Gentlemen at Arms
(1907 July–1911 Mar.).

COLEBROOKE, 1st Lord (Liberal)   SOLE   1911 Mar.–1915 June
                                                 JOINT   1915 June–1922 Oct.
    As Lord in Waiting (1911 Mar.–1911 June) and Captain of Gentlemen at Arms
(1911 June–1922 Oct.).

DEVONSHIRE, 9th Duke of (Conservative)   JOINT   1915 June–1916 July
    As Civil Lord of Admiralty.

HYLTON, 3rd Lord (Conservative)   JOINT   1916 July–1922 Oct.
    As Lord in Waiting (1916 July–1918 May) and Captain of Yeomen of Guard
(1918 May–1922 Oct.).

CLARENDON, 6th Earl of (Conservative)   1922 Nov.–1924 Jan.
    As Captain of Gentlemen at Arms.

MUIR MACKENZIE, 1st Lord (Labour)   1924 Jan.–1924 Nov.
    As Lord in Waiting.

CLARENDON, 6th Earl of (Conservative)   1924 Nov.–1925 June
    As Captain of Gentlemen at Arms.

PLYMOUTH, 2nd Earl of (Conservative)   1925 June–1929 Jan.
    As Captain of Gentlemen at Arms.

LUCAN, 6th Earl of (I) (Conservative)   1929 Jan.–1929 June
    As Captain of Gentlemen at Arms.

DE LA WARR, 9th Earl (Labour)   1929 June–1930 Jan.
    As Lord in Waiting.

MARLEY, 1st Lord (Labour)   1930 Jan.–1931 Aug.
    As Lord in Waiting.

LUCAN, 6th Earl of (I) (cr. Lord BINGHAM (UK)
    26 June 1934) (Conservative)   1931 Aug.–1940 June
    As Captain of Gentlemen at Arms.

TEMPLEMORE, 4th Lord (Conservative)   1940 June–1945 July
    As Captain of Yeomen of Guard.

AMMON, 1st Lord (Labour)   1945 Aug.–1949 July
    As Captain of Gentlemen at Arms.

SHEPHERD, 1st Lord (Labour)   1949 Oct.–1951 Oct.
    As Captain of Gentlemen at Arms. He acted as Chief Whip between July and
Oct. 1949 when holding the office of Captain of Yeomen of Guard.

FORTESCUE, 7th Earl (Conservative)   1951 Oct.–1958 June
    As Captain of Gentlemen at Arms.

ST ALDWYN, 2nd Earl (Conservative)   1958 June–
   As Captain of Gentlemen at Arms.

Conservative Chief Whips

NELSON, 2nd Earl   –1852 Feb.
   It has not been possible to trace any earlier Conservative Whip in the House
of Lords. The only reference to him as Whip is in connection with Colville's
appointment in his place. (Malmesbury, *Memoirs of an Ex-Minister*, i, 303 under
11 Feb. 1852). He took his seat on 4 Feb. 1845 (*LJ*, 77, p. 4).

COLVILLE OF CULROSS, 10th Lord (SR)   1852 Feb.–c. 1870
         Government Chief Whip: 1852 Feb.–1852 Dec. (Chief Equerry and
                          Clerk Marshal)
                          1858 Feb.–1859 June (Chief Equerry and
                          Clerk Marshal)
                          1866 July–1868 Dec. (Master of Buckhounds)

His appointment is mentioned by Malmesbury (*Memoirs of an Ex-Minister*, i, 303 under
11 Feb. 1852). It seems clear from Hardy's Diary that he was still Whip on 22 Feb. 1869
(Gathorne-Hardy, *Life of Lord Cranbrook*, i, 295). If the Tellers in the Division Lists of
the House of Lords are a reliable guide, he remained in office until Session 1870 (*LJ*,
102, passim).

SKELMERSDALE, 2nd Lord (cr. LATHOM,
   1st Earl of, 3 May 1880)   c. 1870–1885 July
         Government Chief Whip: 1874 Feb.–1880 Apr. (Captain of Yeomen of Guard)

H.J. Hanham suggests in a note that he became Whip in 1874 (*Elections and Party
Management*, 373). However it may be inferred from the Division Lists that he succeeded
Colville in 1870 (*LJ*, 102, passim). Two letters of Disraeli's of 11 Jan. and 16 Feb. 1872
indicate that he was already Whip at this time (Buckle, *Life of Disraeli*, v, 174–5). He left
office in July 1885 (Hanham, Notes).

KINTORE, 9th Earl of (S) (KINTORE, 3rd Lord (UK))   1885 July–1889 Feb.
         Government Chief Whip: 1885 July–1886 Feb. (Lord in Waiting)
                          1886 Aug.–1889 Feb. (Captain of Yeomen of Guard)

Succeeded Latham in July 1885 and resigned in Feb. 1889 (Hanham, Notes) on being
appointed Governor of South Australia.

LIMERICK, 3rd Earl of (I) (FOXFORD, 3rd Lord (UK))   1889 Feb.–1896 Aug.
         Government Chief Whip: 1889 Feb.–1892 Aug. (Captain of Yeomen of Guard)
                          1895 June–1896 Aug. (Captain of Yeomen of Guard)

Succeeded Kintore Feb. 1889 (Hanham, Notes). Died 8 Aug. 1896.

WALDEGRAVE, 9th Earl   1896 Aug.–1911 Nov.
         Government Chief Whip: 1896 Aug.–1905 Dec. (Captain of Yeomen of Guard)

Whip 1896–1911 according to *Dod* and *Complete Peerage*, xii, pt 2, 315. For appointment see *The Times*, 19 Jan. 1897. Resigned Nov. 1911 (*The Times*, 30 Nov. 1911).

DEVONSHIRE, 9th Duke of   1911 Nov.–1916 July
    Joint Government Chief Whip: 1915 June–1916 July (Civil Lord of Admiralty)

Became Chief Whip Nov. 1911 (*The Times*, 30 Nov. 1911). In the first full list of Whips in the 1913 edition of Whips he appears as first Unionist Whip. He appears similarly in 1914 and 1915. In the 1916 edition he appears as the first Unionist Whip in the Coalition. He probably resigned on taking up his appointment as Governor-General of Canada in July 1916.

HYLTON, 3rd Lord   1916 July–1922 Nov.
    Joint Government Chief Whip: 1916 July–1922 Nov. (Lord in Waiting 1916
Nov.–1918 May; Captain of Yeomen of Guard 1918 May–1922 Nov.) (*The Times*,
Obituary, 28 May 1945.)

CLARENDON, 6th Earl of   1922 Nov.–1925 June
    Government Chief Whip: 1922 Nov.–1924 Jan. (Captain of Gentlemen at Arms)
                          1924 Nov.–1925 June (Captain of Gentlemen at Arms)
(*The Times*, Obituary, 14 Dec. 1955). Appointed Nov. 1922 (*The Times*, 22 Nov. 1922).

PLYMOUTH, 2nd Earl of   1925 June–1929 Jan.
    Government Chief Whip: 1925 June–1929 Jan. (Captain of Gentlemen at Arms)
(*The Times*, Obituary, 4 Oct. 1943).

LUCAN, 6th Earl of (IR) (cr. BINGHAM, 1st Lord (UK)
    26 June 1934)   1929 Jan.–1940 June
    Government Chief Whip: 1929 Jan.–1929 June (Captain of Gentlemen at Arms)
                       1931 Aug.–1940 June (Captain of Gentlemen at Arms)
(*The Times*, Obituary, 22 Apr. 1949).

TEMPLEMORE, 4th Lord   1940 June–1945 July
    Government Chief Whip: 1940 June–1945 July (Captain of Yeomen of Guard)
(*The Times*, 1 June 1940 for appointment. *The Times*, Obituary, 5 Oct. 1953
wrongly says that he became Chief Whip in 1939).

FORTESCUE, 7th Earl   1945 Aug.–1958 June
    Government Chief Whip: 1951 Oct.–1958 June (Captain of Gentlenen at Arms)
(*The Times*, Obituary, 16 June 1958). Appears to have taken over from L.
Templemore when Conservative Party went into Oppsition in July 1945.

ST ALDWYN, 2nd Earl   1958 June–
    Government Chief Whip: 1958 June– (Captain of Gentlemen at Arms)
(*The Times*, 28 June 1958).

Liberal Chief Whips

FALKLAND, 10th Viscount (S) (HUNSDON, 1st Lord (UK))   1837–1840
    Government Chief Whip: 1837–1840 (Lord in Waiting)

It has not been possible to trace any earlier Whig or Liberal Whip in the House of Lords. The authority in this instance is *Complete Peerage*, v, 244. In 1840 he was appointed Governor of Nova Scotia. He was Captain of Yeomen of Guard July 1846 to Feb. 1848 when he was appointed Governor of Bombay. It is conceivable that he was again Whip during this period.

BESSBOROUGH, 5th Earl of (I) (PONSONBY,
   5th Lord (GB))   1848 May–1880 Jan.
       Government Chief Whip: 1848 May–1852 Feb. (Master of Buckhounds)
                       1852 Dec.–1858 Feb. (Master of Buckhounds)
                       1859 June–1866 July (Master of Buckhounds 1859
                       June–1866 Jan.; Steward of Household 1866
                       Jan.–1866 July)
                       1868 Dec.–1874 Feb. (Steward of Household)

Probably became Whip on his appointment to Buckhounds in May 1848. Was certainly Whip in 1850 (Fitzmaurice, *Life of Lord Granville*, ii, 16). Still Whip 1869 (Fitzmaurice, *Life of Lord Granville*, ii, 16). Did not act as Teller in Divisions after Session 1869 (*LJ*, 101–2). However, according to H.J. Hanham (Notes) he was still Whip in 1874 when he wished Monson to succeed him and 'seems to have carried on until 1879'. In this case it is likely that he remained until his death 28 Jan. 1880. Fitzmaurice (*Life of Granville*, ii, 193) would appear to support this view. Between 1870 and 1880 D. St Albans, E. Cork and Orrery and L. Monson acted as Tellers (*LJ*, passim).

MONSON, 7th Lord (cr. OXENBRIDGE, 1st Viscount
   13 Aug. 1886)   1880 Jan.–1892 Aug.
       Government Chief Whip: 1880 Apr.–1885 June (Captain of Yeomen of Guard)
                       1886 Feb.–1886 Aug. (Captain of Yeomen of Guard)

Presumably followed on death of Bessborough (see above). Was still Whip in Dec. 1887 and Jan. 1888 (Pope-Hennessy, *Life of Lord Crewe*, 27–8) and in 1891 when, on the death of Lord Granville, the election of his successor as Leader took place at Monson's house (Wolf, *Life of Lord Ripon*, ii, 249). It seems likely that he handed over to Kensington at the formation of the Liberal Government in Aug. 1892.

KENSINGTON, 4th Lord (I) (KENSINGTON,
   1st Lord (UK))   1892 Aug.–1896 Oct.
       Government Chief Whip: 1892 Aug.–1895 June (Captain of Yeomen of Guard)

Probably took up position in Aug. 1892 (see above). Was certainly Whip at his death 7 Oct. 1896 (Wolf, *Life of Lord Ripon*, ii, 250).

RIBBLESDALE, 4th Lord   1896–1907 May
       Government Chief Whip: 1905 Dec.–1907 May (Without Office). *Complete Peerage*, x, 773. Resigned May 1907 (*The Times*, 29 May 1907).

DENMAN. 3rd Lord   1907 May–1911 Mar.
       Government Chief Whip: 1907 May–1911 Mar. (Lord in Waiting 1907 May–1907 July; Captain of Gentlemen at Arms 1907 July–1911 Mar.)

Appointed May 1907 (*The Times*, 29 May 1907). Resigned Mar. 1911 (*The Times*, 14 Mar. 1911).

COLEBROOKE, 1st Lord   1911 Mar.–1922 Oct.
Government Chief Whip: 1911 Mar.–1915 June (Lord in Waiting 1911 Mar.– 1911 June; Captain of Gentlemen at Arms 1911 June–1915 June)
Joint Government Chief Whip: 1915 June–1922 Oct. (Captain of Gentlemen at Arms).

Appointed Mar. 1911 (*The Times*, 14 Mar. 1911). From Feb. 1919 was Chief Whip only of Coalition Liberals).

DENMAN, 3rd Lord   1919 Feb.–1924
Became Chief Whip of Independent Liberals 5 Feb. 1919 (*The Times*, 6 Feb. 1919). Appears as such in *Dod*, Editions 1919 to 1923 (published Nov. 1923). In List of Whips in 1924 Edition (published Feb. 1924) appears as first Liberal Whip. It seems that he became Chief Whip of both sections of the Liberal party after the fall of the Coalition in Oct. 1922.

STANMORE, 2nd Lord   1924–1944 Mar.
Chief Liberal Whip supporting the Government 1931 Aug.–1932 Sept. Appears as second Liberal Whip in *Dod* 1924 Second Edition (published Feb. 1924), p. 436, and first Liberal Whip in *Dod* 1925 Edition (published Dec. 1924), p. 434. Ceased to support National Government after Ottawa Agreements. Last appears in List of Whips in *Dod* 1944 Edition (no publication date), p. 326. Appointed Chairman of Committees, House of Lords 29 Mar. 1944 (*LJ*, 176, 80). See *The Times*, Obituary, 15 Apr. 1957.

MERSEY, 2nd Viscount   1944 Mar.–1949 Apr.
Succeeded Stanmore as Chief Whip Mar. 1944 (Mersey, *Journal and Memories*, 36). Ceased to be Chief Whip after 12 Apr. 1949 (Mersey, *Journal and Memories*, 94). First appears in Lists of Whips in *Dod* 1945 Edition (published Dec. 1944), p. 328. Last appears there in 1949 Edition (published Nov. 1948). *Debrett* has 1944–9. *The Times*, Obituary, 21 Nov. 1956 has 1945–9.

WILLINGDON, 2nd Marquess of   1949 Apr.–1950
Succeeded Mersey as Chief Whip after 12 Apr. 1949 (Mersey, *Journal and Memories*, 94). See also *The Times*, 31 Mar. 1949. *Debrett* has 1949–50. Appears as Chief Liberal Whip in Lists of Whips in *Dod* 1950 Edition (published May 1950), p. 476.

MOYNIHAN, 2nd Lord   1950–1950 Nov.
Appears to have succeeded Willingdon in 1950. Resigned Nov. 1950 (*The Times*, 7 Nov. 1950).

REA, 2nd Lord   1950 Nov.–1955 June
Appointed in place of Moynihan Nov. 1950 (*The Times*, 7 Nov. 1950). *Debrett* and *Dod* (Biography) have 1950–5. See also *The Times*, 14 June 1955.

AMULREE, 2nd Lord   1955 June–
    For appointment, see *The Times*, 14 June 1955.

Labour Chief Whips

MUIR MACKENZIE, 1st Lord   1924 Jan.–1924 Nov.
    Government Chief Whip: 1924 Jan.–1924 Nov. (Lord in Waiting)

For his position as Whip in 1924 see List of Whips in *Dod* 1924 Second Edition
(published Feb. 1924), p. 436, and *Lords Debates*, 3rd series, lvi, col. 83 (12 Feb. 1924).
He seems to have retired from position on fall of Government in Nov. 1924 since List
of Whips in *Dod* 1925 Edition (published Dec. 1924), p. 434, gives E. De la Warr as
Chief Labour Whip.

DE LA WARR, 9th Earl   1924 Nov.–1930 Jan.
    Government Chief Whip: 1929 June–1930 Jan. (Lord in Waiting)

First mentioned in List of Whips in *Dod* 1925 Edition (published Dec. 1924), p. 434.
Probably succeeded Muir Mackenzie in Nov. 1924. Appears in Lists of Whips in *Dod*
Editions 1925 to 1929. *Dod* (Biography) states that Marley took office in Jan. 1930 and
De la Warr probably remained Whip until that date.

MARLEY, 1st Lord   1930 Jan.–1937
    Government Chief Whip: 1930 Jan.–1931 Aug. (Lord in Waiting)

Dod (Biography) states that he took office Jan. 1930 and held it 1930–7. Last appears in
Lists of Whips in *Dod* 1938 Edition (published Nov. 1937), p. 308. See also *Debrett*
which has 1930–7 and *The Times*, Obituary, 3 March 1952.

STRABOLGI, 19th Lord   1937 Oct.–1941 Nov.
    Elected 25 Oct. 1937 (*The Times*, 26 Oct. 1937). Held position until
replacement by Listowel in Nov. 1941.

LISTOWEL, 5th Earl of (I) (HARE, 3rd Lord (UK))   1941 Nov.–1944 Oct.
    Elected 12 Nov. 1941 (*The Times*, 13 Nov. 1941). Held position until
appointment as Parliamentary Under-Secretary of State, India and Burma Office
31 Oct. 1944.

SOUTHWOOD, 1st Lord   1944 Nov.–1945 July
    Elected 8 Nov. 1944 (*The Times*, 9 Nov. 1944). Probably held position until
formation of Labour Government in July 1945.

AMMON, 1st Lord   1945 Aug.–1949 July
    Government Chief Whip: 1945 Aug.–1949 July (Captain of Gentlemen at
Arms) (*The Times*, Obituary, 4 Apr. 1960.)

SHEPHERD, 1st Lord (Acting 1949 July–Oct.)   1949 Oct.–1954 Dec.
    Acting Government Chief Whip: 1949 July–1949 Oct. (Captain of Yeomen of
Guard)

Government Chief Whip: 1949 Oct.–1951 Oct. (Captain of Gentlemen at Arms) Died 5 Dec. 1954 (*The Times*, Obituary, 6 Dec. 1954).

LUCAN, 7th Earl of (I) (BINGHAM, 2nd Lord (UK))   1954 Dec.–1964 Jan.
  Became Chief Whip Dec. 1954 (*The Times*, 22 Dec. 1954). Died 22 Jan. 1964.

SHEPHERD, 2nd Lord   1964 Jan.–
  Became Chief Whip Jan. 1964.

Appendix

Minor Parties

Few minor parties have maintained any kind of separate political organisation in the House of Lords. However, the *Liberal Unionists* should be mentioned. The 15th Earl of DERBY became Leader in 1886, continuing until 1891 when the 8th Duke of DEVONSHIRE took over from him on succeeding to the peerage. The Duke accepted office in 1895 and became Leader of the House in 1902. After his resignation in 1903 there was no longer any separate Leader of the Liberal Unionists in the House. The Liberal Unionist Whip was the 2nd Lord LAWRENCE who took up his position possibly in 1886 and almost certainly by 1895, retaining it until his death in 1914 (*Dod*, Lists of Whips). He held office as a Lord in Waiting 1895–1905.

  The *National Liberal party* has never had a separate Leader in the House of Lords, but since 1945 the 1st Lord TEVIOT has been Chief Whip.

Chapter 2. Further Materials from an Unpublished Manuscript of the House of Lords Journal for Sessions 1559 and 1597–8

Preface

The defective character of the printed *Lords Journals* for the reign of Elizabeth was indicated by F.W. Maitland in an article in 1900[1] but it was not until 1913 that the value of the Petyt Manuscripts, preserved in the Inner Temple Library, as a source for the missing portions, was made known by Miss E. Jeffries Davis, who examined them at the suggestion of Professor A.F. Pollard. Miss Davis published a description of the Inner Temple Petyt manuscript numbered 537, vol. 6 and extracts from it to cover twelve sittings of the House in 1559 which do not appear in the printed Journals nor in the manuscript Journals now preserved at the Parliamentary Archives.[2] In 1919 Professor J.E. (now Sir John) Neale drew attention to the value of the same manuscript for filling the gaps which exist in the House of Lords copy of the Journals for Session 1597–8.[3]

An examination of the printed *Lords Journals* for all the Elizabethan parliaments reveals that Sessions 1559 and 1597–8 are the only ones that are defective. For Session 1559 all the missing sittings were transcribed and printed by Miss Davis except two – those on 22nd March (p.m.) and 23rd March 1558–9. For Session 1597–8 none of the eighteen missing sittings has been made available in print.[4] The object of this Memorandum is to make the only known record of these sittings readily available to the student. The accompanying synopsis is designed to relate these sittings to the printed *Journals*.

MS Petyt 537, vol. 6 has already been described by Miss Davis and it is unnecessary to do more here than to draw attention to its characteristics briefly. It is clearly the manuscript mentioned by Sir Simonds D'Ewes, in the Preface to his *Journal*, as collected and transcribed by Robert Bowyer, Clerk of the Parliaments 1609–21. The main differences between the printed *Journals* and Bowyer's Transcript are that the latter

---

[1] *EHR*, xviii, 531.

[2] *EHR*, xxviii, 531–42.

[3] *EHR*, xxxiv, 586–8.

[4] It is worth stressing in this context that D'Ewes' *Journal* of the Elizabethan parliaments frequently omits material that its editor regarded as unimportant, and its value for detailed study is consequently considerably reduced.

usually omits the names of the peers present on each day and the names of the Peers and assistants appointed to serve on Committees. Unlike the *Journals* the Transcript contains marginal numbers for ease of reference. From this it is clear that Bowyer made up the Transcript for the purpose of a kind of procedural reference book, with numbered precedents. D'Ewes was not, however, entirely dependent upon this Transcript, as he himself says, and clearly had access to a version of the *Journals* more complete than is now known to exist, since he is able to provide the names of some of the committees appointed on the days missing from the present MS Lords Journal and not included in the Transcript. It seems clear, therefore, that, at least so far as the Elizabethan parliaments are concerned, the 'Original *Manuscript* or *Journal-Books* of the *Upper House*' which D'Ewes mentions were in a complete state when he examined them. It is most unlikely that he could have forborne to draw attention to the fact if they had not been. This raises a number of unresolved questions about the status of the present MS Journals on which the printed version is founded. An examination of them shows that they must have been transcribed from an already defective version, since the gatherings of the present volumes make it clear that no leaves have fallen out from the existing volumes.

In editing the Transcript Bowyer's own marginal numbers and editorial notes have been included. The manuscript has been collated with D'Ewes' text[5] and, where additional material can be found in the latter, it has been noted. The original spelling has been retained but abbreviations have been expanded and the Latin standardised. The text itself is founded upon a photostatic copy of the manuscript in the Parliamentary Archives and is made available by courtesy of the Librarian and Benchers of the Inner Temple.

Finally I should like to take this opportunity of expressing my thanks to Mr M.F. Bond, Clerk of the Records, for his unfailing help and encouragement at all stages of the preparation of this transcript.

J.C.S.

---

[5] References are to the second edition (1693).

Synopsis: Session 1559

1558/59			1559		
			Apr.	3	⎤
Jan.	25			4	
	28			5	
	30			6	
Feb.	1	⎫		7	⊢ *LJ*, 1, pp. 569–74
	4			8	
	9			10	
	10			12	
	11			13	⎦
	13				
	15			14	*EHR*, xxviii, 536
	16			15	*EHR*, xxviii, 536
	17				
	20			17	⎤
	21			19	⊢ *LJ*, 1, pp. 574–6
	22			20	
	23			22	⎦
	24				
	25			26	*EHR*, xxviii, 537
	27			27	*EHR*, xxviii, 538
	28			28	*EHR*, xxviii, 538–9
Mar.	1	⎬ *LJ*, 1, pp. 543–68		29	*EHR*, xxviii, 539
	2		May	1 (a.m.)	*LJ*, 1, p. 576
	3			1 (p.m.)	
	4			2	*EHR*, xxviii, 540
	5			3	*EHR*, xxviii, 540
	6			5	*EHR*, xxviii, 541
	7			6	*EHR*, xxviii, 541
	8			8 (a.m.)	*LJ*, 1, pp. 577–8
	9			8 (p.m.)	
	10				
	11				
	13				
	15				
	16				
	17				
	18				
	20				
	21 (a.m.)				
	21 (p.m.)				
	22 (a.m.)	⎭			
	22 (p.m.)	see pages 28–9			
	23	see page 29			
	24	*LJ*, 1, p. 568			

Synopsis: Session 1597–8

1597				1597–8		
Oct.	24	⎤		Jan.	11	⎤
	27	⎥			12	⎥
		⎥			13	⎬ *LJ*, 2, pp. 214–18
Nov.	5	⎥			14	⎦
	7	⎥				
	10	⎥			16	see pages 32–3
	12	⎥				
	14	⎬ *LJ*, 2, pp. 192–202			17	⎤
	15	⎥			18	⎬ *LJ*, 2, pp. 218–19
	19	⎥			19	see pages 33–5
	21	⎥			20	see pages 35–6
	22	⎥			21	see pages 36–7
	24	⎥			23	see pages 37–8
	26	⎥			24	*LJ*, 2, pp. 219–20
	28	⎦			25	see pages 38–9
					26	see pages 39–40
Dec.	1				27	see pages 40–1
	3		see pages 29–30		28	*LJ*, 2, pp. 220–1
	5		see pages 30–1		30	see pages 41–2
					31	see pages 42–3
	6	⎤				
	7	⎥		Feb.	1	⎤
	8	⎥			3	⎬ *LJ*, 2, pp. 221–4
	9	⎥			4	⎦
	10	⎥				
	12	⎥			6 (a.m.)	see pages 43–4
	13	⎥			6 (p.m.)	see pages 44–5
	14	⎬ *LJ*, 2, pp. 202–14			7 (a.m.)	see page 45
	15 (a.m.)	⎥			7 (p.m.)	see pages 45–6
	15 (p.m.)	⎥			8	*LJ*, 2, p. 224
	16	⎥			9 (a.m.)	see page 46
	17	⎥			9 (p.m.)	see page 46
	19	⎥				
	20	⎦				

1. Entries for the 1559 Session

[Wednesday, 22 March 1558/59 Afternoon Sitting][6]

[p. 76][7]

91. An act touching Tanners and selling of tanned leather: 2a vice lecta.
    An act for the allowance of sheriffes upon their accomptes: 2a vice lecta.

[6] The headings in brackets have been inserted by J.C. Sainty.
[7] The pagination in brackets is that of the original MS.

92. Fowre Billes weare brought from the commons house vizt.:

An act for the rivivinge of a Statut made anno 23 Henry 8 touchinge the conveienge of horses, geldinges and mares into Scotlande without licence.

An act that carrieng of leather, Tallowe or rawe hydes out of the realme for merchandize to be felony, which was read prima et 2a vice.

An act touching leases to be made by spiritual persons; que prima vice lecta est et commissa attornato domine Regine.

An act revoking divers licences granted for divers thinges prohibited by the Lawe of the realme: prima vice lecta.

93. An act for admitting and consecratinge of Archbishops and Bishops 2a vice lecta.

94. The bill for the Assises to be holden in the towne of Stafford was delivered to the Queenes Attorny and Sollicitor to be carried into the Commons house.

95. Dominus Custos magni Sigilli continuavit presens parliamentum usque in diem crastinum hora octava.

[Thursday, 23 March 1558/59]

96. On thursday the 23 of marche.

The bill for the Assizes to be holden in the towne of Stafford was returned from the commons house, conclusa or Expedita.

97. The bill touching Tanners and sellinge of tanned leather was read 3a vice et conclusa with certaine amendementes to be put to yt: et postea commissa Attornato et Sollicitatori Regine in domum communem deferenda et postea introducta a domo communi, conclusa.

98. Billa for the admitting and consecrating of Archbishops and Bishops; 3a vice lecta est et conclusa.

99. Billa that carrieng leather, Tallowe (or – *interlineated*) rawe hydes out of the realme (for merchandise – *interlineated*) shalbe felonie 3a vice lecta et conclusa dissentiente domino Lumley.

100. Billa touching leases to be made by spiritual persons, 2a vice est lecta.

101. Billa for the explanacion of the Statute against the ingrossinge of dead victualles with a proviso added therunto by the lordes, 3a vice lecta est et conclusa et missa ad Communes per Attornatum et Sollicitatorem Regine.

102. Dominus Custos magni Sigilli continuavit presens parliamentum usque in diem crastinum hora nona . . .

2. *Entries for the 1597–8 Session*

[Saturday, 3 December 1597]

[p. 280]

57. Die Sabbati tertio die Decembris.

Billa an act for establishinge the towne landes of Wanting in the countie of Berkes etc. 3a vice lecta, and sent to the lower house for their consideracion of a proviso thought fitt to be added by the committees. By Mr Serieant drew and Mr Attorny.

58. Five billes sent from the commons house, vizt.

1. An act for the encrease of Mariners and for maintenance of the Navigacion, repealing a former act made in the 23 yeare of hir Maiestys raigne bearing the same title; which Acte was sent to the lower howse from hence for their consideracion and allowance of this title and some amendement in the body of the bill.

2. An acte for erectinge of Hospitalles, or abiding and woorking houses for the poore. prima vice lecta.

3. An acte against forstallers, regrators and engrossers. prima vice lecta.

4. An act for the better execucion of statute made in the 23 yeare of the Queenes Maiestys raigne for the abolishing of Logwood alias Blogwood in the dyeng of cloathe, wooll or yarne. prima vice lecta.

5. An act for Arthur Hatch hir maiestys warde for the enjoying of the Rectorie and Personage of South Molton according to an agreement thereof had betweene him and the Deane and Canons of the King's free chappell of St. George within his Castle of Windsor.

59. Billa an act for the better and safer recording of Fynes to be levied in the court of common pleas. prima vice lecta.

An act for remedie of dilapidacions in the Bishopricke of London. prima vice lecta.

60. Upon the report of Mr Justice Owen and Mr Serieant Drew, unto whome the examinacion of the matter was committed concerning the arrest of Edward Barston, servant to the Lord Chandois, by one Stephenson of London at the suite of one W: Hood being found and iudged to have willfullie offended therin against the [p. 281] priviledge of the house, weare committed and sent unto the prison of the Fleete, there to be kept close Prisoners untill farther direccion should be given by the Lordes of parliament. And whereas [blank in MS][8] weare this day alas brought into the house before the Lordes as supposed partakers of the same offence, they upon examinacion being found not to have willfullie committed anie fault therein, weare dissmissed and order given accordinglie by the lordes for their discharge in that behalfe, As also for the discharge of Edw: Barston out of the prison of the Counter.

61. Dominus Custos magni Sigilli continuavit presens parliamentum usque in diem quintum Novembris hora nona.

[Monday, 5 December 1597]

62. On monday the fift of Decembris.
Sixe bills brought from the common house.

---

[8] According to *D'Ewes*, p. 531 the missing words were 'the two others'.

1. An act for erectinge of houses of correccion and punishment of Rogues and sturdie beggers.
2. An act to restraine Brewers to keepe two coopers and no more. prima vice lecta.
3. An act for naturalizinge certein englishe mens children and others borne beyond the seas.
4. An act giving power and libertie to Sir John spencer knight, Marie his wyfe and Robert spencer esquire, their soon and heir apparant to alienate certaine mannours and landes in the counties of Dorset and Bedford:
5. An act for the establishing of the possessions late of Sir Henry Unton knight deceased for paiment of his debtes.
6. An act for the establishinge of the Hospitall of Queen Elizabeth in Bristoll, and for the releife of the Orphanes and poore there.

63. An act for confirmacion of the iointure of Christian Lady Sandes. prima vice lecta.

Billa an act against Forestallers, Regratours and Engrossers: 2da vice lecta and referred to committees who are appointed to meete at the little councill chamber at the court at Whitehall tomorrowe being the 6 of December at 3 of the clocke in the afternoone.

Billa an act for erectinge of Hospitalles or abiding and woorking houses for the poore: 2da vice lecta, and referred to the former committees with addicion of the Archbishop of Canterbury.

Billa an act for the better execucion of the statute made in the 23th yeare of the Queenes raigne for the abolishinge of Logwood alias Blackwood in the dyenge of cloathe, wooll or yarne 2da vice lecta, and referred to Committees etc. Appointed to meete on wensday in the afternoone about 2 of the clocke at the litle chamber near the inner chamber of Parliament presence.

Billa an act for better and safer recordinge of fynes to be levied in the court of common pleas. 2da vice lecta, referred unto the same committees as before with addicion of the 2 lordes cheife Justices and Mr. Attorney:

The absence of	Earl of Essex Lord Vicount Bindon Earl of Cumberland Lord Scroope Lord Willoughby of Eresby Lord Bishop of Rochester	excused by the	Lord Rich Lord Chandois Lord Wharton Lord Zouch Lord Bishop of Bath etc.

64. Order was given for the release of Stephenson the Serjeant that arrested the Lord Chandois servant.

65. Dominus Custos magni Sigilli continuavit presens parliamentum usque in diem crastinum vizt. 6 Decembris hora nona.

[Monday, 16 January 1597/98]

[p. 292]

140. Die Lunae viz. 16 die Januarii.

Billa an act for the reforminge of sondry abuses committed by soldiers and others used in hir maiestys services concerninge the warres 2da vice lecta and referred to committees etc.

Billa an act for confirmacion of statutes merchantes acknowledged in the cittie of Lincolne and the towne corporate of Nottingham 2da lecta and referred to Committees, etc.[9]

141. Report made to the house by the Lord Archbishop of Canterbury that upon the meetinge of such of the lordes of the higher house as weare appointed this daie to conferre with certaine select knightes and Burgesses of the lower house concerninge the amendementes and provisoes added by their lordships to the bill intituled An act for erectinge of houses of correccion etc. the said knightes and Burgesses do hold them selves satisfied (upon the reason alleaged by their lordships) in somme part of the said amendementes but not in all: vide no. 135.

142. Kirham was called into the house before their lordships and after he had ben herd what he was able to saie in his owne behalfe concerninge the bill the same was read the second tyme, vizt. Billa an act concerninge a lease of greate yearelie valew procured to be passed from hir Maiestie by William Kirkham. 2da vice lecta and commanded to be engrossed: vide antee: no. 131 et postea no. 149.

143. Billa intituled An act for repressing of offences that are of the nature of stealthe etc. was returned to the house by the Earl of Essex firste of the Committees with certaine amendements, which (amendementes – *interlineated*) weare presentlie thrice read and sent by Mr Serieant Drew and Mr Dr stanhope to the lower house for their consideracion.

144. A mocion made that a proviso should be added to the bill concerninge the Bishopprick of Norwich: which proviso was presentlie drawen in the house by Mr Attorny and therupon read; And for the more expedicion in the proceedinge of the bill it was thought meete that the lord Archbishop of Canterbury, Lord Marshall, Lord Admirall, Bishop of London, Lord Chamberlaine and Lord Cobham should conferre with a competent nomber of the lower house about the said proviso: wherupon mr Serieant Drew and mr Attorny weare sent to the lower house to signifie the same; who presentlie assented to a meetinge and made their repaire to their Lordships accordinglie forthwith: vide antea no. 114 et (137 – *deleted*) 128 et no. 137 et no. 150.

145. Billa an act for the avoidinge of bringinge of Pynnes made and wrought in forraine partes beyond the seas into this realme of England. prima vice lecta.

---

[9] According to *D'Ewes*, p. 537 the names of the committees were: Lord Treasurer, Earl of Essex (Earl Marshal), Earl of Nottingham (Lord Admiral), Earl of Northumberland, Earl of Shrewsbury, Bishop of Winchester, Bishop of Bath and Wells, Bishop of Chester, Lord Evers, Lord North, Lord St John and Lord Buckhurst with as assistants the Lord Chief Justice of the Common Pleas, Mr Justice Clench, Serjeant Drew and the Attorney General.

146. Quatuor billae allatae a domo communi, vizt.:

1. An act for costes in a prohibicion. prima vice lecta
2. An act to prevent doble paiment upon shopp bookes prima vice lecta.
3. An act for the enlarging of the statute made for followinge of Hue and crie in the 27 yeare of hir Maiestys raigne in some sort to releive the inhabitantes of the small Hundred of Beyuersh alias Benherst in cases where they are in no voluntarie default and yet are or shalbe charged by the same statute, and by the two auncient statutes, the one made the 13 of King Edward the first, the other in the 28 yeare of King Edward the third for repressing of robberies.
4. An act for confirmacion and better assurance and conveiance of certaine mannours, landes, tenementes and hereditamentes given and intended to an Hospitall or Meason de deiu in Warwick founded and established by the Earl of Leicester. vide postea no. 149.

147. Dominus Custos magni Sigilli continuavit presens Parliamentum usque in diem crastinum. hora 9a.

[Thursday, 19 January 1597/98]

[p. 293]

160. Die Jovis 19° die Januarii.

Billa an act for reformacion of certaine abuses touchinge wine Caske; 2da vice lecta, and referred to committees appointed to meete at the litle counsaile chamber at the court at whitehall by 3 in the after noone.[10]

161. Certaine amendementes and a proviso brought into the house and delivered by the Lord Archbishop of Canterbury, firste of the Committees upon the bill of mainteinance of husbandry etc. and the same twice read and commanded to be engrossed:

[p. 294]

162. Answeare returned in wrightinge from the lower house and delivered by certaine knightes and burgesses sent for that purpose unto the obieccions taken by their lordes [*sic*] to somme pointes of the bill intituled. An act for the encrease of people for the service and defence of the realme, which obieccions also weare formerlie delivered unto them in wrighting upon their request made to their Lordships.

163. Certaine selected persons of the lower house vizt. Sir William Knollis and Sir Edward Hobby Knightes, with divers others comming from the said lower house delivered a message signifienge that the Knightes and burgesses desiered to receave satisfaccion from the lordes concerning an innovacion (as the said knightes and burgesses supposed) Vearie latelie begoon in the upper house in deliverie of an answeare from the lordes by the mouth of the Lord Keeper, in other forme and manner then was pretended by the Knightes and burgesses to have ben in former times used, and as they

---

[10] According to *D'Ewes*, p. 539 the names of the committees were: Lord Burleigh (Lord Treasurer), Earl Marshal, Earl of Nottingham (Lord Admiral), Bishop of Rochester, Bishop of Chichester, Lord North, Lord Buckhurst, Lord Howard de Walden with as assistants Mr Justice Owen and Mr Serjeant Drew.

did interprete it, to the preiudice and derogation of the libertie of the lower house. For whereas on the 14 of this instant, Sir Walter Raleigh Knight with divers others of the lower house weare sent up to the lordes to deliver a certaine message to the house, after consultacion had theron by the lordes and after significacion given to the said Sir Walter Raleigh and the rest (staienge in the owtward roome for aunsweare) that they might comme in to receave the same, yt was thought meete, that the Lord Keeper should deliver the said aunsweare sitting in his place, and all and every of the lordes keeping their places; and not goinge downe to the Barre, as the use and forme is when the lordes receave either Billes or message from the lower howse; and as the Lord Keeper had doon once or twice before by error, or not attendinge the formalitie and order of the howse in that poynt. This was the excepcion taken by the message delivered this daye from the Knightes and Burgesses of the lower howse, wherin they desiered to receave satisfaccion as is above mencioned.

Upon which message the lordes having consulted and delivered their opinions touching the said order and custome of the house as it had ben observed and particularly noated and remembered by some of them that weare the most auncient and of longest continuance in Parliamentes, and especially by the Lord (Treasurer – *deleted*) Burleigh Lord Treasurer the most auncient Parliament man, of any that are at this present either of the upper or lower house, And likewise by the Lord Archbishop of Canterbury and by the Lord Admirall, the Lord North the Lord Buckhurst and others that had ben present in manie Parliamentes; It was resolved that the order and usage of the house was and is That when anie Billes or messages be brought from the lower howse to be preferred to the upper howse, the Lord Keeper and the rest of the Lordes are to arrise from their places, and to go downe to the barre, there to meete such as comme from the lower howse, and from them to receave in that place their messages or Billes: But contrairiwyse when anie aunsweare is to be delivered by the Lord Keeper in the name and behalfe of the house to such Knightes and Burgesses as come from the lower howse; the said Knightes and Burgesses are to receave the same standinge forward the lower ende of the howse without the Barre, And the Lord Keeper is to deliver the same sittinge in his place with his head covered, and all the lordes keepinge their places; and that, whensoever it had ben otherwise doon, the same was an error, and mistaking, and therefore not to be drawen into example or president; as it was acknowledged by the Lord Keeper this day, and the rest of the lordes that the going of the said Lord Keeper and the rest of the lordes from their places to the Barre some fewe daies before once or twice to give answear to somme of the lower howse (wherof the lower howse seemed to take some advantage) was only miscognizance, or rather for want of dew rememberance at that present of the order and custome of the howse, wherunto their lordships (havinge regard rather to dispatch of matters of importance in the house then to formalities) weare not greatlie intentive. This to have ben the auncient usage of the howse, and that the same ought still to be was concluded by common and general consent, and the lordes both upon particuler rememberances and observacions of the like course and order holden afore time by other lordes that held the place in the howse of Lord Chaunceller or Lord Keeper, and also by divers reasons produced and alleaged to prove and shew, that the said order doth best stand with the dignitie and gravitie of the howse and with the conveniencie and aptnesse for dispatch of affaires appertaininge to the Parliament, And that the contrarie course, is both undecent and inconvenient.

[p. 295]

This beinge so resolved and concluded, it was agreed, that Mr Attorny generall and Mr Serieant Drew should goe downe to the lower howse, and signifie from the lordes to the Knightes and Burgesses, that if they would send anie of that howse up to the lordes to receave answeare unto their aforesaid demaunde, aunsweare should be given them, Wherunto the said Knightes and Burgesses returned significacion of their assent, by the said Mr Atturny generall and Mr Serieant Drew And within veary litle tyme after sent upp accordinglie the same persons or divers of them who before had ben sent to demaund satisfaccion But being comme into the howse, and having placed themselves at the lower ende of the roome (as at other times they accustumed) expectinge that the Lord Keeper and the rest of the lordes would comme from their places and meete them at the barre to deliver them aunsweare When the Lord Keeper moved them to comme neerer to receave aunsweare and when they perceaved that the lordes weare resolved not to comme from their places to the barr, they protested by the mouth of Sir William Knowllis that they had no commission to receave aunsweare in that forme, and so refusing to receave any aunsweare departed.

The question and difference thus remayninge betwixt the howses, it was afterward (upon a mocion sent downe from the lordes, to the lower howse) agreed on both partes that a conference should be had, and that the aforesaid selected persons of the lower house or so many of them as should be needefull should meete with divers of the lordes of the upper howse (being nominated by the howse for that purpose) in the owtward great chamber before the Chamber of Parliament presence to debate the matter and bring it to a conclusion, which meetinge and conference beinge assented unto, and afterwards accordinglie there performed on the [blank in MS] of January and the question debated, and the reasons and observacion of former tymes for the aforesaid order and Custom of the howse being alleaged by the Lord Archbishop of Canterbury the Lord Treasurer Lord Admirall, Lord North and the Lord Buckhurst that (had – *interlineated*) ben present in many parliamentes (and especiallie by the Lord Treasurer the most auncient Parliament man) it was found and resolved that the order and custome of the howse was, as is above wrightten, Videlicet, That when any Billes or messages are brought from the lower howse to be presented to the upper howse, The Lord Keeper and the rest of the lordes, are to arrise from their places, and to go downe to the Barr, there to meete such as comme from the lower howse, and from them to receave in that place their messages or Billes, But contrariwise when anie aunsweare is to be delivered by the Lord Keper, in the name and behalfe of the howse, to such Knightes and Burgesses as comme from the lower howse, the said Knightes and Burgesses are to receave the same, standing toward the lower ende of the howse without the barr; and the Lord Keeper is to deliver the same sittinge in his place with (his – *interlineated*) head covered, and all the lordes keeping their places, And hereupon the lower howse was satisfied; and the same forme was afterward kept accordinglie.

164. Dominus Custos magni Sigilli continuavit presens Parliamentum usque in diem crastinum hora nona.

[Friday, 20 January 1597/98]

165. Die Veneris 20 die Januarii.

The aunsweare in wrightinge that came yesterday from the lower howse, to the obiections taken by their lordes to somme pointes of the Bill, intituled An act for the encrease of people, for the service and defence of the realme, was by order of the howse referred and delivered to the lordes Committees formerlie appointed upon that bill, who weare requiered to consider therof, and to make their report of their opinions concerninge the same.

166. Billa, an Act for punishment of Roages, Vagabondes and sturdie Beggers: prima vice lecta.

The former bill of that nature reiected in the lower howse.

Billa an act for the mainteinance of Husbandry and Tillage (3a vice lecta – *interlineated*) and the amendementes and Proviso 3 read together with the bill. Returned to the lower howse for their consideracion of the amendementes and proviso and delivered by Mr Attorny generall and Mr Doctor stanhope.

Billa an act for the reforminge of sondrie abuses committed by soldiers and others in hir maiestys services concerninge the warres. prima vice lecta. The former bill of this nature, having bin considered of by the committees, was by them refused for many defectes found therin, and this preferred to the howse in steede therof.

[p. 296]

167. The howse havinge not tyme to heare the Counsell learned on the behalfe of George Ognell, and those that followe the bill for the Hospitall of Warwick, as was formerlie appointed; a new tyme was appointed for the hearing of the same vizt. monday morninge nexte.

168. Quatuor billae allatae a domo communi presented by Sir William Knollis and others vid.

1. An Act to reforme deceipt and breaches of trust, touching landes given to charitable uses: prima vice lecta.
2. An act for the repealing of a branch of the statut made in the 34 yeare Henry 8 intituled The ordinance for Wales prima vice lecta.
3. An act for Arthur Hatch hir maiestys warde for the enioieng of the Rectori and Parsonage of Southmalton in the county of Devon for certaine yeares, reserving the usuall rent. Returned with their allowance. Expedita.
4. An act for the establishing of the Bishopprick of Norwich and the possessions of the same, against a certaine pretended title made therunto: Returned with their allowance of the Proviso added by the lordes. Expedita.

169. Dominus Custos magni Sigilli continuavit presens Parliamentum usque in diem crastinum, hora nona.

[Saturday, 21 January 1597/98]

170. Die Sabbathi 21 die Januarii.

Billa an act for the reforming of sondry abuses committed by Soldiors and others used in hir maiestys services in the warres: 2da vice lecta and referred to Committees etc.

Billa an act for the repealing of a branch of the Statute made in the 34 yeare Henry 8 intituled the Ordinance of Wales. 2da vice lecta and referred to committees etc.[11]

Billa an act to reforme deceiptes and breaches of trustes touchinge landes given to charitable uses: 2da vice lecta and referred to Committees etc.

Billa an act for punishment of Roages, vagabundes and sturdie beggers 2da vice lecta and referred to the Committees upon the bill of like effect vid. An act for erecting of houses of correccion, and punishment of Roages, vagabundes and sturdie beggers (which was reiected by the lower howse) addinge the Lord Marshall to the former Committees, appointed to meet etc. before the howse sitt in the morninge.

171. The parties on both sides concerning the Bill of Edward Mullineux weare openly herd by their councell learned; and therupon the said bill referred to Committees etc.

172. Dominus Custos magni Sigilli continuavit presens Parliamentum usque in diem Lune viz. 23 Januarii hora nona.

[Monday, 23 January 1597/98]

173. Die Lune 23 die Januarii.

Billa an act for establishing a iointure to Anne Lady Wentwoorth; prima vice lecta.

Billa an act for the confirmacion of statutes acknowledged in the towne corporate of Newcastle upon Tyne. prima vice lecta.

Billa an act for the enlarginge of the statute made for followinge of Hue and Crie in the 27 yeare of hir maiestys raigne in some sort to releeve the Inhabitantes of the small hundred of Beynersh alias Benherst etc. tertia vice lecta et Expedita.

174. Allatae sunt a domo communi quinque billae: vizt.

1. An act for naturalizing of certaine English mens children and others borne beyond the seas; Returned with allowance of the amendementes: Expedita.
2. An act for releife of the poore: Returned with allowance of the amendementes: Expedita.
3. An act for repressing of offences that are of the nature of stealth, and are not felonies, by the lawes of the realme Returned with allowance of the amendementes; Expedita.
4. An act for the revivinge, continuance, explanacion, perfectinge and repealing of divers statutes. Expedita.
5. An act against lewde and wandering persons pretending themselves to be soldiers or mariners. Expedita.

[p. 297]

175. Committees appointed to conferre with a competent number of the lower howse concerninge the bill intituled, An act for the encrease of peaple for the service and defense of the Realme, The meeting desired to be tomorrow morninge the 24 of this

---

[11] According to *D'Ewes*, p. 541 the names of the committees were: Archbishop of Canterbury, Lord Marshal, Earl of Shrewsbury, Earl of Worcester, Bishop of Worcester, Bishop of Landaff, Bishop of Chester, Lord Delawarr, Lord Rich, Lord Chandois and Lord Compton with as assistants the Lord Chief Baron and Mr Baron Evers.

instant before the howse sitt; which the lower howse assented unto: vizt. the Earl of Shrewsburie, Lord Vicount Bindon, 2 Bishops and 2 Barons.

The Committees that weare appointed for conference the 12 of December upon the bill concerninge Tellors Receavors etc: were now appointed to meete (adding the Lord Marshall) tomorrow etc: The meeting allso assented unto by the lower howse with a competent number of them.

176. The Councill learned on the part of George Ognell, and on the behalfe of the hospitall in Warwick etc. weare openly herd in the howse.

177. Excuse made by the Bishop of London for the Bishop of Norwich in regard of his unhealthiness.

The Committees on the bill for punishment of Roages, Vagabondes etc. returned the same to the house with somme amendementes by the Lord Archbishop of Canterbury and the Lord chief Justice requiered to consider of the amendementes.

178. Allatae sunt a domo communi duae billae; presented by Sir Robert Cecill and others:

1. An act that lessees may enioy their leases against all Patentees, their heires and assignees, notwithstanding anie default of paiment of their rentes, duringe the time that the reversion or inheritance remained in the crowne.
2. An act that no person robbinge any house in the day tyme, although no person be therin, shalbe admitted to have the benefitt of his clergie.

179. Dominus Custos magni Sigilli continuavit presens parliamentum usque in diem crastinum hora nona.

[Wednesday, 25 January 1597/98]

[p. 298]

183. Die mercurii 25 die Januarii.

Billa, an act, that no person robbinge anie house in the day tyme, although no person be therin shalbe admitted to have the benefit of his clergie. 2da vice lecta.

Billa an act for revivinge, continuance, explanacion, perfectinge and repealinge of divers statutes. 2da vice lecta and referred to Committees etc.

Billa an act that Lessees may enioie their leases against all Patentees, their heirs and assignees, notwithstandinge anie default of payment of their rentes, duringe the time that the reversion or enheritance remained in the crowne. 2da vice lecta and referred to Committees, vizt. Archbishop of Canterbury, Lord Treasurer, Lord Marshall etc. appointed to meete etc. Lord chief Justice, Lord chief Baron, mr Serieant Drew, mr Attorny generall to attend: Sir Moyle Fynch to be herd by his counceill learned, openly in the house tomorrowe morninge concerninge this bill.

184. Allatae sunt 4 billae a domo communi vizt.

1. An act for mainteinance of husbandry and tillage: Expedita.

2. An act for establishinge an awarde made betweene Edmund Cotton gentleman and Thomas Harvey yoman for the assurance of certaine landes in the countie of Norfolk to Thomas Ponyett and his heirs.

3. An act to restraine the excessive makinge of malt.

4. An act to prohibite the carrienge of the herryinges beyond the seas.

185. An act for reforminge of sondrie abuses committed by Soldiers and others used in hir maiestys services concerning the warres, 3a vice lecta.

Billa an act against lewd and wanderinge persons pretending themselves to be soldiers or mariners: 2da vice lecta, and committed.

186. The Lord marshall enforminge that the Committees upon the bill For the lawfull makinge of Baies etc. had not tyme at the day formerly assigned: and moving for a new day to be appointed for their meeting: the house appointed that the said Committees shall meete for that purpose, this afternoone at the said Lord Marshalls chamber.

Notice given to the house by the Lord Treasurer that the Committees upon the bill concerning Tellors, Receavers etc. had meetinge with a select number of the lower howse to conferre upon the obiections and answeares touching that Bill, yesterday in the afternoone according to the order taken the 23 January. But forasmuch as the said number of the lower howse at the meetinge affirmed that they had no authoritie to undertake the debatinge of the said objections and answeares (otherwise then to speake as the [*sic*] should see cause as private men) and desiered that the aunsweares might be communicated to the lower house in wrightinge; The lordes therefore sent downe the said answeares to the lower house by the handes of Mr Attorny and mr Dr stanhope.

The Committees upon the bill concerninge the drayninge of wast and marsh groundes etc. appointed to meete at the Lord Marshalls chamber, this day by 2 of the clocke in the afternoone.

The amendementes upon the bill for punishment of Roages, vagabundes etc. twice read, and theruppon the bill with the said amendementes commanded to be engrossed:

187. Dominus Custos magni Sigilli continuavit presens parliamentum usque in diem crastinum hora octava.

[Thursday, 26 January 1597/98]

188. Die Jovis 26 die Januarii.

Billa an act for enabling Edmund Molineux to sell landes for the paiment of his debtes etc. was returned to the house by the Lord Marshall 2d of the Committees. And forasmuch as the same could not be determined by the said committees by reason of somme of the kindred of the said Edmund Molineaux, who opposed themselves against the bill: A mocion was therefore made that the cause might be ended by somme arbitrarie course, wheruppon the parties of both sides weare called into the house and moved to that purpose, unto which they assented And made choice of the Earl of Rutland, the Lord Bishop of London and the Lord Mountioy appointed to meete this afternoone etc.

[p. 299]

189. Billa an act to prohibite the carrienge of herringes beyond the seas: prima vice lecta.

Billa an act for the confirmacion, better assurance and conveiance of certaine mannours etc. given or intended to an Hospitall or Meason [sic] de dieu in Warwick founded by the late Earle of Leicester, 3a vice lecta. Expedita.

Billa an act that no person robbing any howse in the day tyme although etc. 3a vice lecta. Expedita.

Billa an act to restraine the excessive makinge of malt. prima vice lecta.

Billa an act for punishment of Roges, vagabundes and sturdy beggars, 3a vice lecta and sent to the lower (house *omitted*) by Sergeant Drew and mr Attorny generall.

Billa, an act against the decaieng of townes and houses of husbandry: prima vice lecta.

Billa an act for the lawfull making of baies etc. returned by the Lord Marshall: 2d of the Committees with a proviso thought meete to be added, which proviso was twice read and commaunded to be engrossed:

Billa an act to reforme deceiptes and breaches of trust towching landes given to charitable uses, returned to the howse by the Lord Archbishop first of the Committees; with somme amendementes and a Proviso, thought meete to be added; which weare twice read, and therupon commaundement given, that the saide amendementes shulde be wrightten in paper and the proviso engrossed in parchment ready for a third readinge.

Upon mocion by the Lord Marshall that the committees on the bill, An act against lewd and wanderinge persones etc.: had not convenient tyme this morninge to perfect the said bill accourding to the order of the howse agreed upon yesterday, their Lordships appointed the said committees to meete againe upon the same to morrow morninge before the house sitt.

The bill intituled, an act for the encrease of people for the service and defence of the realme, returned to the house by the Earl of Shrewsbury first of the Committees; And because it seemed to all the Committees appointed for this bill [together with the Judges] that notwithstanding the conference, with diverse selected persons of the lower house, this bill could not proceede; order was given to the Judges and especially to the Lord chief Justice to draw a new bill; wherupon this new bill following was brought into the house vizt. An act against decaieng of townes and houses of husbandry prima vice lecta.

The bill against carrienge of Peltes etc. returned to the house by the Lord Marshall.

201. Excuse made by the Lord Admyrall for the Earl of Hertfordes absence for want of health: The like excuse by the Lord Chandois for the Lord Lawarr. The Lord Marshall signified to the house that the Lord Mordant and the Lord Sheffeild have leave of hir maiestie for their absence.

202. Dominus Custos magni Sigilli continuavit presens parliamentum usque in diem crastinum hora octava.

[Friday, 27 January 1597/98]

203. Die Veneris 27 die Januarii.

Billa an act to prohibite the carrienge of herringes beyond the seas: 2da vice lecta. nota: no mencion that it was committed.

Billa an act to restraine the excessive making of malt: 2da vice lecta and committed.

Billa an act against the decaieng of townes and howses of husbandrye. 2da vice lecta. Certaine amendementes upon this bill drawen by the Lord chief Justice and allowed by the howse, weare also twice read; and therupon the bill with the said amendementes commanded presently to be engrossed.

Billa an act touchinge the makinge of short, broad, course, colored clothes in the counties of Suffolk and Essex. 2da vice lecta and committed etc. appointed to meete at the Lord Chamberlaines chamber at the court of Whitehall etc.

Billa an act to reforme deceiptes and breaches of trust touching landes given to charitable uses. 3a vice lecta. And returned to the lower house by mr Serieant Drew and mr stanhope for their allowance of the said amendementes.

Billa an act for the explanacion of a branche of a statute of the first yeare of hir maiestys raigne intituled, An act against the carrienge of sheepe skynnes and Peltes over the seas, not being staple ware: 3a vice lecta and reiected.

204. The Lord Treasurer took his place this day as Baron of Burghley betweene the Lord Buckhurst and the Lord Compton: The Lord Admirall his as Earl of Nottingham betweene the Earl of Lincolne and the Lord Viscount Bindon: The Lord Chamberlaine his place (betw – *deleted*) as Baron of Hunsdon betweene the Lord Chandois, and the Lord St. John of Bletsoe.

205. Dominus Custos magni Sigilli continuavit presens parliamentum usque in diem crastinum hora octava.

[Monday, 30 January 1597/98]

[p. 300]

208. Die Lunae 30 die Januarii.

Billa intituled, An act for Retailing Brokers and other pawne takers returned to the house by the Lord Archbishop, first of the Committees. And bicause the committees found manie defectes therin so that they thought the same unfitt to proceede they therfore together with the said bill presented a new bill intituled as the former, which was prima vice lecta.

Billa an act Touching the making of short broad course colored cloathes, returned to the house by the first of the Committees, and therwithall bycause the same was by the said committees thought defective, a new bill of the same title was likewise presented.

Billa an act to prohibite the carrieng of Hearinges beyond the seas. 3 vice lecta; and reiected.

An act for confirmacion of statutes merchantes acknowledge in the towne corporate of Newcastle upon Tyne. 3a vice lecta, and sent to the lower howse by Dr Carey and Dr stanhopp.

209. Seaven billes sent from the commons howse vizt.

1. An act for the lawfull making of Baies in the counties of Essex and Suffolk; returned with allowance of the Proviso added: Expedita.

2. An act to reforme deceiptes and breaches of trust touching landes given to charitable uses returned with like allowance of a proviso: Expedita.

3. An act for punishment of rogues, vagabundes and sturdie beggers, Returned with an amendement which was presentlie thrice read.

4. An act against lewd and wanderinge persons pretending them selves to be soldiers or maryners. Returned with allowance of an amendement which was added by the Lordes.

5. An act concerninge Garrett de Malynes and John Hunger merchant strangers.

6. An act for establishing the landes given by John Bedfords will, to the perpetuall repaire and amendement of the high waies at Alesburie in the countie of Buckingham according to the said will.

7. An act for confirmacion of the Jointure of the Lady Varney, wyfe of Sir Edward Varney knight Prima vice lecta.

210. Sir Robert Cecyll and other Knights and Burgesses that brought the 7 billes last mencioned moved the howse for a conference, concerninge the bill sent from their lordships intituled An act for reforminge of sondrie abuses committed by soldiors and others used in hir maiestys service concerninge the warres; to which conference the lordes assented, the time and place appointed to morrow in the after noone at the greate councill chamber at the court at Whitehall; The same committees that weare formerlie appointed 16 January with addicion of the Earls of Sussex Shrewsbury and Rutland, the Lordes Zouch and Cobham.

The bill intituled an Act for the enablinge of Edmund Mollineux esquire to sell landes etc. returned to the house by the Earl of Rutland first of the Committees or Arbitrators with amendementes which weare twice read, and agreed that the bill should be engrossed.

A new meeting appointed for the committees upon the bill intituled, An act for reformacion of certein abuses touchinge wine caske, The time and place apointed to morrow morninge at the litle chamber neere the parliament presence.

[p. 301]

Dominus Custos magni Sigilli continuavit presens parliamentum usque in diem crastinum hora nona.

[Tuesday, 31 January 1597/98]

Die Martis ultimo die Januarii.

Committees on the bill concerninge Lessees and Patentees appointed to meete to morrow the first of February in the afternoone at the litle chamber neere the parliament presence, and the Judges requiered then to attende: vide 25 Januarii.

Billa an act for retailinge brokers and other pawne takers: 2da vice lecta, And was referred to the committees of the former bill of that title 14 die Decembris with addicion of somme lordes who mette presentlie about the same, and returned the bill with somme amendementes, which weare presentlie twice read and the bill commaunded to be engrossed.

Billa, An act (intituled – *deleted*) for reformacion of certaine abuses touchinge wine caske, returned by the Earl of Nottingham second of the committees with somme amendementes which weare presentlie twice read and the bill commaunded to be ingrossed.

Billa an act for establishing of the landes given by John Bedfords will to the perpetuall repaire of the high waies of Alesbury in the countie of Buckingham according to the said will. prima vice lecta.

Billa an act for the confirmacion of letters patent granted by the Queens maiestie to the maior etc. of the cittie of Lincoln in the 29 of hir raigne for the taking of statutes acknowledgement of statutes marchantes. prima vice lecta.

Billa an act concerning Garrett de Malynes and John Hunger merchant Strangers: prima vice lecta.

Billa intituled An act for establishinge a iointure to Anne Lady Wentwoorth returned to the house by the Earl of Shrewsbury [blank in MS] of the committees with somme amendementes and a proviso, thought meete to be added, which Amendementes and proviso weare twice read, and the bill commanded to be engrossed.

A mocion from the lower house by Sir John Fortescue and others, that somme new tyme might be appointed for conference about the bill intituled An act for reforminge of sondrie abuses committed by soldiers etc. in regard they had appointed somme other meetinge this afternoone for the preparing of a bill of Accomptantes in readines to proceede Their Lordships, having considered of the mocion, made answeare by the Lord Keeper that they wished (for some good consideracions) that the appointed time, vizt. this afternoone might hold for this conference; supposing that if it pleased the committees of the lower house to comme somwhat the sooner this afternoone for this purpose, they might well enough performe both the one and the other.

214. Billa an act for the enhabling of Edmund Mullineux esquire to sell landes for paiment of his debtes and legacies. 3a vice lecta, and sent to the lower house by mr Serieant Drew and Dr Carew:

Billa an act for confirmacion of the iointure of the Lady Varney wife of Sir Edward Varney knight, 2da vice lecta, and committed unto 2 Earls, one Viscount, 3 Bishops and 6 lordes. Serieant Drew to attend, to meete in the litle chamber neere the parliament presence to morrow by 2 in the afternoone.

215. Dominus Custos magni Sigilli continuavit presens Parliamentum usque in diem crastinum hora secunda [*sic*] postmeridianum.

[Monday, 6 February 1597/98]

[p. 303]

233. Die Lunae vizt. (quar – *deleted*) sexto die Februarii.

The bill intituled an act for the confirmacion of letters patent granted by the Queens Maiestie to the Maior etc. of the cittie of Lincoln, etc. returned to the howse by the Earl of Shrewsbury first of the Committees with somme amendementes and a proviso thought meete to be added:

Billa an act, that Lessees may enioye their leases against all Patentees their heires and assignees, returned to the howse by the Lord Archbishop of Canterbury first of the Committees with a proviso thought necessarie to be added:

234. Excuse made by the Lord Marshall for the absence of the Earl of Sussex in regard of his unhealthines. The like excuse made by the Bishop of Roffen, for the Bishop of Coventry and Lichfield.

235. Allatae sunt a domo communi 4 billae presented by Sir William Knollis and others. vizt.

    1. An act for the more speedy paiment of the Queens maiestys debtes, and for the better explanacion of the act made anno 13 of the Queens maiestys raigne intituled An act to make the landes, tenementes, goodes and chattelles of Tellors, Receavors etc. liable to the payment of their debtes. prima vice lecta.

    2. An act against the excesse of apparrell.

    3. An act for confirmacion of the iointure of the Lady Varny, wife of Sir Edward Varney knight returned with their allowance of the amendementes.

    4. An act for the erecting and building of a bridge over the river Wye at Wilton upon Wye neere the towne of Rosse in the countie of Hereford: prima vice lecta.

236. Billa an act for further continuance and explanacion of an act for the necessarie releefe of Soldiers and Maryners made in the 35 yeare of the Queens maiestys raigne. 3a vice lecta, and to the lower howse for their consideracion of somme amendements.

    Billa an act for recovering of 300,000 acres more or lesse etc. in the Isle of Ely and in the counties of Cambridge etc. 3a vice lecta.

    Billa an act concerning the drayning and recoverie from the water of certaine overflowen growndes in the countie of Norfolk: 3a vice lecta.

    The 2 last billes weare sent to the lower house for their consideracion of the amendementes and Provisoes added by their Lordships.

237. Dominus Custos magni Sigilli continuavit presens parliamentum usque in secundam horam post Meridianam.

[Monday, 6 February 1597/98 Afternoon Sitting]

[p. 304]

238. Die Lunae hora secunda postmeridiana 6 Februarii.

    The amendementes and Proviso added by the Committees to the bill for confirmacion of letters patent granted to the Maior etc. of the cittie of Lincolne etc. twice read.

    The proviso added by the lower howse to the bill for confirmacion of the Jointure of Christian Ladie Sandis, read the third tyme, and therupon the bill expedita.

239. Billa an act, for the more speedie paiment of the Queens Maiestys debtes, and for the better explanacion of the act made Anno 13 of the Queens maiestie intituled An act to make the landes, Tenementes, goodes and chattelles of Tellors, Receavors etc. liable to paiment of their debtes. 2da vice lecta.

    An act against excesse of apparell prima vice lecta.

    An act for the erecting and building of a bridge over the river of Wye etc: 2da vice lecta and referred to Committees; appointed to meete at the litle chamber neere the parliament presence to morrowe in the morning before the howse sitt.

240. Dominus Custos magni Sigilli continuavit presens Parliamentum usque in diem crastinum hora nona.

[Tuesday, 7 February 1597/98]

241. Die martis vizt. 7 die Februarii.

Billa an act for the erecting and building of a bridge over the river of Wye etc. returned to the howse by the Lord Marshall first of the Committees, without alteracion, and therupon read 3a vice and Expedita.

Billa an act for the speedie paiment of the Queens maiestys debtes etc. 3a vice lecta and Expedita.

An act against the excesse of apparrell 2da vice lecta and referred to Committees etc. Lord chief Justice, Mr Serieant Drew to attend the lordes appointed to meete presentlie in litle chamber neere the Parliament presence.

242. Tres Billae allatae a domo communi presented by Sir William Knollys, Sir John Fortescue and others, vizt.:

1. An act establishing the landes given by John Bedfordes will to the perpetuall repaire and amendement of the high waies at Alesbury in the countie of Buckingham according to the said will, returned with their allowance of the amendementes and Proviso added by their lordships.
2. An act against the decayeng of townes and howses of husbandry. returned with somme amendementes, which were presentlie once read.
3. An act for amendement of high waies in Sussex, Surrey and Kent: prima vice lecta.

243. Billa an act that leasses maie enioie their leases against all patentees, their heirs and assignees notwithstanding anie default of paiment of their rentes during the time that the reversion or enheritance remayned in the crowne, returned by the Lord chief Justice with some amendementes and a Proviso, thought meete to be added which amendementes and proviso weare once read.

244. A message from their lordships (to the lower howse – *interlineated*) (delivered by mr Serieant Drew and mr Dr Carew) for a conference concerning the bill against Excesse of apparell with a competent nomber of the said howse: The time and place desiered to be this after noone by 2 of the clocke at the great chamber of the upper howse of parliament.

245. Dominus Custos magni Sigilli continuavit presens parliamentum usque in horam secundam postmeridianam.

[Tuesday, 7 February 1597/98 Afternoon Sitting]

246. Die martis bora secunda postmeridiana 7 februarii.

The amendementes on the bill against decayeng of townes and howses of husbandrie, 2da vice lecta.

The amendementes and provisoes thought meete to be added unto the bill concerning Patentees, weare read the second time and therupon commaundement given that the said Provisoes shoulde be engrossed in parchment, and the amendementes wrighten in paper readie for a third readinge.

247. An act for amendement of high waies in the counties of Sussex; Surrey and Kent. 2da vice lecta.

An act for reviving, continuance, explanacion etc. of divers statutes returned, with their allowance of the amendementes and proviso added by their lordships.

248. Dominus Custos magni Sigilli continuavit presens parliamentum usque in diem crastinum.

[Thursday, 9 February 1597/98]

[p. 305]

Die Jovis vizt. 9 Februarii.
Allatae sunt [blank in MS] Billae a domo Communi: vizt.:

1. An act for the further continuance and explanacion of an Act for the necessarie releife of soldiers and maryners made in the 35 yeare of the Queens maiestys raigne that now is, Returned with allowance of the amendementes. Expedita.
2. An act for establishing a iointure to Anne Lady Wentwoorth, now wyfe of William Pope esquire and for the better enabling of the said William Pope to sell certaine of his landes for the paiment of his debtes. Returned with somme amendementes, which weare presentlie 3 read. Expedita.
3. An act for enabling Edmund Molineux esquire to sell landes for the paiment of his debtes and legacies, Returned with somme amendements which weare presentlie thrice read. Expedita.
4. An act for reformacion of retailing Brokers, and other pawne takers. Returned with somme amendementes which weare presently 3 read: Expedita.
5. An act that Leassees maie enioy their leases against all Patentees etc. notwithstanding anie default of paiment of their rentes during the time the reversion etc.: Returned with their allowance of the Amendementes and proviso added by the lordes. Expedita.
6. An act against deceiptfull stretching and taintering of Northern clothe. Returned with their allowance of the amendements and proviso added by their Lordships. Expedita.
7. An act for the Queenes maiestys most gracious and generall and free pardon.

Dominus Custos magni Sigilli continuavit presens parliamentum usque in horam tertiam postmeridianam.

[Thursday, 9 February 1597/98 Afternoon Sitting]

254. Die Jovis hora tertia Postmeridiana 9 Februarii.
Dominus Custos magni Sigilli ex mandato domine Regine tunc [blank in MS] dissolvit presens Parliamentum.

Chapter 3. A List of Representative Peers for Scotland, 1707 to 1963, and for Ireland, 1800 to 1961

Representative Peers for Scotland

The statutory provisions relating to the election of representative peers for Scotland were contained in the Scottish Union with England Act 1707 (1706, c. 7) and the Union with Scotland Act 1707 (6 Ann., c. 78), the Representative Peers (Scotland) Act 1847 (10 and 11 Vict., c. 52) and the Representative Peers (Scotland) Act 1851 (14 and 15 Vict., c. 87). The last election took place in 1959. The representative system was brought to an end by the Peerage Act 1963 (1963, c. 48) which at the same time gave to all peers of Scotland the unrestricted right of membership of the House of Lords.

The representatives were sixteen in number and they were elected for the duration of each parliament. By-elections were held when necessary to fill vacancies when they occurred. The elections were held in Edinburgh with the Lord Clerk Register or the Clerks of Session acting as returning officers. Peers were enabled to vote either in person or by proxy or by sending in a signed list. When the proceedings were complete a return of those elected was sent to the Clerk of the Crown in Chancery for delivery to the House of Lords. The conduct of the elections frequently gave rise to difficulty and controversy, particularly in the eighteenth century and three of the returns were amended by the House of Lords after a review of the proceedings (those for 1708, 1788 (twice) and 1790).

The following list of the 248 Scottish Representative Peers elected at the 167 elections that took place between 1707 and 1959 has been compiled from the returns entered in the House of Lords Journals and the relevant orders of the House amending them. A useful list of dates of elections may be found in J. Fergusson, *The Sixteen Peers of Scotland 1707–1959* (1960), 162–6. Two corrections should, however, be made to this list. The election in 1739 took place on 12 May and not 22 March and that in 1958 took place on 1 October and not 1 September. Where a period of representation ended with a parliament the date of dissolution has been given. Dates of death are given in all cases. Where a peer succeeded to a higher dignity in the peerage of Scotland or obtained by descent or creation a peerage of England, Great Britain or the United Kingdom the relevant details have been noted. Where available, information concerning peers has been taken from *The Complete Peerage*; in other cases from Burke's *Peerage* and from the appropriate volumes of *Who Was Who*.

Representative Peers for Scotland 1707–1963

ABERCORN, 8 E. (cr. V. Hamilton (GB) 24 Aug. 1786)   1761–87
Elected 5 May 1761; 26 Apr. 1768; 15 Nov. 1774; 17 Oct. 1780; 8
    May 1784; adjudged to have ceased to be a representative peer by
    resolution of H.L. 14 Feb. 1787.
Died 9 Oct. 1789.

ABERDEEN, 2 E.   1721–7
 Elected 1 June 1721; 21 Apr. 1722; diss. 5 Aug. 1727.
 Died 30 Mar. 1745.

ABERDEEN, 3 E.   1747–61
 Elected 1 Aug. 1747; 21 May 1754; diss. 20 Mar. 1761.   1774–90
 Elected 15 Nov. 1774; 17 Oct. 1780; 8 May 1784; diss. 11 June 1790.
 Died 13 Aug. 1801.

ABERDEEN, 4 E. (cr. V. Gordon (UK) 1 June 1814)   1806–18
 Elected 4 Dec. 1806; 9 June 1807; 13 Nov. 1812; diss.
  10 June 1818.
 Died 14 Dec. 1860.

ABOYNE, 5 E. (cr. L. Meldrum (UK) 11 Aug. 1815; succ. 1796–1806
  as 9 M. Huntly 28 May 1836)   1807–18
 Elected 30 June 1796; 10 Aug. 1802; diss. 24 Oct. 1806.
 Elected 9 June 1807; 13 Nov. 1812; diss. 10 June 1818.
 Died 17 June 1853.

AIRLIE, 4 E.   1833–49
 Elected 14 Jan. 1833; 10 Feb. 1835; 25 Aug. 1837; 5 Aug. 1841;
  8 Sept. 1847.
 Died 20 Aug. 1849.

AIRLIE, 5 E.   1850–81
 Elected 13 Mar. 1850; 15 July 1852; 14 Apr. 1857; 10 May 1859;
  28 July 1865; 3 Dec. 1868; 18 Feb. 1874; 16 Apr. 1880.
 Died 25 Sept. 1881.

AIRLIE, 6 E.   1885–1900
 Elected 10 Dec. 1885; 20 July 1886; 14 July 1892; 24 July 1895.
 Died 11 June 1900.

AIRLIE, 7 E.   1922–63
 Elected 13 Jan. 1922; 16 Nov. 1922; 10 Dec. 1923; 3 Nov. 1924;
  31 May 1929; 29 Oct. 1931; 15 Nov. 1935; 6 July 1945; 21 Feb.
  1950; 23 Oct. 1951; 23 May 1955; 6 Oct. 1959; representative
  system discontinued 31 July 1963.

ANNANDALE, 1 M.   1709–13
 Name inserted on return for 17 June 1708 by order of H.L. 3 Feb. 1715–21
  1708/09; elected 10 Nov. 1710; diss. 8 Aug. 1713.
 Elected 3 Mar. 1714/15.
 Died 14 Jan. 1720/21.

ARBUTHNOT, 8 V.   1818–20
 Elected 24 July 1818; diss. 29 Feb. 1820.   1821–47
 Elected 2 Aug. 1821; 13 July 1826; 2 Sept. 1830; 3 June 1831; 14 Jan.
  1833; 10 Feb. 1835; 25 Aug. 1837; 5 Aug. 1841; diss. 23 July 1847.
 Died 10 Jan. 1860.

ARBUTHNOT, 14 V. 1945–55
Elected 6 July 1945; 21 Feb. 1950; 23 Oct. 1951; diss. 6 May 1955.
Died 17 Oct. 1960.

ARGYLL, 3 D. see ISLAY, 1 E.

ARGYLL, 4 D. 1761–70
Elected 5 May 1761; 26 Apr. 1768.
Died 9 Nov. 1770.

ATHOLL, 1 D. 1710–15
Elected 10 Nov. 1710; 8 Oct. 1713; diss. 5 Jan. 1714/15.
Died 14 Nov. 1724.

ATHOLL, 2 D. (summ. to H.L. as L. Strange (E) 14 Mar. 1736/37) 1733–41
Elected 21 Sept. 1733; 4 June 1734; diss. 27 Apr. 1741.
Died 8 Jan. 1764.

ATHOLL, 3D. 1766–74
Elected 21 Aug. 1766; 26 Apr. 1768; diss. 30 Sept. 1774.
Died 5 Nov. 1774.

ATHOLL, 4 D. (cr. E. Strange (GB) 18 Aug. 1786) 1780–4
Elected 17 Oct. 1780; diss. 25 Mar. 1784.
Died 29 Sept. 1830.

ATHOLL, 10 D. 1958–63
Elected 1 Oct. 1958; 6 Oct. 1959; representative system
discontinued 31 July 1963.

BALCARRES, 4 E. 1734–6
Elected 4 June 1734.
Died 25 July 1736.

BALCARRES, 6 E. 1784–96
Elected 8 May 1784; 24 July 1790; diss. 20 May 1796. 1802–25
Elected 10 Aug. 1802; 4 Dec. 1806; 9 June 1807; 13 Nov. 1812;
24 July 1818; 11 Apr. 1820.
Died 27 Mar. 1825.

BALFOUR OF BURLEIGH, 6 L. 1876–1921
Elected 22 Dec. 1876; 16 Apr. 1880; 10 Dec. 1885; 20 July 1886;
14 July 1892; 24 July 1895; 5 Oct. 1900; 30 Jan. 1906; 28 Jan.
1910; 15 Dec. 1910; 20 Dec. 1918.
Died 6 July 1921.

BALFOUR OF BURLEIGH, 7 L. 1922–63
Elected 16 Nov. 1922; 10 Dec. 1923; 3 Nov. 1924; 31 May 1929;
29 Oct. 1931; 15 Nov. 1935; 6 July 1945; 21 Feb. 1950; 23 Oct.
1951; 23 May 1955; 6 Oct. 1959; representative system
discontinued 31 July 1963.
Died 4 July 1967.

BALMERINOCH, 4 L.   1710–15
    Elected 10 Nov. 1710; 8 Oct. 1713; diss. 5 Jan. 1714/15.
    Died 13 May 1736.

BELHAVEN AND STENTON, 3 L.   1715–21
    Elected 3 Mar. 1714/15.
    Died 27 Nov. 1721.

BELHAVEN AND STENTON, 8 L. (cr. L. Hamilton (UK)   1819–32
    10 Sept. 1831)
    Elected 18 Mar. 1819; 11 Apr. 1820; 13 July 1826; 2 Sept. 1830;
      3 June 1831; diss. 3 Dec. 1832.
    Died 22 Dec. 1868.

BELHAVEN AND STENTON, 10 L.   1900–20
    Elected 5 Oct. 1900; 30 Jan. 1906; 28 Jan. 1910; 15 Dec. 1910;
      20 Dec. 1918.
    Died 31 Oct. 1920.

BELHAVEN AND STENTON, 11 L.   1922–45
    Elected 13 Jan. 1922; 16 Nov. 1922; 10 Dec. 1923; 3 Nov. 1924;
        31 May 1929; 29 Oct. 1931; 15 Nov. 1935; diss. 15 June 1945.
    Died 26 Oct. 1950.

BLANTYRE, 6 L.   1710–13
    Elected 10 Nov. 1710; diss. 8 Aug. 1713.
    Died 23 June 1723.

BLANTYRE, 11 L.   1806–7
    Elected 4 Dec. 1806; diss. 29 Apr. 1807.
    Died 22 Sept. 1830.

BLANTYRE, 12 L.   1850–92
    Elected 13 Mar. 1850; 15 July 1852; 14 Apr. 1857; 10 May 1859;
      28 July 1865; 3 Dec. 1868; 18 Feb. 1874; 16 Apr. 1880; 10 Dec.
      1885; 20 July 1886; diss. 28 June 1892.
    Died 15 Dec. 1900.

BORTHWICK, 19 L.   1880–5
    Elected 16 Apr. 1880; 10 Dec. 1885.
    Died 24 Dec. 1885.

BORTHWICK, 20 L.   1906–10
    Elected 30 Jan. 1906; 28 Jan. 1910.
    Died 4 Oct. 1910.

BREADALBANE, 1 E.   1713–15
    Elected 8 Oct. 1713; diss. 5 Jan. 1714/15.
    Died 19 Mar. 1716/17.

BREADALBANE, 2 E.   1736–47
    Elected 22 Oct. 1736; 13 June 1741; diss. 18 June 1747.
    Died 23 Feb. 1751/52.

BREADALBANE, 3 E.   1752–68
    Elected 9 July 1752; 21 May 1754; 5 May 1761; diss.   1774–80
      11 Mar. 1768.
    Elected 15 Nov. 1774; diss. 1 Sept. 1780.
    Died 26 Jan. 1782.

BREADALBANE, 4 E. (cr. L. Breadalbane (UK) 13 Nov. 1806;   1784–1806
    M. Breadalbane (UK) 12 Sept. 1831)
    Elected 8 May 1784; 24 July 1790; 30 June 1796; 10 Aug. 1802;
      diss. 24 Oct. 1806.
    Died 29 Mar. 1834.

BREADALBANE, 9 E.   1924–59
    Elected 3 Nov. 1924; 31 May 1929; 29 Oct. 1931;
      15 Nov. 1935; 6 July 1945; 21 Feb. 1950; 23 Oct. 1951;
      23 May 1955.
    Died 5 May 1959.

BUCCLEUCH, 2 D. (rest. as 2 E. Doncaster (E) 22 Mar. 1742/43)   1734–41
    Elected 4 June 1734; diss. 27 Apr. 1741.
    Died 22 Apr. 1751.

BUCHAN, 9 E.   1715–34
    Elected 3 Mar. 1714/15; 21 Apr. 1722; 20 Sept. 1727; diss.
      17 Apr. 1734.
    Died 14 Oct. 1745.

BUTE, 2 E.   1715–23
    Elected 3 Mar. 1714/15; 21 Apr. 1722.
    Died 28 Jan. 1722/23.

BUTE, 3 E.   1737–41
    Elected 14 Apr. 1737; diss. 27 Apr. 1741.   1761–80
    Elected 5 May 1761; 26 Apr. 1768; 15 Nov. 1774; diss.
      1 Sept. 1780.
    Died 10 Mar. 1792.

CAITHNESS, 12 E.   1807–18
    Elected 9 June 1807; 13 Nov. 1812; diss. 10 June 1818.
    Died 16 July 1823.

CAITHNESS, 14 E. (cr. L. Barrogil (UK) 1 May 1866)   1858–68
    Elected 29 June 1858; 10 May 1859; 28 July 1865; diss. 11 Nov.
      1868.
    Died 28 Mar. 1881.

CAITHNESS, 18 E.   1918–29
    Elected 20 Dec. 1918; 16 Nov. 1922; 10 Dec. 1923; 3 Nov. 1924;
      diss. 10 May 1929.
    Died 25 Mar. 1947.

CAITHNESS, 19 E.   1950–63
  Elected 21 Feb. 1950; 23 Oct. 1951; 23 May 1955; 6 Oct. 1959;
  representative system discontinued 31 July 1963.
  Died 8 May 1965.

CARNWATH, 11 E.   1892–1910
  Elected 14 July 1892; 24 July 1895; 5 Oct. 1900; 30 Jan. 1906;
  28 Jan. 1910.
  Died 8 Mar. 1910.

CARNWATH, 13 E.   1935–1941
  Elected 15 Nov. 1935.
  Died 9 Mar. 1941.

CASSILIS, 9 E.   1774–5
  Elected 15 Nov. 1774.
  Died 30 Nov. 1775.

CASSILIS, 10 E.   1776–90
  Elected 14 Nov. 1776; 17 Oct. 1780; 8 May 1784; diss.
  11 June 1790.
  Died 18 Dec. 1792.

CASSILIS, 12 E. (cr. L. Ailsa (UK) 12 Nov. 1806; M. Ailsa (UK)   1796–1806
  10 Sept. 1831)
  Elected 30 June 1796; 10 Aug. 1802; diss. 24 Oct. 1806.
  Died 8 Sept. 1846.

CATHCART, 8 L.   1734–40
  Elected 4 June 1734.
  Died 20 Dec. 1740.

CATHCART, 9 L.   1752–76
  Elected 16 Nov. 1752; 21 May 1754; 5 May 1761; 26 Apr. 1768;
  15 Nov. 1774.
  Died 14 Aug. 1776.

CATHCART, 10 L. (cr. V. Cathcart (UK) 9 Nov. 1807; E. Cathcart   1788–1812
  (UK) 16 July 1814)
  Elected 10 Jan. 1788;[1] 24 July 1790; 30 June 1796; 10 Aug. 1802;
  4 Dec. 1806; 9 June 1807; diss. 29 Sept. 1812.
  Died 16 June 1843.

COLVILLE OF CULROSS, 9 L.   1818–49
  Elected 24 July 1818; 11 Apr. 1820; 13 July 1826; 2 Sept. 1830;
  3 June 1831; 14 Jan. 1833; 10 Feb. 1835; 25 Aug. 1837; 5 Aug.
  1841; 8 Sept. 1847.
  Died 22 Oct. 1849.

---

[1] Name erased from return by order of H.L. 22 Apr. 1788, but restored by further order 28 Apr. 1788.

COLVILLE OF CULROSS, 10 L. (cr. L. Colville of Culross (UK)   1851–85
    31 Dec. 1885; V. Colville of Culross (UK) 12 July 1902)
    Elected 6 Aug. 1851; 15 July 1852; 14 Apr. 1857; 10 May 1859;
        28 July 1865; 3 Dec. 1868; 18 Feb. 1874; 16 Apr. 1880;
        diss. 18 Nov. 1885.
    Died 1 July 1903.

CRAWFORD, 19 E.   1707–10
    Elected 13 Feb. 1706/07; 17 June 1708; diss. 21 Sept. 1710.
    Died 4 Jan. 1713/14.

CRAWFORD, 20 E.   1732–49
    Elected 28 Jan. 1731/32; 4 Jan. 1734; 13 June 1741; 1 Aug. 1747.
    Died 24 Dec. 1749.

DALHOUSIE, 8 E.   1774–87
    Elected 15 Nov. 1774; 17 Oct. 1780; 8 May 1784.
    Died 15 Nov. 1787.

DALHOUSIE, 9 E. (cr. L. Dalhousie (UK) 11 Aug. 1815)   1796–1806
    Elected 30 June 1796; 10 Aug. 1802; diss. 24 Oct. 1806.   1807–18
    Elected 9 June 1807; 13 Nov. 1812; diss. 10 June 1818.
    Died 21 Mar. 1838.

DELORAINE, 1 E.   1715–30
    Elected 3 Mar. 1714/15; 21 Apr. 1722; 20 Sept. 1727.
    Died 25 Dec. 1730.

DUMFRIES, 6 E.   1790–1803
    Elected 24 July 1790; 30 June 1796; 10 Aug. 1802.
    Died 7 Apr. 1803.

DUNDONALD, 4 E.   1713–15
    Elected 8 Oct. 1713; diss. 5 Jan. 1714/15.
    Died 5 June 1720.

DUNDONALD, 11 E.   1879–85
    Elected 11 Mar. 1879; 16 Apr. 1880.
    Died 15 Jan. 1885.

DUNDONALD, 12 E.   1886–1922
    Elected 4 Feb. 1886; 20 July 1886; 14 July 1892; 24 July 1895;
        5 Oct. 1900; 30 Jan. 1906; 28 Jan. 1910; 15 Dec. 1910;
        20 Dec. 1918; diss. 26 Oct. 1922.
    Died 12 Apr. 1935.

DUNDONALD, 13 E.   1941–55
    Elected 8 Jan. 1941; 6 July 1945; 21 Feb. 1950; 23 Oct. 1951;
        diss. 6 May 1955.
    Died 23 May 1958.

DUNDONALD, 14 E.   1959–63
  Elected 6 Oct. 1959; representative system discontinued
    31 July 1963.

DUNMORE, 2 E.   1713–15
  Elected 8 Oct. 1713; diss. 5 Jan. 1714/15.   1727–52
  Elected 20 Sept. 1727; 4 June 1734; 13 June 1741; 1 Aug. 1747.
  Died 18 Apr. 1752.

DUNMORE, 4 E.   1761–74
  Elected 5 May 1761; 26 Apr. 1768; diss. 30 Sept. 1774.   1776–90
  Elected 24 Jan. 1776; 17 Oct. 1780; 8 May 1784; diss. 11 June
    1790.
  Died 25 Feb. 1809.

EGLINTOUN, 9 E.   1710–15
  Elected 10 Nov. 1710; 8 Oct. 1713; diss. 5 Jan. 1714/15.
  Died 18 Feb. 1728/29.

EGLINTOUN, 10 E.   1761–9
  Elected 5 May 1761; 26 Apr. 1768.
  Died 24 Oct. 1769.

EGLINTOUN, 11 E.   1776–96
  Elected 13 June 1776; 17 Oct. 1780; 8 May 1784; 24 July 1790;
    diss. 20 May 1796.
  Died 30 Oct. 1796.

EGLINTOUN, 12 E. (cr. L. Ardrossan (UK) 15 Feb. 1806)   1798–1806
  Elected 15 Aug. 1798; 10 Aug. 1802; diss. 24 Oct. 1806.
  Died 15 Dec. 1819.

ELGIN, 7 E.   1790–1807
  Elected 24 July 1790; 30 June 1796; 10 Aug. 1802; 4 Dec. 1806;   1820–41
    diss. 29 Apr. 1807.
  Elected 11 Apr. 1820; 13 July 1826; 2 Sept. 1830; 3 June 1831;
    14 Jan. 1833; 10 Feb. 1835; 25 Aug. 1837; 5 Aug. 1841.
  Died 14 Nov. 1841.

ELPHINSTONE, 11 L.   1784–94
  Elected 8 May 1784; 24 July 1790.
  Died 19 Aug. 1794.

ELPHINSTONE, 12 L.   1803–7
  Elected 16 June 1803; 4 Dec. 1806; diss. 29 Apr. 1807.
  Died 20 May 1813.

ELPHINSTONE, 13 L. (cr. L. Elphinstone (UK) 21 May 1859)   1833–4
  Elected 14 Jan. 1833; diss. 29 Dec. 1834.   1847–59
  Elected 8 Sept. 1847; 15 July 1852; 14 Apr. 1857; diss. 23 Apr.
    1859.
  Died 19 July 1860.

ELPHINSTONE, 15 L. (cr. L. Elphinstone (UK) 30 Dec. 1885)   1867–85
   Elected 27 Nov. 1867; 3 Dec. 1868; 18 Feb. 1874; 16 Apr. 1880;
   diss. 18 Nov. 1885.
   Died 18 Jan. 1893.

ERROLL, 15 E.   1770–4
   Elected 17 Jan. 1770; diss. 30 Sept. 1774.
   Died 3 July 1778.

ERROLL, 16 E.   1796–8
   Elected 30 June 1796.
   Died 14 June 1798.

ERROLL, 17 E.   1806–7
   Elected 4 Dec. 1806; diss. 29 Apr. 1807.   1818–19
   Elected 24 July 1818.
   Died 26 Jan. 1819.

ERROLL, 18 E. (cr. L. Kilmarnock (UK) 17 June 1831)   1823–31
   Elected 2 Oct. 1823; 13 July 1826; 2 Sept. 1830; diss. 23 Apr.
     1831.
   Died 19 Apr. 1846.

FAIRFAX OF CAMERON, 12 L.   1917–39
   Elected 10 Oct. 1917; 20 Dec. 1918; 16 Nov. 1922; 10 Dec. 1923;
     3 Nov. 1924; 31 May 1929; 29 Oct. 1931; 15 Nov. 1935.
   Died 4 Oct. 1939.

FAIRFAX OF CAMERON, 13 L.   1945–63
   Elected 6 July 1945; 21 Feb. 1950; 23 Oct. 1951; 23 May 1955;
     6 Oct. 1959; representative system discontinued 31 July 1963.
   Died 8 Apr. 1964.

FALKLAND, 10 V. (cr. L. Hunsdon (UK) 15 May 1832)   1831–2
   Elected 3 June 1831; diss. 3 Dec. 1832.
   Died 12 Mar. 1884.

FALKLAND, 12 V.   1894–1922
   Elected 18 July 1894; 24 July 1895; 5 Oct. 1900; 30 Jan. 1906;
     28 Jan. 1910; 15 Dec. 1910; 20 Dec. 1918.
   Died 10 Jan. 1922.

FALKLAND, 13 V.   1922–31
   Elected 16 Nov. 1922; 10 Dec. 1923; 3 Nov. 1924; 31 May 1929;
     diss. 7 Oct. 1931.
   Died 14 July 1961.

FINDLATER, 4 E. see SEAFIELD, 1 E.

FINDLATER, 5 E.   1734–61
   Elected 4 June 1734; 13 June 1741; 1 Aug. 1747; 21 May 1754;
     diss. 20 Mar. 1761.
   Died 9 July 1764.

FORBES, 18 L.   1806–43
  Elected 4 Dec. 1806; 9 June 1807; 13 Nov. 1812; 24 July 1818;
    11 Apr. 1820; 13 July 1826; 2 Sept. 1830; 3 June 1831; 14 Jan.
    1833; 10 Feb. 1835; 25 Aug. 1837; 5 Aug. 1841.
  Died 4 May 1843.

FORBES, 20 L.   1874–1906
  Elected 18 Feb. 1874; 16 Apr. 1880; 10 Dec. 1885; 20 July 1886;
    14 July 1892; 24 July 1895; 5 Oct. 1900; diss. 8 Jan. 1906.
  Died 24 June 1914.

FORBES, 22 L.   1917–24
  Elected 10 Oct. 1917; 20 Dec. 1918; 16 Nov. 1922; 10 Dec. 1923;
    diss. 9 Oct. 1924.
  Died 26 Nov. 1953.

FORBES, 23 D.   1955–63
  Elected 23 May 1955; 6 Oct. 1959; representative system
    discontinued 31 July 1963.

GALLOWAY, 7 E. (cr. L. Stewart of Garlies (GB) 6 June 1796)   1774–90
  Elected 15 Nov. 1774; 17 Oct. 1780; 8 May 1784; diss. 11 June
    1790.
  Died 13 Nov. 1806.

GLASGOW, 1 E.   1707–10
  Elected 13 Feb. 1706/07; 17 June 1708; diss. 21 Sept. 1710.
  Died 31 Oct. 1733.

GLASGOW, 4 E. (cr. L. Ross (UK) 11 Aug. 1815)   1790–1818
  Elected 24 July 1790; 30 June 1796; 10 Aug. 1802; 4 Dec. 1806;
    9 June 1807; 13 Nov. 1812; diss. 10 June 1818.
  Died 6 July 1843.

GLENCAIRN, 14 E.   1780–4
  Elected 17 Oct. 1780; diss. 25 Mar. 1784.
  Died 30 Jan. 1791.

GORDON, 3 D.   1747–52
  Elected 1 Aug. 1747.
  Died 5 Aug. 1752.

GORDON, 4 D. (cr. E. Norwich (GB) 7 July 1784)   1767–84
  Elected 1 Oct. 1767; 26 Apr. 1768; 15 Nov. 1774; 17 Oct. 1780;
    diss. 25 Mar. 1784.
  Died 17 June 1827.

GRAY, 14 L.   1812–41
  Elected 13 Nov. 1812; 24 July 1818; 11 Apr. 1820; 13 July 1826;
    2 Sept. 1830; 3 June 1831; 14 Jan. 1833; 10 Feb. 1835; 25 Aug.
    1837; diss. 23 June 1841.
  Died 20 Aug. 1842.

GRAY, 15 L. 1847–67
  Elected 17 Mar. 1847; 8 Sept. 1847; 15 July 1852; 14 Apr. 1857;
    10 May 1859; 28 July 1865.
  Died 31 Jan. 1867.

HADDINGTON, 6 E. 1716–34
  Elected 28 Feb. 1715/16; 21 Apr. 1722; 20 Sept. 1727; diss.
    17 Apr. 1734.
  Died 28 Nov. 1735.

HADDINGTON, 8 E. 1807–12
  Elected 9 June 1807; diss. 29 Sept. 1812.
  Died 17 Mar. 1828.

HADDINGTON, 10 E. 1859–70
  Elected 10 May 1859; 28 July 1865; 3 Dec. 1868.
  Died 25 June 1870.

HADDINGTON, 11 E. 1874–1917
  Elected 18 Feb. 1874; 16 Apr. 1880; 10 Dec. 1885; 20 July 1886;
    14 July 1892; 24 July 1895; 5 Oct. 1900; 30 Jan. 1906; 28 Jan.
    1910; 15 Dec. 1910.
  Died 11 June 1917.

HADDINGTON, 12 E. 1922–63
  Elected 16 Nov. 1922; 10 Dec. 1923; 3 Nov. 1924; 31 May 1929;
    29 Oct. 1931; 15 Nov. 1935; 6 July 1945; 21 Feb. 1950;
    23 Oct. 1951; 23 May 1955; 6 Oct. 1959; representative system
    discontinued 31 July 1963.

HAMILTON, 4 D. (cr. D. Brandon (GB) 10 Sept. 1711) 1708–12
  Elected 17 June 1708; 10 Nov. 1710.
  Died 15 Nov. 1712.

HOME, 7 E. 1710–13
  Elected 10 Nov. 1710; diss. 8 Aug. 1713.
  Died 1720.

HOME, 8 E. 1741–61
  Elected 13 June 1741; 1 Aug. 1747; 21 May 1754; 5 May 1761.
  Died 28 Apr. 1761.[2]

HOME, 10 E. 1807–41
  Elected 9 June 1807; 13 Nov. 1812; 24 July 1818; 11 Apr. 1820; 13
    July 1826; 2 Sept. 1830; 3 June 1831; 14 Jan. 1833; 10 Feb. 1835;
    25 Aug. 1837; diss. 23 June 1841.
  Died 20 Oct. 1841.

---

[2] The news of his death at Gibraltar on 28 Apr. evidently was not received until after the election had taken place on 5 May.

HOME, 11 E. (cr. L. Douglas (UK) 11 June 1875)   1842–74
   Elected 19 Jan. 1842; 8 Sept. 1847; 15 July 1852; 14 Apr. 1857;
     10 May 1859; 28 July 1865; 3 Dec. 1868; diss. 26 Jan. 1874.
   Died 4 July 1881.

HOPETOUN, 1 E.   1722–42
   Elected 21 Apr. 1722; 20 Sept. 1727; 4 June 1734; 13 June 1741.
   Died 26 Feb. 1741/42.

HOPETOUN, 3 E. (cr. L. Hopetoun (UK) 3 Feb. 1809)   1784–90
   Elected 8 May 1784; diss. 11 June 1790.   1794–96
   Elected 23 Oct. 1794; diss. 20 May 1796.
   Died 29 May 1816.

HYNDFORD, 3 E.   1738–61
   Elected 14 Mar. 1737/38; 13 June 1741; 1 Aug. 1747; 21 May 1754;   1761–7
     diss. 20 Mar. 1761.
   Elected 12 Aug. 1761.
   Died 19 July 1767.

IRWIN, 9 V.   1768–78
   Elected 26 Apr. 1768; 15 Nov. 1774.
   Died 19 June 1778.

ISLAY, 1 E. (succ. as 3 D. Argyll, 4 Oct. 1743)   1707–13
   Elected 13 Feb. 1706/07; 17 June 1708; 10 Nov. 1710; diss. 8 Aug.   1715–61
     1713.
   Elected 3 Mar. 1714/15; 21 Apr. 1722; 20 Sept. 1727;
     4 June 1734; 13 June 1741; 1 Aug. 1747; 21 May 1754;
     diss. 20 Mar. 1761.
   Died 15 Apr. 1761.

KELLIE, 7 E.   1790–6
   Elected 24 July 1790; diss. 20 May 1796.
   Died 8 May 1797.

KELLIE, 9 E.   1804–6
   Elected 14 Nov. 1804; diss. 24 Oct. 1806.   1807–28
   Elected 9 June 1807; 13 Nov. 1812; 24 July 1818; 11 Apr. 1820; 13
     July 1826.
   Died 6 Feb. 1828.

KELLIE, 12 E.   1869–72
   Elected 7 July 1869.
   Died 17 Jan. 1872.

KILSYTH, 3 V.   1710–15
   Elected 10 Nov. 1710; 8 Oct. 1713; diss. 5 Jan. 1714/15. Attainted 17
     Feb. 1715/16.
   Died 12 Jan. 1732/33.

KINNAIRD, 7 L.   1787–90
    Elected 28 Mar. 1787; diss. 11 June 1790.
    Died 11 Oct. 1805.

KINNAIRD, 8 L.   1806–7
    Elected 4 Dec. 1806; diss. 29 Apr. 1807.
    Died 12 Dec. 1826.

KINNOULL, 7 E.   1710–15
    Elected 10 Nov. 1710; 8 Oct. 1713; diss. 5 Jan. 1714/15.
    Died 5 Jan. 1718/19.

LAUDERDALE, 6 E.   1741–4
    Elected 13 June 1741.
    Died 15 July 1744.

LAUDERDALE, 7 E.   1747–61
    Elected 1 Aug. 1747; 21 May 1754; diss. 20 Mar. 1761.   1782–4
    Elected 24 July 1782; diss. 25 Mar. 1784.
    Died 17 Aug. 1789.

LAUDERDALE, 8 E. (cr. L. Lauderdale (UK) 22 Feb. 1806)   1790–6
    Elected 24 July 1790; diss. 20 May 1796.
    Died 15 Sept. 1839.

LAUDERDALE, 11 E.   1867–78
    Elected 21 Mar. 1867; 3 Dec. 1868; 18 Feb. 1874.
    Died 1 Sept. 1878.

LAUDERDALE, 13 E.   1889–1918
    Elected 10 Jan. 1889; 14 July 1892; 24 July 1895; 5 Oct. 1900;
      30 Jan. 1906; 28 Jan. 1910; 15 Dec. 1910; diss. 25 Nov. 1918.
    Died 1 Sept. 1924.

LAUDERDALE, 14 E.   1929–31
    Elected 31 May 1929.
    Died 14 Sept. 1931.

LAUDERDALE, 15 E.   1931–45
    Elected 29 Oct. 1931; 15 Nov. 1935; diss. 15 June 1945.
    Died 17 Feb. 1953.

LEVEN, 5 E.   1707–10
    Elected 13 Feb. 1706/07; 17 June 1708; diss. 21 Sept. 1710.
    Died 6 June 1728.

LEVEN, 7 E.   1747–54
    Elected 1 Aug. 1747; diss. 8 Apr. 1754.
    Died 2 Sept. 1754.

LEVEN, 9 E.   1806–7
    Elected 4 Dec. 1806; diss. 29 Apr. 1807.
    Died 22 Feb. 1820.

LEVEN, 10 E.   1831–60
  Elected 3 June 1831; 14 Jan. 1833; 10 Feb. 1835; 25 Aug. 1837;
    5 Aug. 1841; 8 Sept. 1847; 15 July 1852; 14 Apr. 1857;
    10 May 1859.
  Died 8 Oct. 1860.

LEVEN, 11 E.   1865–76
  Elected 28 July 1865; 3 Dec. 1868; 18 Feb. 1874.
  Died 16 Sept. 1876.

LEVEN, 12 E.   1880–9
  Elected 16 Apr. 1880; 10 Dec. 1885; 20 July 1886.
  Died 22 Oct. 1889.

LEVEN, 13 E.   1891–1906
  Elected 10 Dec. 1891; 14 July 1892; 24 July 1895; 5 Oct. 1900;
    30 Jan. 1906.
  Died 21 Aug. 1906.

LEVEN, 14 E.   1910–13
  Elected 15 Dec. 1910.
  Died 11 June 1913.

LEVEN, 15 E.   1922–47
  Elected 13 Jan. 1922; 16 Nov. 1922; 10 Dec. 1923; 3 Nov. 1924;
    31 May 1929; 29 Oct. 1931; 15 Nov. 1935; 6 July 1945.
  Died 15 Jan. 1947.

LINDSAY, 10 E.   1885–94
  Elected 10 June 1885; 10 Dec. 1885; 20 July 1886; 14 July 1892.
  Died 12 May 1894.

LINDSAY, 12 E.   1917–39
  Elected 10 Oct. 1917; 20 Dec. 1918; 16 Nov. 1922; 10 Dec. 1923;
    3 Nov. 1924; 31 May 1929; 29 Oct. 1931; 15 Nov. 1935.
  Died 14 Jan. 1939.

LINDSAY, 14 E.   1947–59
  Elected 1 July 1947; 21 Feb. 1950; 23 Oct. 1951; 23 May 1955;
    diss. 18 Sept. 1959.

LINLITHGOW, 5 E.   1713–13
  Elected 13 Jan. 1712/13; diss. 8 Oct. 1713.
    Attainted 17 Feb. 1715/16.
  Died 25 Apr. 1723.

LOTHIAN, 2 M.   1707–9
  Elected 13 Feb. 1706/07; 17 June 1708; name erased from return by   1715–22
    order of H.L. 3 Feb. 1708/09.
  Elected 3 Mar. 1714/15.
  Died 28 Feb. 1721/22.

LOTHIAN, 3 M. 1731–61
Elected 19 Feb. 1730/31; 4 June 1734; 13 June 1741; 1 Aug.
1747; 21 May 1754; diss. 20 Mar. 1761.
Died 28 July 1767.

LOTHIAN, 4 M. 1768–74
Elected 21 Dec. 1768; diss. 30 Sept. 1774.
Died 12 Apr. 1775.

LOTHIAN, 5 M. 1778–90
Elected 24 Sept. 1778; 17 Oct. 1780; 8 May 1784; diss.
11 June 1790.
Died 4 Jan. 1815.

LOTHIAN, 6 M. (cr. L. Ker (UK) 17 July 1821) 1817–24
Elected 17 Apr. 1817; 24 July 1818; 11 Apr. 1820.
Died 27 Apr. 1824.

LOUDOUN, 3 E. 1707–31
Elected 13 Feb. 1706/07; 17 June 1708; 10 Nov. 1710; 8 Oct.
1713; 3 Mar. 1714/15; 21 Apr. 1722; 20 Sept. 1727.
Died 20 Nov. 1731.

LOUDOUN, 4 E. 1734–82
Elected 4 June 1734; 13 June 1741; 1 Aug. 1747; 21 May 1754;
5 May 1761; 26 Apr. 1768; 15 Nov. 1774; 17 Oct. 1780.
Died 27 Apr. 1782.

MAR, 23 E. 1707–15
Elected 13 Feb. 1706/07; 17 June 1708; 10 Nov. 1710; 8 Oct.
1713; diss. 5 Jan. 1714/15.
Attainted 17 Feb. 1715/16.
Died May 1732.

MAR, 27 E. 1886–1922
Elected 25 Mar. 1886; 20 July 1886; 14 July 1892; 24 July 1895;
5 Oct. 1900; 30 Jan. 1906; 28 Jan. 1910; 15 Dec. 1910;
20 Dec. 1918; diss. 26 Oct. 1922.
Died 17 June 1930.

MAR AND KELLIE, 13 E. 1876–88
Elected 22 Dec. 1876; 16 Apr. 1880; 10 Dec. 1885; 20 July
1886.
Died 16 Sept. 1888.

MAR AND KELLIE, 14 E. 1892–1950
Elected 14 July 1892; 24 July 1895; 5 Oct. 1900; 30 Jan. 1906;
28 Jan. 1910; 15 Dec. 1910; 20 Dec. 1918; 16 Nov. 1922;
10 Dec. 1923; 3 Nov. 1924; 31 May 1929; 29 Oct. 1931;
15 Nov. 1935; 6 July 1945; diss. 3 Feb. 1950.
Died 3 June 1955.

MAR AND KELLIE, 15 E.   1959–63
Elected 6 Oct. 1959; representative system discontinued
   31 July 1963.

MARCH, 3 E. (succ. as 4 D. Queensberry 22 Oct. 1778;   1761–87
   cr. L. Douglas of Amesbury (GB) 21 Aug. 1786)
Elected 5 May 1761; 26 Apr. 1768; 15 Nov. 1774; 17 Oct. 1780;
   8 May 1784; adjudged to have ceased to be a representative
   peer by resolution of H.L. 14 Feb. 1787.
Died 23 Dec. 1810.

MARCHMONT, 2 E.   1727–34
Elected 20 Sept. 1727; diss. 17 Apr. 1734.
Died 27 Feb. 1739/40.

MARCHMONT, 3 E.   1750–84
Elected 15 Mar. 1749/50; 21 May 1754; 5 May 1761; 26 Apr.
   1768; 15 Nov. 1774; 17 Oct. 1780; diss. 25 Mar. 1784.
Died 10 Jan. 1794.

MARISCHALL, 8 E.   1710–12
Elected 10 Nov. 1710.
Died 27 May 1712.

MONTROSE, 1 D.   1707–10
Elected 13 Feb. 1706/07; 17 June 1708; diss. 21 Sept. 1710.   1715–34
Elected 3 Mar. 1714/15; 21 Apr. 1722; 20 Sept. 1727; diss.
   17 Apr. 1734.
Died 7 Jan. 1741/42.

MORAY, 8 E.   1741–67
Elected 13 June 1741; 1 Aug. 1747; 21 May 1754; 5 May
   1761.
Died 5 July 1767.

MORAY, 9 E. (cr. L. Stuart of Castle Stuart (GB) 4 June 1796)   1784–96
Elected 8 May 1784; 24 July 1790; diss. 20 May 1796.
Died 28 Aug. 1810.

MORTON, 13 E.   1730–8
Elected 17 Nov. 1730; 4 June 1734.
Died 4 Jan. 1737/38.

MORTON, 14 E.   1739–68
Elected 12 May 1739; 13 June 1741; 1 Aug. 1747; 21 May 1754;
   5 May 1761; 26 Apr. 1768.
Died 12 Oct. 1768.

MORTON, 16 E. (cr. L. Douglas of Lochleven (GB) 11 Aug. 1791)   1784–90
Elected 8 May 1784; diss. 11 June 1790.
Died 17 July 1827.

MORTON, 17 E.　　　　　　　　　　　　　　　　　　　　1828–58
　Elected 10 Apr. 1828; 2 Sept. 1830; 3 June 1831; 14 Jan. 1833;
　　10 Feb. 1835; 25 Aug. 1837; 5 Aug. 1841; 8 Sept. 1847;
　　15 July 1852; 14 Apr. 1857.
　Died 31 Mar. 1858.

MORTON, 18 E.　　　　　　　　　　　　　　　　　　　　1859–84
　Elected 10 May 1859; 28 July 1865; 3 Dec. 1868; 18 Feb. 1874;
　　16 Apr. 1880.
　Died 24 Dec. 1884.

MORTON, 19 E.　　　　　　　　　　　　　　　　　　　1886–1935
　Elected 25 Mar. 1886; 20 July 1886; 14 July 1892; 24 July 1895;
　　5 Oct. 1900; 30 Jan. 1906; 28 Jan. 1910; 15 Dec. 1910; 20 Dec.
　　1918; 16 Nov. 1922; 10 Dec. 1923; 3 Nov. 1924; 31 May 1929;
　　29 Oct. 1931.
　Died 8 Oct. 1935.

NAPIER, 8 L.　　　　　　　　　　　　　　　　　　　1796–1806
　Elected 30 June 1796; 10 Aug. 1802; diss. 24 Oct. 1806.　　　1807–23
　Elected 9 June 1807; 13 Nov. 1812; 24 July 1818;
　　11 Apr. 1820.
　Died 1 Aug. 1823.

NAPIER, 9 L.　　　　　　　　　　　　　　　　　　　　1824–32
　Elected 8 July 1824; 13 July 1826; 2 Sept. 1830; 3 June 1831;
　　diss. 3 Dec. 1832.
　Died 11 Oct. 1834.

NORTHESK, 4 E.　　　　　　　　　　　　　　　　　　　1708–15
　Elected 17 June 1708; 10 Nov. 1710; 8 Oct. 1713; diss. 5 Jan.
　　1714/15.
　Died 14 Jan. 1728/29.

NORTHESK, 7 E.　　　　　　　　　　　　　　　　　　1796–1807
　Elected 30 June 1796; 10 Aug. 1802; 4 Dec. 1806; diss.　　　　1830–1
　　29 Apr. 1807.
　Elected 2 Sept. 1830; diss. 23 Apr. 1831.
　Died 28 May 1831.

NORTHESK, 9 E.　　　　　　　　　　　　　　　　　　　1885–91
　Elected 17 Feb. 1885; 10 Dec. 1885; 20 July 1886.
　Died 9 Sept. 1891.

NORTHESK, 10 E.　　　　　　　　　　　　　　　　　　1900–21
　Elected 5 Oct. 1900; 30 Jan. 1906; 28 Jan. 1910; 15 Dec. 1910;
　　20 Dec. 1918.
　Died 5 Dec. 1921.

NORTHESK, 11 E.　　　　　　　　　　　　　　　　　　1959–63
　Elected 6 Oct. 1959; representative system discontinued 31 July 1963.
　Died 7 Nov. 1963.

ORKNEY, 1 E.   1708–37
  Elected 17 June 1708; 10 Nov. 1710; 8 Oct. 1713; 3 Mar.
    1714/15; 21 Apr. 1722; 20 Sept. 1727; 4 June 1734.
  Died 29 Jan. 1736/37.

ORKNEY, 5 E.   1833–74
  Elected 14 Jan. 1833; 10 Feb. 1835; 25 Aug. 1837; 5 Aug. 1841;
    8 Sept. 1847; 15 July 1852; 14 Apr. 1857; 10 May 1859;
    28 July 1865; 3 Dec. 1868; diss. 26 Jan. 1874.
  Died 16 May July 1877.

ORKNEY, 6 E.   1885–9
  Elected 17 Feb. 1885; 10 Dec. 1885; 20 July 1886.
  Died 21 Oct. 1889.

PERTH, 7 E.   1941–51
  Elected 8 Jan. 1941; 6 July 1945; 21 Feb. 1950; 23 Oct. 1951.
  Died 15 Dec. 1951.

PERTH, 8 E.   1952–63
  Elected 2 Apr. 1952; 23 May 1955; 6 Oct. 1959; representative
    system discontinued 31 July 1963.

POLWARTH, 7 L.   1843–67
  Elected 19 July 1843; 8 Sept. 1847; 15 July 1852; 14 Apr. 1857.
    10 May 1859; 28 July 1865.
  Died 16 Aug. 1867.

POLWARTH, 8 L.   1882–1900
  Elected 11 Jan. 1882; 10 Dec. 1885; 20 July 1886; 14 July 1892;
    24 July 1895; diss. 25 Sept. 1900.
  Died 13 July 1920.

POLWARTH, 9 L.   1929–44
  Elected 31 May 1929; 29 Oct. 1931; 15 Nov. 1935.
  Died 24 Aug. 1944.

POLWARTH, 10 L.   1945–63
  Elected 6 July 1945; 21 Feb. 1950; 23 Oct. 1951; 23 May 1955;
    6 Oct. 1959; representative system discontinued 31 July 1963.

PORTMORE, 1 E.   1713–15
  Elected 8 Oct. 1713; diss. 5 Jan. 1714/15.
  Died 2 Jan. 1729/30.

PORTMORE, 2 E.   1734–47
  Elected 4 June 1734; 13 June 1741; diss. 18 June 1747.
  Died 5 July 1785.

QUEENSBERRY, 2 D. (cr. D. Dover (GB) 26 May 1708)   1707–8
  Elected 13 Feb. 1706/07; diss. 15 Apr. 1708.
  Died 6 July 1711.

QUEENSBERRY, 4 D. see MARCH, 3 E.

QUEENSBERRY, 6 M. (cr. L. Solway (UK) 7 June 1833)   1812–32
    Elected 13 Nov. 1812; 24 July 1818; 11 Apr. 1820; 13 July 1826;
      2 Sept. 1830; 3 June 1831; diss. 3 Dec. 1832.
    Died 3 Dec. 1837.

QUEENSBERRY, 9 M.   1872–80
    Elected 7 Mar. 1872; 18 Feb. 1874; diss. 24 Mar. 1880.
    Died 31 Jan. 1900.

QUEENSBERRY, 11 M.   1922–9
    Elected 16 Nov. 1922; 10 Dec. 1923; 3 Nov. 1924; diss. 10 May
      1929.
    Died 27 Apr. 1954.

REAY, 7 L.   1806–7
    Elected 4 Dec. 1806; diss. 29 Apr. 1807.   1835–47
    Elected 10 Feb. 1835; 25 Aug. 1837; 5 Aug. 1841.
    Died 8 July 1847.

REAY, 13 L.   1955–9
    Elected 23 May 1955; diss. 18 Sept. 1959.
    Died 10 Mar. 1963.

ROLLO, 8 L.   1841–6
    Elected 5 Aug. 1841.
    Died 24 Dec. 1846.

ROLLO, 9 L.   1847–52
    Elected 8 Sept. 1847; diss. 1 July 1852.
    Died 8 Oct. 1852.

ROLLO, 10 L. (cr. L. Dunning (UK) 29 June 1869)   1860–8
    Elected 15 Nov. 1860; 28 July 1865; diss. 11 Nov.
      1868.
    Died 3 Oct. 1916.

ROSEBERY, 1 E.   1707–15
    Elected 13 Feb. 1706/07; 17 June 1708; 10 Nov. 1710;
      8 Oct. 1713; diss. 5 Jan. 1714/15.
    Died 20 Oct. 1723.

ROSEBERY, 3 E.   1768–84
    Elected 26 Apr. 1768; 15 Nov. 1774; 17 Oct. 1780; diss. 25 Mar.
      1784.
    Died 25 Mar. 1814.

ROSEBERY, 4 E. (cr. L. Rosebery (UK) 26 Jan. 1828)   1818–30
    Elected 24 July 1818; 11 Apr. 1820; 13 July 1826; diss.
      24 July 1830.
    Died 4 Mar. 1868.

ROSS, 12 L.   1715–22
  Elected 3 Mar. 1714/15; diss. 10 Mar. 1721/22.
  Died 15 Mar. 1737/38.

ROTHES, 9 E.   1708–10
  Elected 17 June 1708; diss. 21 Sept. 1710.   1715–22
  Elected 3 Mar. 1714/15; 21 Apr. 1722.
  Died 9 May 1722.

ROTHES, 10 E.   1723–34
  Elected 13 June 1723; 20 Sept. 1727; diss. 17 Apr. 1734.   1747–67
  Elected 1 Aug. 1747; 21 May 1754; 5 May 1761.
  Died 10 Dec. 1767.

ROTHES, 13 E.   1812–17
  Elected 13 Nov. 1812.
  Died 11 Feb. 1817.

ROTHES, 19 E.   1906–23
  Elected 8 Nov. 1906; 28 Jan. 1910; 15 Dec. 1910; 20 Dec.
    1918; 16 Nov. 1922; diss. 16 Nov. 1923.
  Died 29 Mar. 1927.

ROTHES, 20 E.   1931–59
  Elected 29 Oct. 1931; 15 Nov. 1935; 6 July 1945; 21 Feb.
    1950; 23 Oct. 1951; 23 May 1955; diss. 18 Sept. 1959.

ROXBURGHE, 1 D.   1707–10
  Elected 13 Feb. 1706/07; 17 June 1708; diss. 21 Sept. 1710.   1715–27
  Elected 3 Mar. 1714/15; 21 Apr. 1722; diss. 5 Aug. 1727.
  Died 27 Feb. 1740/41.

ROXBURGHE, 5 D.   1818–20
  Elected 24 July 1818; diss. 29 Feb. 1820.
  Died 19 July 1823.

SALTOUN, 17 L.   1807–53
  Elected 9 June 1807; 13 Nov. 1812; 24 July 1818; 11 Apr. 1820;
    13 July 1826; 2 Sept. 1830; 3 June 1831; 14 Jan. 1833; 10 Feb.
    1835; 25 Aug. 1837; 5 Aug. 1841; 8 Sept. 1847; 15 July 1852.
  Died 18 Aug. 1853.

SALTOUN, 18 L.   1859–86
  Elected 10 May 1859; 28 July 1865; 3 Dec. 1868; 18 Feb. 1874;
    16 Apr. 1880; 10 Dec. 1885.
  Died 1 Feb. 1886.

SALTOUN, 19 L.   1890–1933
  Elected 6 Jan. 1890; 14 July 1892; 24 July 1895; 5 Oct. 1900; 30 Jan.
    1906; 28 Jan. 1910; 15 Dec. 1910; 20 Dec. 1918; 16 Nov. 1922;
    10 Dec. 1923; 3 Nov. 1924; 31 May 1929; 29 Oct. 1931.
  Died 19 June 1933.

SALTOUN, 20 L.   1935–63
   Elected 15 Nov. 1935; 6 July 1945; 21 Feb. 1950; 23 Oct. 1951;
     23 May 1955; 6 Oct. 1959; representative system discontinued
     31 July 1963.

SEAFIELD, 1 E. (succ. as 4 E. Findlater, 1711)   1707–10
   Elected 13 Feb. 1706/07; 17 June 1708; diss. 21 Sept. 1710.   1712–15
   Elected 14 Aug. 1712; 8 Oct. 1713; diss. 5 Jan. 1714/15.   1722–30
   Elected 15 Aug. 1722; 20 Sept. 1727.
   Died 15 Aug. 1730.

SEAFIELD, 6 E.   1841–53
   Elected 5 Aug. 1841; 8 Sept. 1847; 15 July 1852.
   Died 30 July 1853.

SEAFIELD, 7 E. (cr. L. Strathspey (UK) 14 Aug. 1858)   1853–9
   Elected 16 Nov. 1853; 14 Apr. 1857; diss. 23 Apr. 1859.
   Died 18 Feb. 1881.

SELKIRK, 2 E.   1713–15
   Elected 8 Oct. 1713; diss. 5 Jan. 1714/15.   1722–39
   Elected 21 Apr. 1722; 20 Sept. 1727; 4 June 1734.
   Died 13 Mar. 1738/39.

SELKIRK, 4 E.   1787–90
   Elected 28 Mar. 1787; diss. 11 July 1790.   1793–6
   Name inserted on return for 24 July 1790 by order of H.L.
     10 June 1793; diss. 20 May 1796.
   Died 26 May 1799.

SELKIRK, 5 E.   1806–18
   Elected 4 Dec. 1806; 9 June 1807; 13 Nov. 1812; diss.
     10 June 1818.
   Died 8 Apr. 1820.

SELKIRK, 6 E.   1831–85
   Elected 3 June 1831; 14 Jan. 1833; 10 Feb. 1835; 25 Aug. 1837;
     5 Aug. 1841; 8 Sept. 1847; 15 July 1852; 14 Apr. 1857;
     10 May 1859; 28 July 1865; 3 Dec. 1868; 18 Feb. 1874;
     16 Apr. 1880.
   Died 11 Apr. 1885.

SELKIRK, 10 E.   1945–63
   Elected 6 July 1945; 21 Feb. 1950; 23 Oct. 1951; 23 May 1955;
     6 Oct. 1959; representative system discontinued 31 July 1963.

SEMPILL, 18 L.   1910–34
   Elected 28 Jan. 1910; 15 Dec. 1910; 20 Dec. 1918;
     16 Nov. 1922; 10 Dec. 1923; 3 Nov. 1924; 31 May 1929;
     29 Oct. 1931.
   Died 28 Feb. 1934.

SEMPILL, 19 L.   1935–63
    Elected 15 Nov. 1935; 6 July 1945; 21 Feb. 1950; 23 Oct. 1951;
       23 May 1955; 6 Oct. 1959; representative system discontinued
       31 July 1963.
    Died 30 Dec. 1963.

SINCLAIR, 4 L.   1807–31
    Elected 9 June 1807; 13 Nov. 1812; 24 July 1818; 11 Apr. 1820;   1833–59
       13 July 1826; 2 Sept. 1830; diss. 23 Apr. 1831.
    Elected 14 Jan. 1833; 10 Feb. 1835; 25 Aug. 1837; 5 Aug. 1841;
       8 Sept. 1847; 15 July 1852; 14 Apr. 1857; diss. 23 Apr. 1859.
    Died 30 Sept. 1863.

SINCLAIR, 5 L.   1868–80
    Elected 3 Dec. 1868; 18 Feb. 1874; diss. 24 Mar. 1880.
    Died 24 Oct. 1880.

SINCLAIR, 6 L.   1885–1922
    Elected 10 Dec. 1885; 20 July 1886; 14 July 1892; 24 July 1895;
       5 Oct. 1900; 30 Jan. 1906; 28 Jan. 1910; 15 Dec. 1910;
       20 Dec. 1918.
    Died 25 Apr. 1922.

SINCLAIR, 7 L.   1923–57
    Elected 10 Dec. 1923; 3 Nov. 1924; 31 May 1929; 29 Oct. 1931;
       15 Nov. 1935; 6 July 1945; 21 Feb. 1950; 23 Oct. 1951;
       23 May 1955.
    Died 25 Nov. 1957.

SINCLAIR, 8 L.   1959–63
    Elected 6 Oct. 1959; representative system discontinued
       31 July 1963.

SOMERVILLE, 12 L.   1741–7
    Elected 13 June 1741; diss. 18 June 1747.
    Died 14 Dec. 1765.

SOMERVILLE, 13 L.   1793–6
    Elected 7 Aug. 1793.
    Died 16 Apr. 1796.

SOMERVILLE, 14 L.   1796–1807
    Elected 30 June 1796; 10 Aug. 1802; 4 Dec. 1806; diss.
       29 Apr. 1807.
    Died 5 Oct. 1819.

STAIR, 2 E.   1707–8
    Elected 13 Feb. 1706/07; diss. 15 Apr. 1708.   1715–34
    Elected 3 Mar. 1714/15; 21 Apr. 1722; 20 Sept. 1727;   1744–7
       diss. 17 Apr. 1734.
    Elected 12 Oct. 1744.
    Died 9 May 1747.

STAIR, 5 E. 1771–4
  Elected 2 Jan. 1771; diss. 30 Sept. 1774.
  Died 13 Oct. 1789.

STAIR, 6 E. 1793–1807
  Name inserted on return for 24 July 1790 by order of H.L. 1820–1
    10 June 1793; elected 30 June 1796; 10 Aug. 1802;
    4 Dec. 1806; diss. 29 Apr. 1807.
  Elected 11 Apr. 1820.
  Died 1 June 1821.

STORMONT, 7 V. (succ. as 2 E. Mansfield (GB) 20 Mar. 1793) 1754–96
  Elected 21 May 1754; 5 May 1761; 26 Apr. 1768; 15 Nov.
    1774; 17 Oct. 1780; 8 May 1784; 24 July 1790; diss. 20
    May 1796.
  Died 1 Sept. 1796.

STRATHALLAN, 6 V. 1825–51
  Elected 2 June 1825; 13 July 1826; 2 Sept. 1830; 3 June 1831;
    14 Jan. 1833; 10 Feb. 1835; 25 Aug. 1837; 5 Aug. 1841;
    8 Sept. 1847.
  Died 14 May 1851.

STRATHALLAN, 7 V. 1853–86
  Elected 7 Sept. 1853; 14 Apr. 1857; 10 May 1859; 28 July 1865;
    3 Dec. 1868; 18 Feb. 1874; 16 Apr. 1880; 10 Dec. 1885.
  Died 23 Jan. 1886.

STRATHALLAN, 8 V. 1890–3
  Elected 6 Jan. 1890; 14 July 1892.
  Died 5 Dec. 1893.

STRATHMORE, 7 E. 1767–76
  Elected 1 Oct. 1767; 26 Apr. 1768.
  Died 7 Mar. 1776.

STRATHMORE, 8 E. (cr. L. Bowes (UK) 7 Aug. 1815) 1796–1806
  Elected 30 June 1796; 10 Aug. 1802; diss. 24 Oct. 1807–12
    1806.
  Elected 9 June 1807; diss. 29 Sept. 1812.
  Died 3 July 1820.

STRATHMORE, 10 E. 1852–65
  Elected 15 July 1852; 14 Apr. 1857; 10 May 1859; diss.
    6 July 1865.
  Died 13 Sept. 1865.

STRATHMORE, 11 E. (cr. L. Bowes (UK) 1 July 1887) 1870–92
  Elected 4 Aug. 1870; 18 Feb. 1874; 16 Apr. 1880; 10 Dec.
    1885; 20 July 1886; diss. 28 June 1892.
  Died 16 Feb. 1904.

SUTHERLAND, 16 E.   1707–8
   Elected 13 Feb. 1706/07; diss. 15 Apr. 1708.   1715–33
   Elected 3 Mar. 1714/15; 21 Apr. 1722; 20 Sept. 1727.
   Died 27 June 1733.

SUTHERLAND, 17 E.   1734–47
   Elected 4 June 1734; 13 June 1741; diss. 18 June 1747.
   Died 7 Dec. 1750.

SUTHERLAND, 18 E.   1763–6
   Elected 8 Mar. 1763.
   Died 16 June 1766.

TORPHICHEN, 9 L.   1790–1802
   Elected 24 July 1790; 30 June 1796; diss. 29 June
      1802.
   Died 7 June 1815.

TORPHICHEN, 12 L.   1894–1910
   Elected 18 July 1894; 24 July 1895; 5 Oct. 1900; 30 Jan. 1906;   1910–15
      diss. 10 Jan. 1910. Elected 15 Dec. 1910.
   Died 20 July 1915.

TWEEDDALE, 2 M.   1707–8
   Elected 13 Feb. 1706/07; diss. 15 Apr. 1708.
   Died 20 May 1713.

TWEEDDALE, 3 M.   1715–15
   Elected 3 Mar. 1714/15.
   Died 15 Dec. 1715.

TWEEDDALE, 4 M.   1722–34
   Elected 21 Apr. 1722; 20 Sept. 1727; diss. 17 Apr. 1734.   1742–62
   Elected 30 Apr. 1742; 1 Aug. 1747; 21 May 1754;
      5 May 1761.
   Died 9 Dec. 1762.

TWEEDDALE, 7 M.   1796–1804
   Elected 30 June 1796; 10 Aug. 1802.
   Died 9 Aug. 1804.

TWEEDDALE, 8 M.   1818–76
   Elected 24 July 1818; 11 Apr. 1820; 13 July 1826; 2 Sept. 1830;
      3 June 1831; 14 Jan. 1833; 10 Feb. 1835; 25 Aug. 1837; 5 Aug.
      1841; 8 Sept. 1847; 15 July 1852; 14 Apr. 1857; 10 May 1859; 28
      July 1865; 3 Dec. 1868; 18 Feb. 1874.
   Died 10 Oct. 1876.

WEMYSS, 4 E.   1707–10
   Elected 13 Feb. 1706/07; 17 June 1708; diss. 21 Sept. 1710.
   Died 15 Mar. 1719/20.

The statutory provisions relating to the election of representative peers for Ireland were contained in an act of the Irish parliament (40 Geo. III, c. 29) and the Union with Ireland Act 1800 (39 and 40 Geo. III, c. 67). These provisions were subsequently modified by the Representative Peers (Ireland) Act 1857 (20 and 21 Vict., c. 33) and the Election of Representative Peers (Ireland) Act 1882 (45 and 46 Vict., c. 26). The last election took place in 1919. On 24 November 1966 the House of Lords agreed to a report of the Committee for Privileges to the effect that the provisions relating to the election of Irish Representative Peers ceased to be effective on the passing of the Irish Free State (Agreement) Act 1922 (12 and 13 Geo. V, c. 4) and that the right to elect representatives no longer existed.

The representatives were 28 in number and were elected for life. The election of the original 28 peers took place on 2 August 1800 in the Irish House of Lords. All subsequent elections were conducted by post through the agency of the Clerk of the Crown and Hanaper in Ireland. In each case the Clerk made out a return which he delivered to the House of Lords. As stated above, the last election took place in 1919 and no vacancies were filled up after the creation of the Irish Free State in 1922 although those peers already elected remained members of the House of Lords until their deaths. The last representative peer, the 4th Earl of Kilmorey, died in 1961.

The following list of the 159 Irish Representative Peers elected at the 131 elections that took place between 1800 and 1919 has been compiled from the returns entered in the House of Lords Journals. The date of the first election on 2 August 1800 has been taken from the entry in the Journals of the House of Lords of Ireland. The dates of all subsequent elections have been taken from the returns delivered by the Clerk of the Crown and Hanaper. Where a peer was advanced in the peerage of Ireland or had conferred upon him a peerage of the United Kingdom the relevant details have been noted. Where available, information concerning the peers has been taken from *The Complete Peerage*; in other cases from Burke's *Peerage* and from the appropriate volumes of *Who Was Who*.

Representative Peers for Ireland 1800–1961

ALTAMONT, 3 E. (cr. M. Sligo 29 Dec. 1800; L. Monteagle (UK) 20   1800–9
    Feb. 1806)
    Elected 2 Aug. 1800.
    Died 2 Jan. 1809.

ANNESLEY, 4 E.   1867–74
    Elected 15 Oct. 1867.
    Died 10 Aug. 1874.

ANNESLEY, 5 E.   1877–1908
    Elected 28 Apr. 1877.
    Died 15 Dec. 1908.

ASHTOWN, 3 L.   1908–46
   Elected 4 Nov. 1908.[3]
   Died 20 Mar. 1946.

BANDON, 1 V. (cr. E. Bandon 29 Aug. 1800)   1800–1830
   Elected 2 Aug. 1800.
   Died 26 Nov. 1830.

BANDON, 2 E.   1835–1856
   Elected 31 July 1835.
   Died 31 Oct. 1856.

BANDON, 3 E.   1858–1877
   Elected 21 Aug. 1858.
   Died 17 Feb. 1877.

BANDON, 4 E.   1881–1924
   Elected 6 June 1881.
   Died 18 May 1924.

BANGOR, 4 V.   1855–1881
   Elected 9 Jan. 1855.
   Died 14 Sept. 1881.

BANGOR, 5 V.   1886–1911
   Elected 12 Jan. 1886.
   Died 23 Feb. 1911.

BANGOR, 6 V.   1913–50
   Elected 7 Mar. 1913.
   Died 17 Nov. 1950.

BANTRY, 2 E.   1854–68
   Elected 1 July 1854.
   Died 16 July 1868.

BANTRY, 3 E.   1869–84
   Elected 6 July 1869.
   Died 15 Jan. 1884.

BECTIVE, 2 E. (cr. M. Headfort 30 Dec. 1800)   1800–29
   Elected 2 Aug. 1800.
   Died 24 Oct. 1829.

BELLEW, 3 L.   1904–11
   Elected 1 Aug. 1904.
   Died 15 July 1911.

---

[3] The return showed that Lords Ashtown and Farnham had received an equal number of votes. This equality was resolved in favour of the former at the Table of the House of Lords in accordance with the procedure laid down by the Act of Union.

BELLEW, 4 L. 1914–35
 Elected 20 Apr. 1914.
 Died 15 June 1935.

BELMORE, 2 E. 1819–41
 Elected 5 May 1819.
 Died 18 Apr. 1841.

BELMORE, 4 E. 1857–1913
 Elected 13 Jan. 1857.
 Died 6 Apr. 1913.

BLAYNEY, 12 L. 1841–74
 Elected 12 June 1841.
 Died 18 Jan. 1874.

BLESINGTON, 1 E. see MOUNTJOY, 2 V.

CAHER, 10 L. (cr. E. Glengall 22 Jan. 1816) 1800–19
 Elected 2 Aug. 1800.
 Died 30 Jan. 1819.

CALEDON, 2 E. 1804–39
 Elected 26 Nov. 1804.
 Died 8 Apr. 1839.

CALEDON, 3 E. 1841–55
 Elected 8 May 1841.
 Died 30 June 1855.

CALEDON, 4 E. 1877–98
 Elected 30 Oct. 1877.
 Died 27 Apr. 1898.

CALLAN, 1 L. 1800–15
 Elected 2 Aug. 1800.
 Died 29 Oct. 1815.

CARBERY, 6 L. 1824–45
 Elected 30 Jan. 1824.
 Died 12 May 1845.

CARBERY, 8 L. 1891–94
 Elected 3 Aug. 1891.
 Died 7 Nov. 1894.

CARLETON, 1 V. 1800–26
 Elected 2 Aug. 1800.
 Died 25 Feb. 1826.

CARRICK, 3 E. 1819–38
 Elected 13 Mar. 1819.
 Died 4 Feb. 1838.

CASTLEMAINE, 3 L.   1841–69
  Elected 6 July 1841.
  Died 4 July 1869.

CASTLEMAINE, 4 L.   1874–92
  Elected 9 May 1874.
  Died 26 Apr. 1892.

CASTLEMAINE, 5 L.   1898–1937
  Elected 7 Mar. 1898.
  Died 6 July 1937.

CAVAN, 10 E.   1915–46
  Elected 24 Sept. 1915.
  Died 28 Aug. 1946.

CHARLEMONT, 2 E. (cr. L. Charlemont (UK) 13 Feb. 1837)   1806–63
  Elected 12 Dec. 1806.
  Died 26 Dec. 1863.

CHARLEMONT, 8 V.   1918–49
  Elected 19 Aug. 1918.
  Died 30 Aug. 1949.

CHARLEVILLE, 1 V. (cr. E. Charleville 16 Feb. 1806)   1801–35
  Elected 2 Nov. 1801.
  Died 31 Oct. 1835.

CHARLEVILLE, 2 E.   1838–51
  Elected 13 Apr. 1838.
  Died 14 July 1851.

CLANCARTY, 2 E. (cr. L. Trench (UK) 4 Aug. 1815;   1808–37
      V. Clancarty (UK) 8 Dec. 1823)
  Elected 16 Dec. 1808.
  Died 24 Nov. 1837.

CLANRICARDE, 13 E.   1800–8
  Elected 2 Aug. 1800.
  Died 27 July 1808.

CLARINA, 3 L.   1849–72
  Elected 16 Apr. 1849.
  Died 18 Nov. 1872.

CLARINA, 4 L.   1888–97
  Elected 31 Dec. 1888.
  Died 16 Dec. 1897.

CLONBROCK, 3 L.   1838–93
  Elected 20 Feb. 1838.
  Died 4 Dec. 1893.

CLONBROCK, 4 L. 1895–1917
 Elected 21 Jan. 1895.
 Died 12 May 1917.

CLONMELL, 4 E. 1874–91
 Elected 10 Nov. 1874.
 Died 22 June 1891.

CONYNGHAM, 1 E. (cr. M. Conyngham 15 Jan. 1816; 1800–32
 L. Minster (UK) 17 July 1821)
 Elected 2 Aug. 1800.
 Died 28 Dec. 1832.

CROFTON, 2 L. 1840–69
 Elected 21 Jan. 1840.
 Died 27 Dec. 1869.

CROFTON, 3 L. 1873–1912
 Elected 11 Feb. 1873.
 Died 22 Sept. 1912.

CROFTON, 4 L. 1916–42
 Elected 10 Jan. 1916.
 Died 15 June 1942.

CURZON, 1 L. (cr. E. Curzon of Kedleston (UK) 2 Nov. 1911; 1908–25
 M. Curzon of Kedleston (UK) 28 June 1921)
 Elected 21 Jan. 1908.
 Died 20 Mar. 1925.

DARNLEY, 8 E. 1905–27
 Elected 10 Mar. 1905.
 Died 10 Apr. 1927.

DE VESCI, 2 V. 1839–55
 Elected 19 Jan. 1839.
 Died 19 Oct. 1855.

DE VESCI, 3 V. 1857–75
 Elected 10 Jan. 1857.
 Died 23 Dec. 1875.

DE VESCI, 5 V. 1909–58
 Elected 13 Feb. 1909.
 Died 16 Aug. 1958.

DECIES, 5 L. 1912–44
 Elected 18 Nov. 1912.
 Died 31 Jan. 1944.

DESART, 1 E. 1800–4
 Elected 2 Aug. 1800.
 Died 9 Aug. 1804.

DESART, 3 E.   1846–65
   Elected 11 Dec. 1846.
   Died 1 Apr. 1865.

DONERAILE, 3 V.   1830–54
   Elected 15 Mar. 1830.
   Died 27 Mar. 1854.

DONERAILE, 4 V.   1855–87
   Elected 2 May 1855.
   Died 26 Aug. 1887.

DONOUGHMORE, 1 V. (cr. E. Donoughmore 31 Dec. 1800;   1800–25
   V. Hutchinson (UK) 14 July 1821)
   Elected 2 Aug. 1800.
   Died 22 Aug. 1825.

DOWNES, 2 L.   1833–63
   Elected 30 Mar. 1833.
   Died 26 July 1863.

DROGHEDA, 9 E.   1899–1908
   Elected 31 Mar. 1899.
   Died 28 Oct. 1908.

DROGHEDA, 10 E. (cr. L. Moore (UK) 30 Jan. 1954)   1913–57
   Elected 21 Nov. 1913.
   Died 22 Nov. 1957.

DUFFERIN, 2 L.   1820–36
   Elected 7 Oct. 1820.
   Died 8 Aug. 1836.

DUNALLEY, 2 L.   1828–54
   Elected 19 Dec. 1828.
   Died 19 Oct. 1854.

DUNALLEY, 4 L.   1891–1927
   Elected 9 Oct. 1891.
   Died 5 Aug. 1927.

DUNBOYNE, 14 L.   1868–81
   Elected 11 Jan. 1868.
   Died 22 Mar. 1881.

DUNBOYNE, 16 L.   1901–13
   Elected 4 Jan. 1901.
   Died 29 Aug. 1913.

DUNGANNON, 3 V.   1855–62
   Elected 11 Sept. 1855.
   Died 11 Aug. 1862.

DUNRAVEN, 2 E.   1839–50
    Elected 21 Sept. 1839.
    Died 6 Aug. 1850.

DUNSANDLE, 2 L.   1851–93
    Elected 23 Sept. 1851.
    Died 11 Jan. 1893.

DUNSANY, 14 L.   1836–48
    Elected 18 Jan. 1836.
    Died 11 Dec. 1848.

DUNSANY, 15 L.   1850–2
    Elected 19 Nov. 1850.
    Died 7 Apr. 1852.

DUNSANY, 16 L.   1864–89
    Elected 8 Mar. 1864.
    Died 22 Feb. 1889.

DUNSANY, 17 L.   1893–9
    Elected 6 Mar. 1893.
    Died 16 Jan. 1899.

ENNISKILLEN, 2 E. (cr. L. Grinstead (UK) 11 Aug. 1815)   1804–40
    Elected 13 Oct. 1804.
    Died 31 Mar. 1840.

ERNE, 1 E.   1800–28
    Elected 2 Aug. 1800.
    Died 15 Sept. 1828.

ERNE, 3 E. (cr. L. Fermanagh (UK) 13 Jan. 1876)   1845–85
    Elected 24 July 1845.
    Died 3 Oct. 1885.

FARNHAM, 2 E.   1816–23
    Elected 2 Mar. 1816.
    Died 23 July 1823.

FARNHAM, 5 L.   1825–38
    Elected 17 Dec. 1825.
    Died 20 Sept. 1838.

FARNHAM, 7 L.   1839–68
    Elected 2 July 1839.
    Died 20 Aug. 1868.

FARNHAM, 10 L.   1898–1900
    Elected 22 July 1898.
    Died 22 Nov. 1900.

FARNHAM, 11 L.   1908–57
  Elected 18 Dec. 1908.
  Died 5 Feb. 1957.

FRANKFORT DE MONTMORENCY, 3 V.   1900–2
  Elected 5 June 1900.
  Died 7 May 1902.

GLANDORE, 2 E.   1800–15
  Elected 2 Aug. 1800.
  Died 23 Oct. 1815.

GLENGALL, 2 E.   1829–58
  Elected 1 Sept. 1829.
  Died 22 June 1858.

GLENGALL, 1 E., see CAHER, 10 L.

GLENTWORTH, 2 L. (cr. V. Limerick 29 Dec. 1800;   1800–44
    E. LIMERICK 1 Jan. 1803; L. Foxford (UK)
    11 Aug. 1815)
  Elected 2 Aug. 1800.
  Died 7 Dec. 1844.

GORT, 2 V.   1824–42
  Elected 30 Jan. 1824.
  Died 11 Nov. 1842.

GORT, 3 V.   1865
  Elected 13 June 1865.
  Died 20 Oct. 1865.

GOSFORD, 2 E. (cr. L. Worlingham (UK) 13 June 1835)   1811–49
  Elected 19 Aug. 1811.
  Died 27 Mar. 1849.

HAWARDEN, 3 V.   1836–56
  Elected 31 Oct. 1836.
  Died 12 Oct. 1856.

HAWARDEN, 4 V. (cr. E. De Montalt (UK) 9 Sept. 1886)   1862–1905
  Elected 2 Dec. 1862.
  Died 9 Jan. 1905.

HEADFORT, 1 M, see BECTIVE, 2 E.

HEADLEY, 3 L.   1868–77
  Elected 28 Sept. 1868.
  Died 30 July 1877.

HEADLEY, 4 L.   1883–1913
  Elected 20 Dec. 1883.
  Died 13 Jan. 1913.

INCHIQUIN, 13 L.   1863–72
 Elected 20 Oct. 1863.
 Died 22 Mar. 1872.

INCHIQUIN, 14 L.   1873–1900
 Elected 5 Apr. 1873.
 Died 9 Apr. 1900.

INCHIQUIN, 15 L.   1900–29
 Elected 23 Nov. 1900.
 Died 9 Dec. 1929.

KILMAINE, 3 L.   1849–73
 Elected 22 June 1849.
 Died 13 Jan. 1873.

KILMAINE, 4 L.   1890–1907
 Elected 21 Feb. 1890.
 Died 9 Nov. 1907.

KILMAINE, 5 L.   1911–46
 Elected 14 Apr. 1911.
 Died 27 Aug. 1946.

KILMOREY, 3 E.   1881–1915
 Elected 31 Dec. 1881.
 Died 28 July 1915.

KILMOREY, 4 E.   1916–61
 Elected 14 Feb. 1916.
 Died 11 Jan. 1961.

KINGSTON, 3 E. (cr. L. Kingston (UK) 17 July 1821) 1807–39
 Elected 11 July 1807.
 Died 18 Oct. 1839.

KINGSTON, 8 E.   1887–96
 Elected 24 Oct. 1887.
 Died 13 Jan. 1896.

KINGSTON, 9 E.   1917–46
 Elected 13 July 1917.
 Died 11 Jan. 1946.

LANDAFF, 1 E.   1800–6
 Elected 2 Aug. 1800.
 Died 30 July 1806.

LANESBOROUGH, 5 E.   1849–66
 Elected 14 Aug. 1849.
 Died 7 July 1866.

LANESBOROUGH, 6 E.   1870–1905
  Elected 5 Apr. 1870.
  Died 12 Sept. 1905.

LANESBOROUGH, 7 E.   1913–29
  Elected 2 June 1913.
  Died 18 Aug. 1929.

LANGFORD, 4 L.   1884–1919
  Elected 14 Mar. 1884.
  Died 29 Oct. 1919.

LEITRIM, 1 E.   1800–4
  Elected 2 Aug. 1800.
  Died 27 July 1804.

LIFFORD, 4 V.   1856–87
  Elected 23 Jan. 1856.
  Died 20 Nov. 1887.

LIMERICK, 1 E & 1 V. see GLENTWORTH, 2 L.

LONDONDERRY, 1 E. (cr. M. Londonderry 13 Jan. 1816)   1800–21
  Elected 2 Aug. 1800.
  Died 6 Apr. 1821.

LONGFORD, 2 E. (cr. L. Silchester (UK) 17 July 1821)   1800–35
  Elected 2 Aug. 1800.
  Died 24 May 1835.

LONGUEVILLE, 1 L. (cr. V. Longueville 29 Dec. 1800)   1800–11
  Elected 2 Aug. 1800.
  Died 23 May 1811.

LORTON, 1 V.   1823–54
  Elected 8 Feb. 1823.
  Died 20 Nov. 1854.

LUCAN, 2 E.   1800–39
  Elected 2 Aug. 1800.
  Died 30 June 1839.

LUCAN, 3 E.   1840–88
  Elected 22 June 1840.
  Died 10 Nov. 1888.

LUCAN, 4 E.   1889–1914
  Elected 19 Apr. 1889.
  Died 5 June 1914.

LUCAN, 5 E. (cr. L. Bingham (UK) 26 June 1934)   1914–49
  Elected 10 Aug. 1914.
  Died 20 Apr. 1949.

MASSY, 6 L.   1876–1915
    Elected 14 Mar. 1876.
    Died 28 Nov. 1915.

MAYO, 4 E.   1816–49
    Elected 2 Mar. 1816.
    Died 23 May 1849.

MAYO, 5 E.   1852–67
    Elected 22 June 1852.
    Died 12 Aug. 1867.

MAYO, 7 E.   1890–1927
    Elected 14 July 1890.
    Died 31 Dec. 1927.

MILLTOWN, 6 E.   1881–90
    Elected 23 Aug. 1881.
    Died 30 May 1890.

MOUNTCASHELL, 2 E.   1815–22
    Elected 24 Mar. 1815.
    Died 27 Oct. 1822.

MOUNTCASHELL, 4 E.   1826–83
    Elected 1 July 1826.
    Died 10 Oct. 1883.

MOUNTJOY, 2 V. (cr. E. Blesington 12 Jan. 1816)   1809–29
    Elected 15 Apr. 1809.
    Died 25 May 1829.

MUSKERRY, 4 L.   1892–1929
    Elected 13 June 1892.
    Died 9 June 1929.

NORMANTON 1 E, see SOMERTON, 1 L.

NORTHLAND, 1 V.   1800–18
    Elected 2 Aug. 1800.
    Died 5 Nov. 1818.

O'NEILL, 2 V. (cr. E. O'Neill Aug. 1800)   1800–41
    Elected 2 Aug. 1800.
    Died 25 Mar. 1841.

O'NEILL, 3 V.   1843–55
    Elected 31 Jan. 1843.
    Died 12 Feb. 1855.

ORANMORE AND BROWNE, 2 L.   1869–1900
    Elected 6 Sept. 1869.
    Died 15 Nov. 1900.

ORANMORE AND BROWNE, 3 L. (cr. L. Mereworth (UK)   1902–27
 19 Jan. 1926)
 Elected 11 July 1902.
 Died 30 June 1927.

OXMANTOWN, 1 V. (cr. E. Rosse 3 Feb. 1806)   1800–7
 Elected 2 Aug. 1800.
 Died 20 Apr. 1807.

PORTARLINGTON, 3 E.   1855–89
 Elected 24 Oct. 1855.
 Died 1 Mar. 1889.

PORTARLINGTON, 5 E.   1896–1900
 Elected 20 Mar. 1896.
 Died 31 Aug. 1900.

POWERSCOURT, 5 V.   1821–3
 Elected 3 Aug. 1821.
 Died 9 Aug. 1823.

POWERSCOURT, 7 V. (cr. L. Powerscourt (UK) 27 June 1885)   1865–1904
 Elected 26 Dec. 1865.
 Died 5 June 1904.

RATHDONNELL, 2 L.   1889–1929
 Elected 8 Apr. 1889.
 Died 22 May 1929.

RODEN, 2 E.   1800–20
 Elected 2 Aug. 1800.
 Died 29 June 1820.

RODEN, 8 E.   1919–56
 Elected 22 Dec. 1919.
 Died 30 Oct. 1956.

ROSSE, 1 E, see OXMANTOWN, 1 V.

ROSSE, 2 E.   1809–41
 Elected 22 Oct. 1809.
 Died 24 Feb. 1841.

ROSSE, 3 E.   1845–67
 Elected 24 Feb. 1845.
 Died 31 Oct. 1867.

ROSSE, 4 E.   1868–1908
 Elected 22 Dec. 1868.
 Died 29 Aug. 1908.

ROSSE, 5 E.   1911–18
 Elected 9 Oct. 1911.
 Died 10 June 1918.

ROSSMORE, 1 L.   1800–1
   Elected 2 Aug. 1800.
   Died 6 Aug. 1801.

SLIGO, 1 M, see ALTAMONT, 3 E.

SOMERTON, 1 L (cr. V. Somerton 30 Dec. 1800;   1800–9
   E. Normanton 4 Feb. 1806)
   Elected 2 Aug. 1800.
   Died 14 July 1809.

TEMPLETOWN, 3 V.   1866–90
   Elected 14 Sept. 1866.
   Died 4 Jan. 1890.

TEMPLETOWN, 4 V.   1894–1939
   Elected 29 Jan. 1894.
   Died 30 Sept. 1939.

THOMOND, 2 M (cr. L. Tadcaster (UK) 3 July 1826)   1816–46
   Elected 2 Mar. 1816.
   Died 21 Aug. 1846.

TYRAWLEY, 1 L.   1800–21
   Elected 2 Aug. 1800.
   Died 15 June 1821.

VENTRY, 4 L.   1871–1914
   Elected 10 July 1871.
   Died 8 Feb. 1914.

WESTMEATH, 7 E.   1800–14
   Elected 2 Aug. 1800.
   Died 30 Dec. 1814.

WESTMEATH, 1 M.   1831–71
   Elected 26 Feb. 1831.
   Died 5 May 1871.

WESTMEATH, 11 E.   1901–33
   Elected 4 Feb. 1901.
   Died 12 Dec. 1933.

WICKLOW, 2 V. (succ. as 2 E. Wicklow 7 Mar. 1807)   1800–15
   Elected 2 Aug. 1800.
   Died 23 Oct. 1815.

WICKLOW, 4 E.   1821–69
   Elected 10 Nov. 1821.
   Died 22 Mar. 1869.

WICKLOW, 5 E.   1872–81
   Elected 19 June 1872.
   Died 20 June 1881.

WICKLOW, 6 E.   1888–91
 Elected 23 Jan. 1888.
 Died 24 July 1891.

WICKLOW, 7 E.   1905–46
 Elected 27 Nov. 1905.
 Died 11 Oct. 1946.

Chapter 4. The Origin of the Office of Chairman of Committees in the House of Lords

The office of Chairman of Committees in the House of Lords is one of considerable significance in the administrative structure of Parliament. Its history is of interest both on its own account and also because the chairman attained a position of influence and authority, particularly in the field of private legislation, at a much earlier date than his counterpart in the House of Commons, the Chairman of Ways and Means.[1] The post first received official sanction in 1800 when its basic duties were defined in resolutions of the House. Thereafter the Chairman of Committees was appointed on a sessional basis and, once appointed, automatically took the chair in all committees unless the House ordered otherwise.[2] However, although the events of 1800 were important, they should not be allowed to obscure the fact that the post had a previous semi-official existence dating back to the earlier part of the eighteenth century. Some light was thrown on this earlier history by Edmund Gosse, then librarian of the House, who summarised the results of his researches in a letter to *The Times* in 1911. This letter was reprinted by F.H. Spencer as an appendix to his book *Municipal Origins* in which he discussed the role of the Chairman of Committees in the supervision of private legislation.[3] Spencer evidently accepted Gosse's conclusions without question. Investigation has shown, however, that they are in need of serious revision in a great many respects. The purpose of this memorandum is to look again at the available evidence concerning the origin and development of the office.

On only one occasion before 1800 do the records of the House or the reports of parliamentary debates throw any direct light on the position of the Chairman of Committees. On 2 February 1778 the House had, on the motion of the Duke of Richmond, a leading opposition lord, agreed to resolve itself into a committee on the state of the nation in order to consider the papers laid by the government relating to the conduct of the American war. A conflict then arose on the question whether the Duke of Portland, Richmond's nominee, or Lord Scarsdale, the candidate of the government or 'Lords in administration', should take the chair.[4] Richmond's action was designed to embarrass the government and he and his supporters were anxious to make as much capital out of the incident as they could. Nevertheless, the interesting feature of the debate in the present context is that, while the interpretation which the two sides placed on the facts of the situation differed, there was a significant degree of agreement about

---

[1] O.C. Williams, *The Historical Development of Private Bill Procedure and Standing Orders of the House of Commons* (1948–9), i, 91–105.

[2] *LJ*, xlii, 636, resolutions of 23 July 1800.

[3] F.H. Spencer, *Municipal Origins* (1911). The letter is printed on pp. 327–9; the chairman's role is discussed on pp. 95–113.

[4] *Parliamentary History*, xix, cols 651–3; *LJ*, xxxv, 287.

the facts themselves. Richmond justified his nomination of the Duke of Portland on the ground that 'it was always usual for the person who moved for the committee of the whole house to be complimented with the nomination of the chairman'. On the other hand, Lord Dudley stated 'that in the other House it was usual for the member who moved for the committee, to name the chairman, but in that House (the Lords) the usage had been uniformly otherwise; because the chairman in committees of the whole House, if present, is looked upon in the light of perpetual chairman'. Supporting Richmond, the Duke of Grafton said that 'there was no resolution of the House which entitled one Lord to be chairman more than another but that, in strict duty, each of their Lordships ought to discharge the office in his turn'. But no speaker contradicted Earl Gower who stated that 'the usage of the House was in favour of the noble Lord (Scarsdale), who always presided in committees of the whole house'. Similarly, the Earl of Denbigh expressed the view that 'as the business of the committee would be arduous, and the noble Lord (Scarsdale) had been for years used to do the duty, . . . he was the fittest person to preside then'.

Of particular interest is the testimony of the Earl of Sandwich who said that 'it was a rule of that House (the Lords) for one person always to take the chair on such occasions. Lord Scarsdale had often presided with great dignity and credit to himself, and it would imply a tacit idea of his not having discharged his duty to the satisfaction of their Lordships, if he were now set aside'. Sandwich went on to say that 'he had, for a great many years, sat in that House; that he remembered when Lord Delawarr was the constant Chairman of Committees, and he never knew an instance of their Lordships appointing a new chairman when the old one was present'. The curious aspect of Sandwich's contribution to this debate is that, although he had succeeded to the peerage as long ago as 1729, he had not been able to take his seat until 1740, shortly after he attained his majority. Consequently he could have had no personal experience of Delawarr's tenure of the chair, which, as will be seen, came to an end in 1734. However, this does not diminish the significance of the fact that Delawarr's activities as chairman made enough of an impression on the House for the memory of them to endure for more than forty years.

It is clear from the debate of 1778 that, while there was no resolution of the House to regulate his position, it had for long been accepted that there should be one lord who, if present, took the chair in all committees of the whole house. It follows that, in the absence of more specific information, an analysis of the lords who acted as chairmen of such committees before 1800 is likely to provide the most reliable means of discovering the period at which the convention of having a permanent chairman came to be accepted, and also the identity of those lords who held the position. In order to obtain this basic statistical evidence an analysis was made of the lords who reported from all committees in each session from 1701 to 1800. The committees were divided into two categories, committees of the whole house and select committees, in order to see whether any significantly different patterns emerged for the two types.[5] The information was derived exclusively from the *Lords Journals* where the names of the lords reporting from committees are recorded. During the period under consideration neither the

---

[5] A copy of this analysis has been placed in the Parliamentary Archives. In the following remarks no account has been taken of the short sessions of 1707, 1714 (2), 1721, 1727 (2), 1754 and 1768 in each of which only four or fewer committees were appointed. Cf. Appendix.

proceedings in committees of the whole house nor those in select committees are recorded in the *Journals*. The relevant details may be found in the manuscript minute books and the manuscript committee minute books.[6] An examination of the procedure observed in committees of both types makes it clear that it is correct to identify the peer who reported from a committee with the lord who acted as its chairman.

A word should be said at this point about committee procedure in the eighteenth century. By 1700 the committee of the whole house was well established in the procedure of the House. During the eighteenth century as now, its principal use was for the consideration of public bills after second reading. However, on relatively infrequent occasions it was used for the consideration of important matters of public interest. Examples include the conduct of the war in Spain (1711), the state of public credit (1721), the conduct of the American war (1778) and the resolutions concerning the union with Ireland (1800). The committee was constituted by the House agreeing to the motion that it do resolve itself into committee. It sat in the chamber and all those peers who happened to be present formed its membership. Proceedings in committee of the whole house differed from those in the House itself in three main respects. The decisions taken by the committee were only provisional and had to be reported to and agreed to by the House before achieving finality.[7] In the event of a division in the committee of the whole house the use of proxies was not permitted. Finally, the presiding officer in the committee was not the speaker on the woolsack but the chairman in the chair at the table of the House.

As to the procedure for appointing the chairman, there is no guidance apart from that provided by the incident in 1778 already described. There is no other case either in the *Journals* or in the manuscript minute books where the relevant proceedings are recorded. Nevertheless, there must, at least by implication, have been a decision with regard to the chairman on each occasion that the House went into committee. In 1778 this question was decided by the House immediately after the question to resolve itself into committee had been agreed to but before the House had actually gone into committee. In ordinary circumstances, however, the question was evidently regarded simply as one of form and was not thought worthy of record in the minutes or *Journals*.

There were, apart from committees of the whole house, committees of a distinct type which have been described for the purposes of this enquiry as 'select committees' for want of a more satisfactory term. Originally the appointment of committees to sit elsewhere than in the chamber had involved a conscious process of selection which would have entitled them to be described as select committees in the modern sense.[8] By 1700, however, the principle of conscious selection had been abandoned. Where a committee of the whole house was not employed, bills or matters were simply committed to 'a committee' whose membership was composed of those lords who happened to be present in the House on the day of its appointment. Usually these committees were not accorded any particular designation in the records of the House although on rare occasions, when it was found necessary to transfer the consideration of bills from a

---

[6] For these records see M.F. Bond, *Guide to the Records of Parliament* (1971), 33, 43.

[7] For the principle involved, see *LJ*, ii, 707.

[8] See *LJ*, xiii, 582.

committee of the whole house to a committee off the floor of the chamber, they were distinguished by the name of 'select' or 'private' committees.[9] However, select committees in the modern sense were, so far as the House of Lords was concerned, a development of the nineteenth century. The committees in question were used principally for the consideration of local and private bills of which the main categories were inclosure, road, navigation, estate and naturalisation bills. They were also used for the framing of addresses to the crown, although after 1714 the proceedings in this connection were of an increasingly formalised kind, the text of the addresses having been drafted by the government well in advance of any action in the House. Occasionally other matters were referred to these committees. Such matters were usually of a procedural or domestic character although sometimes questions of any general kind were considered by them as was the case with the committees on public records of 1704–6 and the dearness of provisions in 1765.[10] Originally the chair in these committees was taken by the senior peer or the 'first of the committees'.[11] However, by 1700 it seems to have been generally accepted that the members had the power to choose their own chairman without regard to seniority.

The analysis of peers reporting from committees showed that while certain members of the House undertook more committee work than others between 1701 and 1714, no single lord clearly emerged from amongst his fellows as the usual chairman during this period. From 1714, however, a succession of lords can be established whose performance as chairman both of committees of the whole house and of select committees outstrips that of all others, a fact that must be due to more than statistical chance. The first lord to emerge in this connection is the third Earl of Clarendon.[12] Clarendon was the grandson of the Lord Chancellor and nephew of the Earl of Rochester, the leading tory politician. As Lord Cornbury, Clarendon had sat in the Commons 1685–7 and 1689–1701, and had been governor of New York and New Jersey from 1701 to 1708. On his father's death in 1709, he returned from America and took his seat in the House of Lords. Before long he was active in committee work. He first chaired a select committee on 2 March 1711 and a committee of the whole house on 16 April following. In session 1711–12 he led the field as chairman both of committees of the whole house and of select committees. In session 1713 and session 1714 (1) his performance was less remarkable but still significant. From session 1715–16 to session 1722–3 he was by a substantial margin the peer most frequently selected as chairman of committees of both types in every session. Clarendon last acted as chairman on 21 March 1723, after which he did not attend the House again before his death which occurred on 31 March 1724. In spite of Clarendon's striking record no reference has been found to indicate that he was thought to occupy any special position as Chairman of Committees.

---

[9] See, for example, *LJ*, xvii, 344, 384; xviii, 429; xx, 632; xxi, 242, 319; xxxv, 224.

[10] The committee for privileges constitutes a special case. It customarily sat in the chamber and its menbership was, in practice, unlimited. Technically it was not a committee of the whole house. For the purpose of the analysis its sittings have been included under the head of select committees. No special conventions were observable in relation to its chairmanship and the number of its sittings was not sufficiently large to import any significant distortion into the figures.

[11] See, for example, *LJ*, ii, 385.

[12] Unless otherwise noted, information relating to peers is taken from *Complete Peerage*, ed. G.E. Cokayne (2nd edn, 1910–59).

The reason for the emergence of a permanent chairman at this point can only be a matter for speculation. On general grounds there were clear advantages in having a single individual who would, if present, normally act as chairman. Indeed it is perhaps surprising that it took so long for this convention to become established given the fact that the system of annual parliamentary sessions had been introduced as long ago as 1689. One explanation for the delay may have been that before Clarendon no suitable candidate had emerged. What was required was a lord who had no commitments which would prevent his attending the House regularly and who would be content to apply himself seriously to the relatively humdrum business of chairing committees. Once such a person had emerged, it was obvious that his role would make an important contribution to the smooth conduct of business in the House and there would have been a natural tendency on the part of the government to encourage such a development. Clarendon started taking an active part in the proceedings of the House shortly after the tories replaced Godolphin's administration and it may be that he began to devote himself seriously to its business at the suggestion of his uncle, Rochester, who until his death in May 1711 was a leading member of the new ministry. It was to the same ministry that Clarendon owed his appointment as a privy counsellor in December 1711 and as envoy extraordinary to Hanover in June 1714. However, the support which he enjoyed was evidently more than partisan since his career as chairman survived the collapse of the tory government in 1714 and his position was consolidated under successive whig ministries thereafter. Why Clarendon was content to accept the drudgery involved in the chairmanship is another question. It may have been on account of his financial position. This was precarious in spite of generous provision from the crown. Clarendon was given a pension of £1,000 from the secret service in 1710 which he enjoyed until 1713.[13] In the latter year this was replaced by another of £2,000 on the Irish establishment which was confirmed to him in 1715.[14] It is conceivable that this continued support was in some way connected with his services in the chair. Nevertheless Clarendon was said to have died 'in obscurity, and deeply in debt'.

Following Clarendon's withdrawal from the House in 1723 no single lord emerged as his successor for the remainder of the session, the chairmanship of committees of the whole house being shared between the sixth Earl of Westmorland and the sixth Lord Delawarr. However, the analysis showed that, during the course of the following session, Clarendon's role was assumed by the seventh Lord Delawarr. The son of the sixth Lord Delawarr, the seventh Lord had sat in the Commons as the Hon. John West from 1715 until he succeeded his father on 26 May 1723. A firm supporter of successive ministries, Delawarr served as a lord of the bedchamber 1725–7 and as treasurer of the household 1731–7, being appointed a privy counsellor in 1731. He took a leading part in the proceedings of the House and was appointed speaker in the absence of the Lord Chancellor in 1733 and 1754,[15] a function usually reserved for the presiding judges of the courts of law. Delawarr seems almost to have been predestined for the position of chairman. Taking his seat on 9 January 1724 he first chaired a select committee on 10 March 1724 and a committee of the whole house on 14 April following. With the

[13] *Calendar of Treasury Books*, xxviii, 487, 497.
[14] *Calendar of Treasury Books*, xxviii, 135, 314; xxix, 585.
[15] *LJ*, xxiv, 237; xxviii, 249.

exception of session 1727 (1), when his place as chairman of committees of the whole house was taken by the second Lord Waldegrave, he acted as chairman of committees of both types more frequently than any other lord until the end of session 1733. Thereafter, while he continued to take the chair from time to time he ceased to play the prominent part although he once again led the field as chairman in 1737. Delawarr's performance, measured in these terms, amply confirms Sandwich's recollection of his position in his speech of 1778 which has already been quoted.

During the course of session 1734 Delawarr's position as chairman was taken over by the eighth Earl of Warwick. Warwick had succeeded his cousin in the Earldoms of Warwick and Holland in 1721. He appears to have inherited nothing besides the titles and to have belonged to the category of poor lords who looked to the crown to support their dignities. He was granted a civil list pension of £800 a year shortly after succeeding[16] and was accorded a private allowance of £500 a year from the secret service money at about the same time.[17] He enjoyed both these annuities until his death. Whether there was any implied contract between the crown and Warwick that the latter would attend the House regularly in return for this financial support is unknown, but the later case of Viscount Saye and Sele suggests that this may have been the case.[18] In any event Warwick was regular in his attendance from the time that he took his seat. However, it was not until session 1731 that he acted as a chairman, taking the chair in one committee of the whole house and in one select committee. He chaired one select committee in 1732 but no committee of either kind in 1733. He appears first to have been accepted as the regular chairman of committees of the whole house in April 1734.[19] Warwick remained chairman until his death which occurred on 7 September 1759. During the last two sessions of his life, those of 1757–8 and 1758–9, he was absent for much of the time, presumably on account of sickness, and his place as chairman of committees of the whole house was taken by the fifth Lord Willoughby of Parham and the third Earl of Marchmont respectively. Otherwise his record was remarkable. With the exception of session 1737, when he was replaced by Delawarr, he chaired committees of the whole house more frequently than any other lord in each session from 1734 to 1756–7. Over the same period he acted in respect of select committees more frequently than any other lord except in eight sessions.[20]

There is no reference during Warwick's lifetime to the special position which he occupied but there seems little doubt that certain conventions came to be accepted during the twenty-five years that he acted as chairman if indeed they had not already been established before his appointment. At any rate it was recognised on his death that an office had been vacated which would have to be filled. This is evident from the correspondence relating to his successor, the fifth Lord Willoughby of Parham, which survives amongst the Hardwicke papers.[21] In a letter to Lord Royston of 11 September

---

[16] TNA, T. 52/31, pp. 316–17, warrant 12 Oct. 1721. The pension was renewed by George II; see T. 52/35, pp. 202–3, warrant 16 Oct. 1727.

[17] BL, Add. MS 32896, f. 431.

[18] L.B. Namier, *The Structure of Politics at the Accession of George III* (2nd edn, 1957), 179 n. 1.

[19] *LJ*, xxiv, 423–4.

[20] Those of 1734, 1735, 1737, 1741–2, 1742–3, 1744–5, 1751 and 1753–4.

[21] My attention was drawn to this material by Mr P.J.W. Higson's article 'Lord Willoughby of Parham: A Neglected Society President', *Antiquaries Journal*, lii (1972), 169–84.

1759 Daniel Wray announced that 'Lord Warwick . . . is dead' and asked 'Who will succeed to the business he did in the House of Lords?'[22] On 22 September Thomas Birch informed the same correspondent that 'Lord Warwick's death makes a vacancy in the post of Chairman of the House of Lords . . .'.[23] On the following day, Wray told Royston that Willoughby 'contrary to all expectation . . . appeared seriously interested in the succession to the seat filled by that Lord (Warwick)', going on to say that 'What emoluments, and how arising, attend the acting in that capacity his lordship and we here are equally ignorant'.[24] Writing to Birch on 23 October Royston gave it as his view that 'Lord Hardwicke's good offices have prevailed and . . . our friend (Willoughby) will inherit Lord Warwick's mantle'.[25] The matter had apparently been finally settled by 12 November when Willoughby wrote to Hardwicke to thank him for 'recommending me to the Duke of Newcastle as a proper person to succeed the late Earl of Warwick'.[26]

The language used by the writers just quoted makes it plain that Warwick had occupied a clearly recognised position in the House of Lords and that Willoughby would, as chairman, have to take over the business which he had done. Unfortunately the correspondence does not specify the nature of this business. Royston and Hardwicke had apparently conflicting views about the arduousness of the duties attached to the post. The former referred to 'the easy business of the function' while the latter hoped that Willoughby would 'have no objection . . . to the confinement which this service may confine him to'.[27]

Willoughby of Parham was an interesting figure whose scholarly interests were recognised in his election to the office of President of the Society of Antiquaries which he held from 1754 until his death. He was, like Warwick, a poor lord who looked to the crown to support his dignity. He succeeded to the peerage as an infant in 1715 and from 1718 was in receipt of an annuity of £200 payable by the paymaster of pensions.[28] He took his seat in the House in 1734 and it was possibly from this date that he began to receive the secret service allowance of £400 a year which he is known to have enjoyed from at least 1754.[29] In the session following that in which he took his seat, he chaired one committee of the whole house, but it was not until session 1739–40 that he began to play a significant role in committee work. By the time of Warwick's death in 1759 he had had nearly twenty years' continuous experience as a chairman and was a natural choice as his successor. In connection with his employment Willoughby asked for the secret service allowance of £500 previously enjoyed by Warwick to be trans-ferred to him.[30] In the event he did not secure this particular allowance which was divided between Warwick's widow and daughter.[31] He did, however, obtain an

[22] BL, Add. MS 35401, f. 233.

[23] BL, Add. MS 35399, f. 106.

[24] BL, Add. MS 35401, f. 236.

[25] BL, Add. MS 35399, f. 123.

[26] BL, Add. MS 35596, f. 38.

[27] BL, Add. MS 35399, f. 108; Add. MS 35352, f. 123.

[28] *Calendar of Treasury Books*, xxxii, 550.

[29] Namier, *Structure of Politics*, 429, 436, 441, 449, 456, 462, 467, 474, 479.

[30] BL, Add. MS. 35352, f. 123; Add. MS 35606, f. 305.

[31] Namier, *Structure of Politics*, 222 n. 2.

additional £500 a year from the paymaster of pensions.[32] This brought his total income from the government to £1,100. Willoughby continued to occupy the position of chairman until his death which occurred on 21 January 1765, leading the field as chairman of committees of the whole house throughout the period and taking the chair in select committees more frequently than any other lord except in session 1761–2.[33]

In the absence of any corroborative evidence, the analysis provided the only indication of the identity of the chairmen of committees during the decade following Willoughby's death. From this it is evident that his immediate successor was Lord Delamer who had succeeded his cousin, the Earl of Warrington, as fourth baron in 1758. Like his two predecessors as chairman, Delamer was a poor lord which explains the fact that he was accorded a secret service allowance of £800 a year in 1761.[34] He was assiduous in his attendance from the time of his succession. He first acted as chairman in 1760 and chaired a total of seventeen committees before taking over from Willoughby at the beginning of session 1765. Rockingham's secret service accounts reveal that Delamer's allowance from this source had been raised from £800 to £1,200 by October 1765.[35] The most likely explanation of this development would appear to be that the £400 allowance from the secret service formerly received by Willoughby was transferred to Delamer on his appointment. Delamer remained chairman until his death on 9 January 1770, taking the leading part as chairman of committees of the whole house in each session except that of 1766–7 when he was absent for most of the time, probably on account of sickness, and his place was taken by the fourth Lord Botetourt. So far as select committees were concerned he acted more frequently than any other peer except in sessions 1765–6 and 1766–7.

Delamer's successor, as revealed by the analysis, was the first Viscount Wentworth. Succeeding as ninth Lord Wentworth in 1745, he was created a viscount in 1762. Before his appointment he had never played a large part in committee work, chairing only sixteen committees between 1756 and 1770, nor had he attended the House very regularly. He was not, like his three predecessors, a poor lord and the reasons for his selection remain obscure. Once appointed he took a leading part as chairman in sessions 1770 and 1770–1. Thereafter his attendance declined, possibly on account of ill health. In session 1772 he was absent except in May, attending only seventeen out of a possible seventy-eight sittings. Nevertheless, he chaired a majority of the committees of the whole house in that session. In his absence the first Lord Boston almost invariably acted as chairman of committees of both types. In session 1772–3 Wentworth attended

---

[32] TNA, T. 52/50, p. 292, warrant 21 Dec. 1759; the pension was renewed by George III; see T. 52/52, pp. 113–22, warrant 3 Apr. 1761.

[33] During Willoughby's period of office the Irish House of Lords began to entrust its committee business to a permanent chairman. In 1768 the fourth Viscount Ranelagh was granted £1,000 in respect of his services since October 1761. Thereafter the chairman received a series of sessional grants which varied from £1,000 to £2,000 until 1789 when he was given a fixed annual allowance of £1,443 6s on the Irish establishment. Ranelagh died in 1797 and was succeeded by the first Earl of Portarlington (1797–8) and then by the fourth Earl of Mayo who acted until the abolition of the Irish Parliament in 1800 (*LJ (Ireland)*, iv, 487, 530, 608, 725, 813; v, 26, 148, 255–6, 417, 585–6, 704; vi, 66, 197, 273–4; vii, 549, 570, viii, 137, 211; E.M. Johnston, *Great Britain and Ireland 1760–1800: A Study in Political Administration* (Edinburgh, 1963), 307.

[34] Namier, *Structure of Politics*, 222, 223, 473, 475, 477, 479.

[35] Sherffield City Libary, Rockingham Ms R. 15/1, payments of 30 Oct. 1765, 26 Apr. and 17 July 1766. I am grateful to Mr J. Bebbington for providing me with this information.

fifty-nine out of a possible 106 sittings. He played the leading part as chairman of select committees but chaired only twenty committees of the whole house while Boston chaired thirty. Although he did not die until 31 October 1774, Wentworth did not attend the House after 19 June 1773 and was therefore absent for the whole of session 1774 when Boston once again acted as chairman. It is impossible to say with certainty whether Wentworth was still regarded as chairman at his death or whether Boston took over this position after 1773. It may well be that Boston was regarded as acting as his deputy until such time as he was fit to attend the House again in the same way as Botetourt acted during session 1766–7 in the absence of Delamer. There is no evidence to indicate what remuneration, if any, Wentworth received as chairman.

Wentworth's death took place during the parliamentary recess. At the beginning of the next session which opened on 29 November 1774 Boston usually took the chair although it is not clear whether he was regarded as the permanent chairman or was acting on an interim basis until a successor to Wentworth could be found. He last chaired a committee on 23 December 1774 and died on 30 March 1775. Before his death a permanent chairman had already emerged in the person of Lord Scarsdale, who first took the chair on 8 February 1775. As Nathaniel Curzon, Scarsdale had sat in the Commons from 1748 to 1761 when he was elevated to the peerage. He was a rather surprising choice for the post of chairman. During his fourteen years' membership he had rarely attended the House of Lords and had never chaired a committee. A possible clue to the reason for his selection may have been his financial difficulties. His estate was considerably encumbered on account of his vast building programme at Kedleston.[36] There is reliable evidence that he enjoyed a sessional allowance of £1,500 from the secret service money as chairman of committees from at least 1778–9.[37] It is impossible to say when this allowance began to be paid. The last chairman whose sources of income from the government are known is Delamer who received a total of £1,200 a year during his period as chairman. It may be that the sessional allowance of £1,500 was provided in the first instance for Wentworth on his appointment in 1770 but, in the absence of the relevant accounts, it is impossible to be certain. Conceivably the fact that this relatively large allowance was attached to the post induced Scarsdale to seek the appointment in 1775.

Scarsdale remained chairman until the end of session 1788–9. While he can be seen to have undertaken the bulk of the committee work during this period, he was not especially assiduous in the performance of his duties. In the early part of each session he was invariably active but he only rarely attended the House after the end of May with the result that in three out of a total of sixteen sessions – those of 1780–1, 1782–3 and 1784 – other lords, Sandys, Chedworth and Walsingham respectively, actually chaired committees of the whole house more frequently than he did. On the other hand his record for select committees was better and he surpassed the performance of any other lord in each session throughout his period of office. However Scarsdale's conduct is viewed, the report of the debate of 1778 already quoted provides clear evidence that the chairman had a recognised place in the conduct of the business of the House at this period. An indication that it could be thought of as a potentially influential office is to

[36] For Scarsdale's career, see L.B. Namier and J. Brooke, *The History of Parliament: The House of Commons 1754–1790* (1964), ii, 287–8.
[37] BL, Add. MS 37836, ff. 68, 80, 114, 138.

be found in the fact that in 1783 Lord Walsingham was seeking to succeed him. The significance of this fact will be considered later. That the chairmanship was now regarded as having a permanent character is illustrated by the fact that Scarsdale was granted a pension on his retirement in 1789. As already noted, he enjoyed an allowance of £1,500 as chairman of committees. This sum continued to be paid from the secret service until the reforms brought about by Burke's Civil List Establishment Act in 1782. It was then transferred to the special service account from which successive chairmen received their remuneration until 1799.[38] Scarsdale was paid the allowance until 1789. In 1790 he was granted a civil list pension of £1,200 for life payable from 5 July 1789, the quarter day nearest to the date on which the session of 1788–9 had been prorogued.[39] The most plausible explanation of this pension is that in 1789, when Scarsdale had reached the age of 62, he or the government decided that the time had come for him to vacate the chair in favour of a younger man and that Scarsdale was able to persuade the government that the post of chairman had enough of a permanent character to justify the grant of a retiring allowance.

The choice of Scarsdale's successor fell upon the tenth Lord Cathcart.[40] Cathcart had studied law at Dresden and Glasgow, and had been admitted a member of the faculty of advocates in February 1776. He succeeded to the Scottish peerage of his father on the latter's death in August of the same year. In the following year he entered the army, serving with distinction in America until October 1780 when ill health obliged him to return to England. In March 1787 he failed to secure election as a Scottish Representative Peer and wrote to Pitt asking for a British peerage, stating in the course of his letter[41] that 'I believe that you are convinced that my object in wishing to get into Parliament was to endeavour to come forward in Business, to be useful, and therefore to be employed'. He characterised his predicament in the following terms:

A Lawyer until I succeeded to the Title, a Soldier, but in a Profound Peace, and a Peer, not in the House of Lords, not rich enough to undertake an ordinary Foreign Mission, such is my damned Situation!

In January 1788 Cathcart was elected a Representative Peer. However, the problem of obtaining a post for him still remained. In July he wrote to Pitt seeking military promotion[42] and in October he was asking to succeed James Stuart Mackenzie, who was rumoured to be dying, in the office of keeper of the privy seal of Scotland. He told Pitt that the possession of this post:

would effectually enable me to relieve my estate of all its Embarrassments, I mean those by which it is overburthened: But what would make it beyond all others an

---

[38] 22 Geo. III, c. 82, s. 29. Payments to Scarsdale may be traced in TNA, T. 38/741, ff. 23, 27, 49, 68, 95, 109, 124, 137.

[39] TNA, T. 52/78, p. 398, warrant 7 May 1790.

[40] Except where otherwise noted the details of Cathcart's life have been taken from the article in the *Dictionary of National Biography*.

[41] TNA, 30/8/121, f. 226.

[42] TNA, 30/8/121, ff. 228–9.

object of the last Importance to me would be the Hope that you would not allow it to remain a sinecure but that in time you might find means to call for the services of the holder of that office.[43]

However, Stuart Mackenzie survived and no vacancy occurred.

In the House of Lords Cathcart was a firm ministerial supporter, being selected to second the address in reply to the speech from the throne in March 1789.[44] His reward came with his appointment as Chairman of Committees at the beginning of the following session when he had been in the House for less than two years and after he had chaired only one of its committees. It is clear from the evidence already cited that Cathcart intended to take his duties seriously. For four sessions – until the end of that of 1793 – he was by a large margin the peer most frequently chosen to fill the chair in committees of the whole house. His record for select committees was less remarkable. He chaired these committees more frequently than any other lord in his first three sessions of office although he increasingly left this work to the Bishop of Bangor. In session 1792–3 the bishop actually played the leading part as chairman of select committees. Out of a total of 234 such committees he chaired 102 as opposed to Cathcart who chaired only fifty-eight.

The outbreak of war with France transformed Cathcart's situation. He evidently found the prospect of resuming his active military career more attractive than that of remaining chairman. In November 1793 he was made a brigadier general and appointed to command a brigade in the army then assembling for embarkation to France. From then on he was out of the country for long periods. In session 1794 he was present on only five occasions and took the chair only once, his place as chairman both of committees of the whole house and of select committees being taken at other times on a temporary basis by the Bishop of Bangor.[45] However, Cathcart received the allowance for session 1794 and remained chairman, at least formally, until prorogation in July 1794.[46] Cathcart's delay in finally relinquishing office may have been due partly to uncertainty about the duration of the war. Another factor may have been the need to find a suitable means of compensating him for loss of office. A solution to this problem was eventually found in January 1795 when he was granted the post of vice admiral of Scotland, a sinecure with a salary of £1,000.[47] At the same time it was proposed that his wife should be given a pension to make up the difference between the salaries attached to the two offices.[48]

Cathcart's successor was the second Lord Walsingham who took over as chairman at the beginning of session 1794–5 and served for twenty years until his retirement in

---

[43] TNA, 30/8/121, f. 230.

[44] *Parliamentary History*, xxvii, cols 1300–1.

[45] Writing to Pott on 27 Dec. 1794 the Bishop of Bangor assured him that 'he would be very ready to serve the House of Lords as Chairman of the Committees during the approaching (1794–5) Session in the same Manner as he did all last (1794) Session, unless he finds that a different Arrangement is to take place'. TNA, 30/8/87, f. 63. I am grateful to Mr M. McCahill for this reference.

[46] For the payment of Cathcart's allowance, see TNA, T. 38/741, ff. 150, 163, 177, 186; T. 38/742, f. 2. See also *Gentleman's Magazine* (1843), cxiii, 314.

[47] TNA, H.C.A. 50/12, f. 28, warrant 7 Jan. 1795.

[48] *The Later Correspondence of George III*, ed. A. Aspinall (Cambridge, 1962–70), ii, 262.

1814.[49] As Thomas de Grey, he had sat in the Commons from 1774 until he succeeded his father in 1781 at the age of thirty-two.[50] An important politician of the second rank, Walsingham was sworn of the privy council in 1783 and made joint postmaster general in 1787. His occupancy of this office was the immediate cause of his appointment as chairman. As part of the complex arrangements made by Pitt in July 1794 for the admission of the Portland whigs into the government, it was agreed that William Windham should be made secretary at war. This involved displacing Sir George Yonge who had to be compensated with another office that was compatible with a seat in the Commons. Yonge was, therefore, made master of the mint, displacing in his turn the Earl of Leicester who was accommodated with Walsingham's place of joint postmaster general.[51] Finally provision had to be made for Walsingham. On 7 July Pitt wrote to him in the following terms:

> In order to facilitate an extensive Arrangement which is at this Time of great Importance to the King's Service, I am induced to mention to your Lordship that it will be a very essential Accommodation to open the Office which your Lordship holds of Joint Postmaster General. There is a Situation vacant which I flatter myself it may not be disagreeable to you to accept in Exchange, which is that of Chairman of the Committees of the House of Lords, the duties of which I understand you have already occasionally had the goodness to discharge. *No Idea can certainly be entertained, that by acceding to this Arrangement for the Convenience of Government, your Lordship should suffer any Diminution of Income.* I therefore hope you will allow me to recommend a Pension *equal to the difference* of Value *in the two* Situations to any Part of your family whom you may think proper to name.[52]

Walsingham acquiesced in this proposal. The discrepancy between the salaries attached to the two posts – £2,500 in the case of the joint postmaster general and £1,500 in that of the chairman – was duly made good by the grant of a pension of £1,200 in trust for his two sons, the largest sum that could be made available without recourse to an address from parliament.[53]

In spite of this generous provision Walsingham was not entirely pleased with the manner in which his appointment had been handled. Writing to him on 19 July 1795 George Rose, the secretary of the Treasury, was at pains to stress that, in making the arrangement 'Mr. Pitt was not actuated by the slightest Disinclination towards your Lordship'.[54] In fact the office of chairman was one in which Walsingham had earlier shown an interest and, as is clear from the letter already quoted, this was one of the reasons why Pitt decided to appoint him. Walsingham had been a member of the House of Lords for only two years when, in July 1783, his aspirations were characterised in the

[49] *LJ*, l, 8, 20, 22, 27; Hansard, *Parl. Debs*, 1st ser., xxix, cols 27–8, 91–2.

[50] For Walsingham's earlier career, see Namier and Brooke, *House of Commons 1754–90*, ii, 307–8.

[51] Norfolk and Norwich RO, Walsingham Papers, Box XLVIII/2: George Rose to Walsingham, 19 July 1795. I am grateful to Lord Walsingham for permission to make use of these papers.

[52] Norfolk and Norwich RO, Walsingham Papers, Box XLVIII/2: Pitt to Walsingham 7 July 1794.

[53] Norfolk and Norwich RO, Walsingham Papers, Box XLVIII/2: Rose to Walsingham, 11 July 1794; 22 Geo. III, c. 82, s. 17; TNA, T. 52/81, warrants of 15 and 27 July 1794.

[54] Norfolk and Norwich RO, Walsingham Papers, Box XLVIII/2: Rose to Walsingham, 19 July 1795.

following terms: 'Speculates, Wishes for Lord Scarsdale's place'.[55] This comment is interesting in that it shows that the office of chairman could at that date be the object of the attention of a young and energetic man who had already made his mark in politics. Possibly his interest in the post was first aroused as a result of his marriage in 1772 to the daughter of Lord Boston who, as has been seen, acted as chairman of committees during the absence of Lord Wentworth. It is evident that Walsingham did not regard it simply as an office with merely routine duties to which a reasonable salary was attached. On the contrary, his subsequent career suggests that he may already have seen it as a position of consequence in the House of Lords and in Parliament with potentially important responsibilities in connection with the legislative process.

In the event eleven years were to elapse before Walsingham obtained the appointment. In the meantime he gained a certain amount of relevant experience, chairing fifty-eight committees of the whole house and six select committees between 1781 and 1794. On becoming chairman he at once set a distinctive mark on the post, chairing eighty-seven out of a possible eighty-nine committees of the whole house in session 1794–5 and every single such committee in the five following sessions up to 1800. His record for select committees was equally impressive. In session 1794–5 he chaired 148 such committees out of a total of 190, the Bishop of Bangor acting in thirty-seven instances. In the next session Walsingham chaired 173 out of a possible 184 select committees, the bishop's total being reduced to eight. In the four following sessions Walsingham chaired 801 out of a possible 817 select committees. Walsingham's record is in striking contrast to even his most assiduous predecessors and it is clear that his appointment marked a turning point in the evolution of the office. How far this development was due to Walsingham's own qualities and how far it resulted from a deliberate move to invest the post with a more comprehensive authority it is impossible to say in the present state of the evidence although, as will be seen, recent developments in the field of private bill procedure lend some support to the view that the latter consideration was not without its importance.

While it was not until 1800 that the office of Chairman of Committees was finally recognised in resolutions of the House there is no reason to suppose that these resolutions did anything more than give official sanction to conventions that were already well established. It is interesting to note that the office had already received a degree of public recognition before 1800. When the resolutions relating to the promulgation of the statutes were formulated in 1797 the Chairman of Committees was one of those accorded a set of sessional acts by virtue of his office.[56] From the same year Walsingham was styled Chairman of Committees in the *Royal Kalendar*.[57]

The reasons which prompted the adoption of the resolutions of 1800 are not entirely clear, given that Walsingham was not invested with any functions or duties as a result of them which he had not in practice exercised before. The only procedural effect which they had was to place the Chairman of Committees automatically in the chair both of committees of the whole house and of select committees whereas before a question had, at least in theory, to be resolved in each case before this result could be

---

[55] *Complete Peerage*, ed. Cokayne, xii pt 2, 334 n.

[56] *LJ*, xli, 265.

[57] *Royal Kalendar* (1797), 14.

secured. One possible explanation of the resolutions is that they were prompted by the need to regulate the chairman's position before he was accorded an increased, and publicly acknowledged, salary. Until 1799 Walsingham received an allowance of £1,500 a session from the special service account like his two predecessors.[58] In June of that year he began to press the government for an increase in remuneration. Two proposals were put forward: one was that the chairman should be accorded a fee on private bills and the other was that he should receive an increase in his allowance. During the course of the next year the matter was considered by Pitt, Loughborough, the Lord Chancellor and Grenville, who, in addition to being Foreign Secretary, acted as 'leader' of the House of Lords. In the event Pitt came down decisively against the proposal for a fee and in favour of an increase in the allowance.[59] The necessary address to the crown was agreed to on 23 July 1800, immediately after the resolutions regulating the office had been passed. In the following month the Treasury gave authority for the allowance to be increased by £1,000 to £2,500.[60] This very substantial increase in remuneration is a significant indication of the importance now attached to the post.

The resolutions of 1800 make no reference to what has long been regarded as the most distinctive and important function of the Chairman of Committees – the detailed supervision of private legislation.[61] Nevertheless it is clear from the exchange of remarks between Lord Grenville and Walsingham which took place in the House when the resolutions were moved on 23 July 1800 that it was this aspect of the chairman's duties which was foremost in the minds of the lords. In view of their intrinsic interest and of the fact that they are not recorded in the *Parliamentary History* these remarks are worth quoting at some length.[62] In introducing the resolutions on behalf of the government Grenville said that:

the office of Chairman of the Committees (both public and private) was an office that required great ability, great industry, and a perfect knowledge of parliamentary forms, and the rules of proceeding; and that no noble Lord could be found who possessed a larger share of those qualifications than the noble Lord who now, so highly to his own credit, and so much to the advantage of the House and the Public, held that office, the duties of which he discharged with singular diligence, correctness and propriety.

In reply Walsingham said:

that whoever undertakes the trust which the House is pleased thus to repose in him, undertakes no light or trivial concern. If we consider the weight of property of

[58] For the payment of Walsingham's allowance, see TNA, T. 38/742, ff. 16, 24, 36, 48, 63.

[59] Norfolk and Norwich RO, Walsingham Papers, Box XLVIII/2: Rose to Walsingham, 24 June 1799, 21 Mar. 1800.

[60] *LJ*, xlii, 636, 647; TNA, T. 29/76, p. 539. Treasury minute 13 Aug. 1800; T. 52/86, p. 156, warrant 2 Oct. 1800. The sessional allowance to the chairman of ways and means in the House of Commons was raised from £500 to £1,200 at the same time (*The Diary and Correspondence of Charles, Lord Colchester*, ed. Lord Colchester (1861), i, 200; TNA, T. 38/742, f. 63; *CJ*, lv, 790, 792).

[61] For a description of the chairman's role in this connection see Williams, *Private Bill Procedure*, i, 55–6, 92–103; *The Clerical Organisation of the House of Commons 1660–1850* (Oxford, 1954), 156–7; S. Lambert, *Bill and Acts* (Cambridge, 1971), 92–5.

[62] The report of this discussion is to be found in J. Debrett, *Parliamentary Register*, xii, 475–6.

which we have already cognizance in these Committees, and that of which we shall now have cognizance, we shall agree that we are all deeply interested in paying as much attention to this part of our public duty as to any other, and the House judge wisely ... in providing that one and the same person shall be constantly and permanently in the chair, whose more immediate duty it shall be to take care that these bills proceed upon one settled and uniform principle, that no innovation shall be made upon the long-established usage and practice of Parliament, and that the property of individuals shall be improved without injury to the public.

... if it is true, and ... I really believe it is so, (for it is no merit of mine,) that these bills are now passed in a way which gives general satisfaction to the public, it is owing to the constant and ready attendance which is given by your Lordships in these Committees, insomuch that I verily believe not a single day has been lost in the course of this session for want of attendance; and I look forward to a continuation of the support which I have constantly and uniformly met from so many of your Lordships, upon whose wisdom and experience I know I may safely rely, in pref-erence to my own frail and fallible judgment ... it will be the object of my life to deserve the confidence and protection of the House, and it will give me the greatest satisfaction if by any industry or attention of mine (which is all I have to give) I can be instrumental in settling these bills, with a view as well to the private and local benefit of those who solicit them as to the general interest which the public may have in them.

The language used on this occasion makes it abundantly clear that the role of the chairman in private legislation was universally understood and accepted by 1800. The origin of his functions in this respect remain obscure. They were, of course, never conferred upon him in any formal sense by the House. However, once it became accepted that one peer should undertake the bulk of the work of chairing private bill committees, it was natural that that peer should evolve certain principles for his own guidance. When the promoters of private bills became aware of this development it was inevitable that they should endeavour to save themselves trouble and expense by drafting their measures in a manner that they knew would be acceptable to the chairman and that they should consult him on difficult points at an early stage in their progress. It was only a step from this for promoters of bills in the Commons, where no figure comparable to the chairman had yet emerged, to do the same. This process is illustrated by a letter written by Walsingham to Lord Hawkesbury in May 1796 in which he said that 'they send to me all the private Bills whilst they are in the House of Commons that I may suggest any alterations I think fit lest such alterations should lose the Bill in the Committee of the Lords'.[63]

Of course, the authority of the chairman rested on no more than convention at this date. He himself had no formal power to disallow any provision in advance but all parties were aware that, should the matter be taken to the House, his decision would in all probability be upheld. In the nature of the case this would have been an evolutionary process. Any evaluation of the role of earlier chairmen in supervising private legislation will have to await the discovery of further evidence. However, it seems beyond dispute

[63] BL, Add. MS 38231, f. 31. See also Spencer, *Municipal Origins*, 102–4.

that Walsingham greatly extended the functions of the office in this direction. The year 1793 had witnessed the introduction of new standing orders to tighten up the procedure relating to canal bills which had been found to be inadequate in the light of the experience of the 'canal mania' of the early 1790s. Similar regulations were made for other classes of private bill during Walsingham's chairmanship.[64] While there is no direct evidence to connect Walsingham's appointment with the standing orders of 1793 it may well be that it was felt that the effective enforcement of parliamentary control over private legislation demanded the services of a chairman who would devote substantially more attention to his duties than any of Walsingham's predecessors had been prepared to do.[65]

One aspect of the matter which remains somewhat obscure is the question with whom the right of selecting the chairman rested. From 1800, when the practice of appointing him by sessional resolution was instituted, the necessary motion was customarily moved by the lord who managed the business on behalf of the government, or leader of the House as he later came to be called. It seems reasonable to infer from this fact that the responsibility for selecting the chairman when a vacancy occurred had previously fallen to the government. There was an obvious government interest in regulating the arrangements with regard to the chairmanship since, by this means, the orderly passage of its own business was facilitated. The provision of a sessional allowance payable out of public funds was a reflection of this fact. That the 'Lords in administration' felt a responsibility to sustain the regular chairman when his position was called in question is evident from the debate of 1778. Such evidence as survives relating to the selection of chairmen points in the same direction. Although the Hardwickes were instrumental in obtaining the post for Willoughby in 1759, the decision to appoint him rested in the last analysis with the First Lord of the Treasury, the Duke of Newcastle, and it was Pitt, the Prime Minister, who offered the office to Walsingham in 1794.

The analysis established beyond reasonable doubt that it was the general rule for there to be one lord who, if present, took the chair in committees of the whole house. That this was the distinctive characteristic of the Chairman of Committees is confirmed by the statements made in the debate of 1778. The analysis also made it clear that, while there was no question until the time of Walsingham of the chairman taking the chair in all select committees, it was the rule for him to take a leading part in this field as well. Obviously, actual practice must have varied considerably according to the conscientiousness of particular chairmen and inevitably, absence on account of sickness must have affected their record. In any event there is a substantial number of occasions when a lord other than the regular chairman is found acting. Such lords fall into two broad categories. On the one hand there is a large group, each member of which chaired a relatively small number of committees, some as few as one a

<hr>

[64] *LJ*, xxxix, 556–7; H.S. Cobb, *Sources for Economic History amongst the Parliamentary Records in the House of Lords Record Office* (House of Lords Record Office Memorandum no. 50, 1973), 8.

[65] Walsingham was also credited in some quarters with considerable influence over the fate of public legislation. Writing to Spencer Perceval on 23 May 1805 about the Irish Post Roads Bill, Lord Redesdale said that 'I cannot but blame Vansittart (chief secretary for Ireland) for suffering this bill to be hurried through the House of Lords. A single word to Lord Walsingham would have stopped it'. Gloucestershire RO, Redesdale Paper, T. 3030/7/73. I am grateful to Dr A.P.W. Malcomson for this reference.

session. The reasons for the selection of the lords in this group as chairmen must have varied considerably. In some cases it may have been the mere fact of availability and willingness to serve. There is little evidence of specialisation according to the type of bill or matter being considered although bishops were occasionally selected for committees on bills dealing with ecclesiastical concerns and Scots lords sometimes served as chairmen of committees dealing with Scottish questions. In the case of the various types of local bills there is some evidence that lords with relevant territorial interests were chosen as chairmen when they were available and sufficiently concerned. Occasionally lords related to the parties affected took the chair in committees on estate bills. An evaluation of the importance of the work of the peers in this group is outside the scope of this enquiry and must await the outcome of more detailed research than has yet been undertaken.

In relation to the total number of committees in the eighteenth century the contribution of the lords in the category just described was not, in numerical terms, very important. Much more significant was the performance of a handful of peers whose activities can only be explained in terms of a strong inclination towards the business of the House generally rather than to the particular character of the bills or matters actually being considered by the committees. The work of this group of lords may be best summarised in the form of a table:

Lord	Limits of Service	Committees of whole house	Select committees	Total	Remarks
Willoughby of Parham, 5th Lord	1735–59	58	227	285	Appointed Chairman of Committees 1759
Sandys, 1st Lord	1744–70	17	551	568	Died 1770
Marchmont, 3rd Earl of	1751–80	45	231	276	Ceased to be representative peer 1784
Botetourt, 4th Lord	1765–8	63	175	238	Appointed Governor of Virginia 1768
Boston, 1st Lord	1762–75	114	411	525	Died 1775
St Davids/Bangor, Bishop of (Warren)	1783–97	67	413	480	Died 1800

Although only one of these lords, Willoughby, ever achieved the position of Chairman of Committees itself, the frequency with which they all acted almost entitles them to be regarded as deputy or associate chairmen. Their principal contribution was in the field of select committees but four of them also acted as chairmen of committees of the whole house in the absence of the regular chairmen. These were Willoughby, Botetourt, Boston and the Bishop of Bangor who acted in the absence of Warwick, Delamer,

Wentworth and Cathcart respectively. Marchmont, during his long membership of the House, tended to confine himself more exclusively to select committees. There seems little doubt that his extensive activities as chairman were linked with his known interest in the history and records of the House, to which his chairmanship of the committee which was responsible for supervising the printing of the journals and rolls of parliament testifies.[66] Sandys confined himself even more than Marchmont to the chairmanship of select committees. The intimate knowledge of the proceedings of the House that he would thus have acquired was probably an important factor in his selection to act as speaker of the House during session 1756–7 while the great seal was in commission.[67] As already noted in connection with Delawarr, this was a function normally reserved for one of the presiding judges of the courts of law.

The early history of the office of Chairman of Committees remains in many respects obscure, but, on the basis of the evidence presented here, it is clear that from the time of Clarendon (c. 1715–23) there was a regular succession of lords who were recognised as holding the post. This development appears to have been encouraged by the government and was, no doubt, found convenient by the House generally. From the time of the appointment of Warwick in 1734 until the death of Delamer in 1770 the post was occupied by lords who were entirely dependent on the crown for financial support and who received annual sums of varying amounts from the government. Thereafter the office passed into the hands of lords who, while not necessarily affluent, were less dependent upon support of this kind. Possibly from the time of Wentworth (1770–4) and certainly from that of Scarsdale (1775–89), a sessional allowance was paid to the Chairman of Committees as such. From the chairmanship of Warwick (1734–59) the post was evidently understood to be permanent in character, the holder remaining in office until his death or until some financial provision was made for his retirement. Of the functions of the chairmen before 1800, insofar as they went beyond the immediate business of presiding over the committees themselves, little can be said in the present state of knowledge. It has been suggested above that the role of the chairman in the supervision of private legislation, while extended and consolidated by Walsingham, was to some degree exercised by his predecessors. It is hoped that, now that it has proved possible to identify these predecessors more securely than was the case before, detailed research will be undertaken so that their contribution to the process of legislation in the eighteenth century may be correctly evaluated.

[66] *LJ*, xxxiii, 214; xxxiv, 728.
[67] *LJ*, xxix, 4.

Appendix

Table indicating the names of all lords who reported from committees of the whole house and from select committees on three or more occasions in each session from 1701 to 1800.[68]

Note. In the table the following abbreviations have been used:

Abp	Archbishop
Bp	Bishop
D.	Duke
E.	Earl
(GB)	Peerage of Great Britain
L.	Lord
M.	Marquess
(S)	Peerage of Scotland
V.	Viscount

Session	Whole House		Select	
1701–2	Longueville, 1 V.	44	Longueville, 1 V.	15
	Halifax, 1 L.	5	Jeffreys, 2 L.	8
	Herbert, 1 L.	4	Warrington, 2 E.	6
	Lucas, 3 L.	4	Ferrers, 7 L.	5
	Ferrers, 7 L.	3	Delawarr, 6 L.	4
	Stamford, 2 E.	3	Peterborough, 3 E.	4
	7 Others	9	Guilford, 2 L.	3
			Herbert, 1 L.	3
			12 Others	16
	Total	**72**	**Total**	**64**
1702–3	Longueville, 1 V.	11	Devonshire, 1 D.	7
	Herbert, 1 L.	10	Stamford, 2 E.	6
	1 Other	1	Bolton, 2 D.	5
			London, Bp	5
			Somerset, 6 D.	5
			Townshend, 2 V.	4
			Warrington, 2 E.	4
			Delawarr, 6 L.	3
			Hereford, Bp	3
			Howard of Escrick, 4 L.	3
			Longueville, 1 V.	3
			Rochester, 1 E.	3
			12 Others	16
	Total	**22**	**Total**	**67**

[68] No account has been taken of the short sessions 1707, 1714 (2), 1721, 1727 (2), 1754 and 1768 in each of which only four or fewer committees were appointed.

Session	Whole House		Select	
1703–4	Salisbury, Bp	5	Stamford, 2 E.	14
	Ferrers, 7 L.	4	Rochester, 1 E.	13
	Herbert, 1 L.	3	Winchilsea, 4 E.	8
	9 Others	13	Somers, 1 L.	6
			Delawarr, 6 L.	5
			Manchester, 4 E.	5
			Somerset, 6 D.	5
			Herbert, 1 L.	4
			Halifax, 1 L.	3
			Salisbury, Bp	3
			18 Others	21
	Total	**25**	**Total**	**87**
1704–5	Herbert, 1 L.	7	Stamford, 2 E.	22
	Stamford, 2 E.	6	Bolton, 2 D.	8
	Sunderland, 3 E.	6	Rochester, 1 E.	7
	Halifax, 1 L.	4	Herbert, 1 L.	6
	6 Others	7	Salisbury, Bp	6
			Halifax, 1 L.	3
			Howard of Escrick, 4 L.	3
			Orford, 1 E.	3
			Winchilsea, 4 E.	3
			12 Others	15
	Total	**30**	**Total**	**76**
1705–6	Stamford, 2 E.	11	Rochester, I E.	22
	Herbert, 1 L.	8	Stamford, 2 E.	15
	9 Others	10	Somers, 1 L.	8
			Halifax, 1 L.	7
			Kingston, 5 E.	6
			Bolton, 2 D.	5
			Herbert, 1 L.	5
			Guilford, 2 L.	4
			Winchilsea, 4 E.	4
			Somerset, 6 D.	3
			Townshend, 2 V.	3
			I3 Others	14
	Total	**29**	**Total**	**96**
1706–7	Stamford, 2 E.	9	Rochester, 1 E.	22
	Herbert, 1 L.	8	Stamford, 2 E.	11
	Salisbury, Bp	6	Oxford, Bp	9
	5 Others	7	Salisbury, Bp	5
			Halifax, 1 L.	4
			Townshend, 2 V.	3
			12 Others	15
	Total	**30**	**Total**	**69**

Session	Whole House		Select	
1707–8	Herbert, 1 L.	32	Rochester, 1 E.	7
	Salisbury, Bp	7	Bolton, 2 D.	7
	Stamford, 2 E.	7	Somers, 1 L.	7
	Rochester, 1 E.	4	Halifax, 1 L.	5
	Guilford, 2 L.	3	Salisbury, Bp	4
	Halifax, 1 L.	3	Stamford, 2 E.	4
	5 Others	6	Warrington, 2 E.	4
			Devonshire, 2 D.	3
			Herbert, 1 L.	3
			Townshend, 2 V.	3
			9 Others	12
	Total	**62**	**Total**	**59**
1708–9	Stamford, 2 E.	13	Derby, 10 E.	6
	Halifax, 1 L.	5	Stamford, 2 E.	6
	Winchilsea, 4 E.	3	Rochester, 1 E.	5
	11 Others	16	Dorset, 7 E.	4
			Guilford, 2 L.	4
			Halifax, 1 L.	4
			Townshend, 2 V.	3
			14 Others	17
	Total	**37**	**Total**	**49**
1709–10	Delawarr, 6 L.	6	Rochester, 1 E.	20
	Stamford, 2 E.	3	Wharton, 1 E.	3
	7 Others	9	13 Others	17
	Total	**18**	**Total**	**40**
1710–11	Abingdon, 2 E.	12	Clarendon, 3 E.	8
	Delawarr, 6 L.	10	Delawarr, 6 L.	8
	Clarendon, 3 E.	9	Rochester, 1 E.	4
	Stamford, 2 E.	5	Stamford, 2 E.	4
	Ferrers, 7 L.	4	Chester, Bp	3
	Guilford, 2 L.	4	Ferrers, 7 L.	3
	10 Others	12	12 Others	17
	Total	**56**	**Total**	**47**
1711–12	Clarendon, 3 E.	19	Clarendon, 3 E.	18
	Delawarr, 6 L.	13	Nottingham, 2 E.	3
	Ferrers, 1 E.	6	Trevor, 1 L.	3
	Winchilsea, 4 E.	5	14 Others	22
	Abingdon, 2 E.	3		
	15 Others	18		
	Total	**64**	**Total**	**46**
1713	Delawarr, 6 L.	9	Clarendon, 3 E.	6
	Clarendon, 3 E.	4	Delawarr, 6 L.	6
	4 Others	5	Chester, Bp	4
			Yarmouth, 2 E.	4
			11 Others	13
	Total	**18**	**Total**	**33**

Session	Whole House		Select	
1714 (1)	Clarendon, 3 E.	8	Delawarr, 6 L.	5
	Yarmouth, 2 E.	6	Rochester, 2 E.	4
	London, Bp	4	Clarendon, 3 E.	3
	Delawarr, 6 L.	3	Cowper, 1 L.	3
	North, 6 L.	3	17 Others	21
	York, Abp	3		
	9 Others	10		
	Total	**37**	**Total**	**36**
1715–16	Clarendon, 3 E.	41	Clarendon, 3 E.	28
	Delawarr, 6 L.	18	Delawarr, 6 L.	6
	Carleton, 1 L.	4	Stamford, 2 E.	4
	Stamford, 2 E.	3	Bolton, 2 D.	3
	11 Others	15	Carlisle, Bp	3
			Nottingham, 2 E.	3
			Warrington, 2 E.	3
			12 Others	15
	Total	**81**	**Total**	**65**
1717	Clarendon, 3 E.	23	Clarendon, 3 E.	21
	Torrington, 1 L.	4	Trevor, 1 L.	3
	1 Other	1	12 Others	15
	Total	**28**	**Total**	**39**
1717–18	Clarendon, 3 E.	20	Clarendon, 3 E.	25
	1 Other	1	7 Others	9
	Total	**21**	**Total**	**34**
1718–19	Clarendon, 3 E.	43	Clarendon, 3 E.	33
	1 Other	2	8 Others	9
	Total	**45**	**Total**	**42**
1719–20	Clarendon, 3 E.	26	Clarendon, 3 E.	44
	2 Others	2	Delawarr, 6 L.	8
			7 Others	9
	Total	**28**	**Total**	**61**
1720–1	Clarendon, 3 E.	42	Clarendon, 3 E.	46
			Delawarr, 6 L.	4
			Warrington, 2 E.	3
			Westmorland, 6 E.	3
			6 Others	6
	Total	**42**	**Total**	**62**
1721–2	Clarendon, 3 E.	30	Clarendon, 3 E.	40
			2 Others	2
	Total	**30**	**Total**	**42**

Session	Whole House		Select	
1722–3	Clarendon, 3 E.	10	Clarendon, 3 E.	18
	Westmorland, 6 E.	6	Yarmouth, 2 E.	8
	Delawarr, 6 L.	4	Delawarr, 6 L.	6
	2 Others	2	Dorset, 1 D.	5
			5 Others	8
	Total	**22**	**Total**	**45**
1724	Delawarr, 7 L.	7	Yarmouth, 2 E.	9
	4 Others	6	Delawarr, 7 L.	7
			Findlater, 4 E.	7
			Bristol, Bp	3
			9 Others	11
	Total	**13**	**Total**	**37**
1724–5	Delawarr, 7 L.	18	Delawarr, 7 L.	30
	4 Others	6	Norwich, Bp	13
			Findlater, 4 E.	5
			Yarmouth, 2 E.	4
			Guilford, 2 L.	3
			Warrington, 2 E.	3
			7 Others	7
	Total	**24**	**Total**	**65**
1726	Delawarr, 7 L.	11	Delawarr, 7 L.	24
	Norwich, Bp	6	Norwich, Bp	24
	1 Other	1	6 Others	10
	Total	**18**	**Total**	**58**
1727 (1)	Waldegrave, 2 L.	8	Norwich, Bp	35
	Delawarr, 7 L.	6	Delawarr, 7 L.	16
	Norwich, Bp	3	Waldegrave, 2 L.	3
	1 Other	1	7 Others	8
	Total	**18**	**Total**	**62**
1728	Delawarr, 7 L.	12	Delawarr, 7 L.	37
	Westmorland, 6 E.	4	Peterborough, Bp	5
			Falmouth, 1 V.	3
			Findlater, 4 E.	3
			4 Others	5
	Total	**16**	**Total**	**53**
1729	Delawarr, 7 L.	27	Delawarr, 7 L.	35
	Findlater, 4 E.	3	Findlater, 4 E.	6
	2 Others	2	8 Others	8
	Total	**32**	**Total**	**49**

Session	Whole House		Select	
1730	Delawarr, 7 L.	13	Delawarr, 7 L.	13
	Findlater, 4 E.	3	Findlater, 4 E.	12
	1 Other	1	Bath & Wells, Bp	5
			Bathurst, 1 L.	3
			Wilmington, 1 L.	3
			10 Others	12
	Total	**17**	**Total**	**48**
1731	Delawarr, 7 L.	10	Delawarr, 7 L.	24
	Falmouth, 1 V.	6	Falmouth, 1 V.	8
	Dorset, 1 D.	3	Wilmington, 1 E.	6
	Westmorland, 6 E.	3	Strafford, 1 E.	4
	3 Others	4	11 Others	12
	Total	**26**	**Total**	**54**
1732	Delawarr, 7 L.	18	Delawarr, 7 L.	22
	Falmouth, 1 V.	10	Falmouth, 1 V.	22
	1 Other	2	12 Others	15
	Total	**30**	**Total**	**59**
1733	Delawarr, 7 L.	14	Delawarr, 7 L.	22
	Falmouth, 1 V.	10	Falmouth, 1 V.	11
	Lovell, 1 L.	3	Strafford, 1 E.	4
	2 Others	2	13 Others	14
	Total	**29**	**Total**	**51**
1734	Warwick, 8 E.	8	Strafford, 1 E.	8
	Delawarr, 7 L.	3	Delawarr, 7 L.	6
	5 Others	8	Bathurst, 1 L.	4
			Shaftesbury, 4 E.	4
			15 Others	15
	Total	**19**	**Total**	**37**
1735	Warwick, 8 E.	7	Delawarr, 7 L.	9
	Delawarr, 7 L.	4	Warwick, 8 E.	6
	1 Other	2	Wilmington, 1 E.	5
			15 Others	24
	Total	**13**	**Total**	**44**
1736	Warwick, 8 E.	14	Warwick, 8 E.	28
	Delawarr, 7 L.	3	Portland, 2 D.	7
	4 Others	5	Macclesfield, 2 E.	4
			Shaftesbury, 4 E.	3
			12 Others	17
	Total	**22**	**Total**	**59**
1737	Delawarr, 7 L.	16	Delawarr, 7 L.	17
	Warwick, 8 E.	10	Warwick, 8 E.	13
	1 Other	1	Findlater, 5 E.	5
			15 Others	21
	Total	**27**	**Total**	**56**

Session	Whole House		Select	
1738	Warwick, 8 E.	9	Warwick, 8 E.	34
	Delawarr, 7 L.	8	Cholmondeley, 3 E.	7
	Findlater, 5 E.	3	Findlater, 5 E.	4
	3 Others	3	9 Others	16
	Total	**23**	**Total**	**51**
1739	Warwick, 8 E.	16	Warwick, 8 E.	19
	Delawarr, 7 L.	8	Portland, 2 D.	7
	1 Other	1	Findlater, 5 E.	6
			Delawarr, 7 L.	4
			15 Others	21
	Total	**25**	**Total**	**57**
1739–40	Warwick, 8 E.	14	Warwick, 8 E.	8
	Findlater, 5 E.	4	Findlater, 5 E.	6
	Delawarr, 7 L.	3	Delawarr, 7 L.	5
	2 Others	2	9 Others	15
	Total	**23**	**Total**	**34**
1740–1	Warwick, 8 E.	21	Warwick, 8 E.	15
	2 Others	3	Leeds, 4 D.	8
			Findlater, 5 E.	7
			Delawarr, 7 L.	5
			Oxford, 2 E.	5
			15 Others	18
	Total	**24**	**Total**	**58**
1741–2	Warwick, 8 E.	24	Findlater, 5 E.	11
	Delawarr, 7 L.	4	Norwich, Bp	5
	Findlater, 5 E.	3	Portland, 2 D.	5
			Sandwich, 4 E.	5
			Delawarr, 7 L.	4
			Oxford, 3 E.	4
			Warwick, 8 E.	4
			18 Others	20
	Total	**31**	**Total**	**58**
1742–3	Warwick, 8 E.	10	Willoughby of Parham, 5 L.	11
	Willoughby of Parham, 5 L.	8	Warwick, 8 E.	5
	2 Others	2	25 Others	30
	Total	**20**	**Total**	**46**
1743–4	Warwick, 8 E.	21	Warwick, 8 E.	23
	1 Other	1	Willoughby of Parham, 5 L.	7
			Portland, 2 D.	5
			20 Others	27
	Total	**22**	**Total**	**62**

Session	Whole House		Select	
1744–5	Warwick, 8 E.	26	Sandys, 1 L.	11
	1 Other	1	Warwick, 8 E.	7
			Willoughby of Parham, 5 L.	7
			Shaftesbury, 4 E.	6
			10 Others	12
	Total	**27**	**Total**	**43**
1745–6	Warwick, 8 E.	32	Warwick, 8 E.	14
	2 Others	3	Sandys, 1 L.	5
			Willoughby of Parham, 5 L.	5
			Monson, 1 L.	4
			12 Others	19
	Total	**35**	**Total**	**47**
1746–7	Warwick, 8 E.	24	Warwick, 8 E.	25
	Delawarr, 7 L.	3	Shaftesbury, 4 E.	6
	1 Other	1	Ward, 5 L.	6
			Findlater, 5 E.	5
			12 Others	18
	Total	**28**	**Total**	**60**
1747–8	Warwick, 8 E.	23	Warwick, 8 E.	17
	2 Others	2	Willoughby of Parham, 5 L.	14
			Ward, 5 L.	4
			7 Others	11
	Total	**25**	**Total**	**46**
1748–9	Warwick, 8 E.	21	Warwick, 8 E.	32
	Delawarr, 7 L.	3	Willoughby of Parham, 5 L.	15
	2 Others	2	Shaftesbury, 4 E.	8
			Oxford, 3 E.	4
			9 Others	17
	Total	**26**	**Total**	**76**
1749–50	Warwick, 8 E.	26	Warwick, 8 E.	22
	1 Other	1	Willoughby of Parham, 5 L.	11
			Delawarr, 7 L.	5
			9 Others	12
	Total	**27**	**Total**	**50**
1751	Warwick, 8 E.	17	Willoughby of Parham, 5 L.	29
	Willoughby of Parham, 5 L.	6	Warwick, 8 E.	12
	Findlater, 5 E.	4	Findlater, 5 E.	8
	Delawarr, 7 L.	3	Shaftesbury, 4 E.	6
	5 Others	6	15 Others	17
	Total	**36**	**Total**	**72**

Session	Whole House		Select	
1751–2	Warwick, 8 E.	27	Warwick, 8 E.	23
	Macclesfield, 2 E.	3	Willoughby of Parham, 5 L.	14
	1 Other	1	Sandys, 1 L.	11
			Shaftesbury, 4 E.	6
			Portland, 2 D.	4
			13 Others	20
	Total	**31**	**Total**	**78**
1753	Warwick, 8 E.	27	Warwick, 8 E.	31
	Findlater, 5 E.	5	Willoughby of Parham, 5 L.	22
	Willoughby of Parham, 5 L.	4	Sandys, 1 L.	13
	Sandys, 1 L.	3	Findlater, 5 E.	9
			Shaftesbury, 4 E.	9
			Portland, 2 D.	8
			Folkestone, 1 V.	5
			9 Others	18
	Total	**39**	**Total**	**115**
1753–4	Warwick, 8 E.	6	Willoughby of Parham, 5 L.	16
	Willoughby of Parham, 5 L.	6	Warwick, 8 E.	11
	Sandys, 1 L.	5	Sandys, 1 L.	9
	2 Others	2	Findlater, 5 E.	6
			15 Others	21
	Total	**19**	**Total**	**63**
1754–5	Warwick, 8 E.	71	Warwick, 8 E.	30
	Portland, 2 D.	4	Sandys, 1 L.	24
	Willoughby of Parham, 5 L.	4	Willoughby of Parham, 5 L.	24
	1 Other	1	10 Others	14
	Total	**26**	**Total**	**92**
1755–6	Warwick, 8 E.	26	Warwick, 8 E.	35
	Delawarr, 7 L.	5	Sandys, 1 L.	30
	Willoughby of Parham, 5 L.	3	Willoughby of Parham, 5 L.	16
	2 Others	4	Shaftesbury, 4 E.	6
			Oxford, 4 E.	4
			15 Others	21
	Total	**38**	**Total**	**112**
1756–7	Warwick, 8 E.	33	Warwick, 8 E.	45
			Willoughby of Parham, 5 L.	12
			Shaftesbury, 4 E.	11
			Marchmont, 3 E.	6
			18 Others	23
	Total	**33**	**Total**	**97**

Session	Whole House		Select	
1757–8	Willoughby of Parham, 5 L.	11	Marchmont, 3 E.	18
	Findlater, 5 E.	6	Sandys, 1 L.	12
	Warwick, 8 E.	6	Findlater, 5 E.	11
	Romney, 2 L.	5	Willoughby of Parham, 5 L.	5
	Delawarr, 7 L.	3	Scarbrough, 4 E.	4
	Fauconberg, 1 E.	3	16 Others	27
	6 Others	8		
	Total	**42**	**Total**	**77**
1758–9	Marchmont, 3 E.	12	Sandys, 1 L.	34
	Warwick, 8 E.	9	Willoughby of Parham, 5 L.	16
	Willoughby of Parham, 5 L.	8	Marchmont, 3 E.	15
	3 Others	3	Kinnoull, 8 E (S) (Hay, 2 L. (GB))	5
			Shaftesbury, 4 E.	5
			14 Others	22
	Total	**32**	**Total**	**97**
1759–60	Willoughby of Parham, 5 L.	22	Willoughby of Parham, 5 L.	37
	Sandys, I L.	4	Sandys, 1 L.	35
	Shaftesbury, 4 E.	3	Marchmont, 3 E.	7
	1 Other	1	St. Asaph, Bp	4
			15 Others	19
	Total	**30**	**Total**	**102**
1760–1	Willoughby of Parham, 5 L.	22	Willoughby of Parham, 5 L.	28
			Sandys, 1 L.	23
			Marchmont, 3 E.	14
			6 Others	6
	Total	**22**	**Total**	**71**
1761–2	Willoughby of Parham, 5 L.	15	Marchmont, 3 E.	50
	Marchmont, 3 E.	9	Willoughby of Parham, 5 L.	31
	Delamer, 4 L.	6	Shaftesbury, 4 E.	11
	5 Others	5	Kinnoull, 8 E. (S) (Hay, 2 L. (GB))	10
			Boston, 1 L.	7
			Abercorn, 8 E.	5
			Walpole, 2 L.	3
			17 Others	21
	Total	**35**	**Total**	**138**
1762–3	Willoughby of Parham, 5 L.	14	Willoughby of Parham, 5 L.	34
	Shaftesbury, 4 E.	8	Marchmont, 3 E.	15
	Marchmont, 3 E.	3	Sandys, 1 L.	12
			Delamer, 4 L.	4
			Kinnoull, 8 E. (S) (Hay, 2 L. (GB))	3
			St. John of Bletso, 11 L.	3
			11 Others	11
	Total	**25**	**Total**	**82**

Session	Whole House		Select	
1763–4	Willoughby of Parham, 5 L.	34	Willoughby of Parham, 5 L.	56
	2 Others	2	Sandys, 1 L.	48
			Marchmont, 3 E.	12
			Winchilsea, 8 E.	6
			Bedford, 4 D.	3
			Delamer, 4 L.	3
			13 Others	19
	Total	**36**	**Total**	**147**
1765	Delamer, 4 L.	42	Delamer, 4 L.	61
	Marchmont, 3 E.	3	Sandys, 1 L.	52
	2 Others	2	Botetourt, 4 L.	19
			Marchmont, 3 E.	18
			Boston, 1 L.	11
			Abercorn, 8 E.	5
			Winchlilsea, 8 E.	5
			12 Others	14
	Total	**47**	**Total**	**185**
1765–6	Delamer, 4 L.	40	Sandys, 1 L.	64
	Botetourt, 4 L.	12	Delamer, 4 L.	40
			Botetourt, 4 L.	36
			Llandaff, Bp	3
			Wentworth, 1 V.	3
			8 Others	9
	Total	**52**	**Total**	**155**
1766–7	Botetourt, 4 L.	50	Botetourt, 4 L.	89
	Delamer, 4 L.	9	Sandys, 1 L.	54
			Delamer, 4 L.	12
			Marchmont, 3 E.	7
			Oxford, 4 E.	4
			3 Others	5
	Total	**59**	**Total**	**171**
1767–8	Delamer, 4 L.	28	Delamer, 4 L.	38
			Botetourt, 4 L.	31
			Sandys, 1 L.	31
			Marchmont, 3 E.	5
			2 Others	2
	Total	**28**	**Total**	**107**

Session	Whole House		Select	
1768–9	Delamer, 4 L.	28	Delamer, 4 L.	73
	Abercorn, 8 E.	4	Sandys, 1 L.	57
	1 Other	2	Saye & Sele, 6 V.	10
			Boston, 1 L.	7
			Marchmont, 3 E.	6
			Wentworth, 1 V.	6
			Sandwich, 4 E.	4
			Gower, 2 E.	3
			10 Others	12
	Total	**34**	**Total**	**178**
1770	Wentworth, 1 V.	36	Wentworth, 1 V.	103
	3 Others	3	Boston, 1 L.	21
			Marchmont, 3 E.	20
			Sandys, 1 L.	12
			Oxford, 4 E.	8
			Walpole, 2 L.	3
			7 Others	7
	Total	**39**	**Total**	**174**
1770–1	Wentworth, 1 V.	26	Wentworth, 1 V.	74
	Boston, 1 L.	8	Sandys, 1 L.	50
	2 Others	2	Boston, 1 L.	44
			Abercorn, 8 E.	6
			Rosebery, 3 E.	5
			4 Others	7
	Total	**36**	**Total**	**186**
1772	Wentworth, 1 V.	24	Boston, 1 L.	100
	Boston, 1 L.	18	Wentworth, 1 V.	59
	Sandys, 1 L.	4	Sandys, 1 L.	14
	Denbigh, 6 E.	3	Oxford, 4 E.	8
	Falmouth, 2 V.	3	Abercorn, 8 E.	5
	4 Others	5	Westmorland, 9 E.	5
			Denbigh, 6 E.	3
			5 Others	6
	Total	**57**	**Total**	**200**
1772–3	Boston, 1 L.	30	Wentworth, 1 V.	78
	Wentworth, 1 V.	20	Boston, 1 L.	62
	3 Others	4	Westmorland, 9 E.	30
			Marchmont, 3 E.	3
			7 Others	7
	Total	**54**	**Total**	**180**

Session	Whole House		Select	
1774	Boston, 1 L.	56	Boston, 1 L.	153
	Bruce, 2 L.	3	Buckinghamshire, 2 E.	3
	7 Others	7	Cathcart, 9 L.	3
			Abercorn, 8 E.	3
			6 Others	7
	Total	**66**	**Total**	**169**
1774–5	Scarsdale, 1 L.	27	Scarsdale, 1 L.	97
	Galloway, 7 E.	4	Marchmont, 3 E.	16
	4 Others	7	Chandos, 3 D.	5
			Montfort, 2 L.	3
			9 Others	10
	Total	**38**	**Total**	**131**
1775–6	Scarsdale, 1 L.	30	Scarsdale, 1 L.	136
	Marchmont, 3 E.	7	Cathcart, 9 L.	6
	Abercorn, 8 E.	4	Sandys, 2 L.	5
	2 Others	3	Dalhousie, 8 E.	4
			Chandos, 3 D.	3
			Marchmont, 3 E.	3
			10 Others	15
	Total	**44**	**Total**	**172**
1776–7	Scarsdale, 1 L.	23	Scarsdale, 1 L.	173
	Polwarth, L. (Hume, 1 L. (GB))	19	Polwarth, L. (Hume, 1 L. (GB))	23
	Sandys, 2 L.	4	Rosebery, 3 E.	3
	Brownlow, 1 L.	3	Willoughby of Parham, 14 L.	3
	2 Others	2	7 Others	10
	Total	**51**	**Total**	**212**
1777–8	Scarsdale, 1 L.	33	Scarsdale, 1 L.	145
	Sandys, 2 L.	6	Oxford, 4 E.	13
	Dudley and Ward, 2 V.	5	Sandys, 2 L.	10
	9 Others	12	Le Despencer, 11 L.	5
			Dalhousie, 8 E.	4
			Dudley and Ward, 2 V.	4
			Willoughby of Parham, 14 L.	3
			5 Others	5
	Total	**56**	**Total**	**189**
1778–9	Scarsdale, 1 L.	44	Scarsdale, 1 L.	118
	Chesterfield, 5 E.	10	Willoughby of Parham, 14 L.	12
	Willoughby of Parham, 14 L.	7	Sandys, 2 L.	7
	Effingham, 3 E.	4	Oxford, 4 E.	5
	Marchmont, 3 E.	4	Portland, 3 D.	5
	Sandys, 2 L.	4	Marchmont, 3 E.	4
	Abercorn, 8 E.	3	Gower, 2 E.	3
	7 Others	9	10 Others	16
	Total	**85**	**Total**	**170**

Session	Whole House		Select	
1779–80	Scarsdale, 1 L.	22	Scarsdale, 1 L.	85
	Galloway, 7 E.	7	Fitzwilliam, 4 E.	4
	Abercorn, 8 E.	6	King, 6 L.	3
	Dudley and Ward, 2 V.	5	Marchmont, 3 E.	3
	Dartmouth, 2 E.	3	12 Others	15
	Le Despencer, 11 L.	3		
	Oxford, 4 E.	3		
	4 Others	5		
	Total	**54**	**Total**	**110**
1780–1	Sandys, 2 L.	30	Scarsdale, 1 L.	62
	Scarsdale, 1 L.	15	Bagot, 1 L.	6
	Walsingham, 2 L.	6	Sandys, 2 L.	5
	Abercorn, 8 E.	4	Chandos, 3 D.	4
	Dudley and Ward, 2 V,	3	St. Davids, Bp	3
	Galloway, 7 E	3	9 Others	13
	Hillsborough, 1 E.	3		
	3 Others	3		
	Total	**67**	**Total**	**93**
1781–2	Scarsdale, 1 L.	45	Searsdale 1 L.	65
	Galloway, 7 E.	8	Bagot, 1 L.	3
	Walsingham, 2 L.	3	Bristol, Bp	3
	8 Others	11	Radnor, 2 E.	3
			Sandys, 2 L.	3
			Walsingham, 2 L.	3
			8 Others	11
	Total	**67**	**Total**	**91**
1782–3	Chedworth, 4 L.	23	Scarsdale, 1 L.	67
	Scarsdale, 1 L.	22	Chedworth, 4 L.	7
	Fitzwilliam, 4 E.	5	Sydney, 1 L.	6
	6 Others	9	Sandwich, 4 E.	4
			Dudley and Ward, 2 V.	3
			5 Others	6
	Total	**59**	**Total**	**93**
1783–4	Scarsdale, 1 L.	7	Scarsdale, 1 L.	29
	1 Other	1	3 Others	4
	Total	**8**	**Total**	**33**
1784	Walsingham, 2 L.	27	Scarsdale, 1 L.	20
	Scarsdale, 1 L.	6	Rawdon, 1 L.	11
	Galloway, 7 E.	4	Effingham, 3 E.	6
	Howard de Walden, 4 L.	4	Walsingham, 2 L.	3
	4 Others	6	9 Others	13
	Total	**47**	**Total**	**53**

Session	Whole House		Select	
1785	Scarsdale, 1 L.	46	Scarsdale, 1 L.	100
	Hawke, 2 L.	25	Bangor, Bp	3
	Chedworth, 4 L.	5	Chedworth, 4 L.	3
	4 Others	6	Galloway, 7 E.	3
			Shaftesbury, 5 E.	3
			9 Others	13
	Total	**82**	**Total**	**125**
1786	Scarsdale, 1 L.	73	Scarsdale, 1 L.	104
	Chedworth, 4 L.	9	Hawke, 2 L.	18
	3 Others	3	Dudley and Ward, 2 V.	9
			Bristol, Bp	3
			5 Others	5
	Total	**85**	**Total**	**139**
1787	Scarsdale, 1 L.	44	Scarsdale, 1 L.	82
	Galloway, 7 E.	4	King, 6 L.	6
			Bangor, Bp	3
			Kinnaird, 7 L.	3
			7 Others	9
	Total	**48**	**Total**	**103**
1787–8	Scarsdale, 1 L.	40	Scarsdale, 1 L.	68
	Chedworth, 4 L.	7	Bangor, Bp	16
	Hawkesbury, 1 L.	4	Hawke, 2 L.	10
	Walsingham, 2 L.	4	Hopetoun, 3 E.	4
	Hawke, 2 L.	3	Macclesfield, 3 E.	4
	2 Others	3	Morton, 16 E.	3
			13 Others	18
	Total	**61**	**Total**	**123**
1788–9	Scarsdale, I L.	19	Scarsdale, 1 L.	77
	Walsingham, 2 L.	8	Hopetoun, 3 E.	9
	Hopetoun, 3 E.	7	Somers, 1 L.	9
	Chcdworth, 4 L.	5	Bagot, 1 L.	7
	Sandwich, 5 E.	5	Hawke, 2 L.	6
	5 Others	6	Rawdon, 1 L.	6
			Radnor, 2 E.	4
			19 Others	20
	Total	**50**	**Total**	**138**
1790	Cathcart, 10 L.	36	Cathcart, 10 L.	110
	Hawkesbury, L.	7	Bangor, Bp	12
			Sandwich, 5 E.	3
			4 Others	5
	Total	**43**	**Total**	**130**

Session	Whole House		Select	
1790–1	Cathcart, 10 L.	46	Cathcart, 10 L.	82
	Middleton, 5 L.	5	Bangor, Bp	30
	6 Others	7	Gloucester, Bp	12
			Sandwich, 5 E.	11
			Hawke, 2 L.	6
			Coventry, 6 E.	4
			Rawdon, 1 L.	4
			Bristol, Bp	3
			10 Others	12
	Total	**58**	**Total**	**164**
1792	Cathcart, 10 L.	44	Cathcart, 10 L.	75
	Chedworth, 4 L.	6	Bangor, Bp	39
	Kellie, 7 E.	3	Portland, 3D.	11
	Stanhope, 3 E.	3	Scarsdale, 1 L.	9
	5 Others	6	Rawdon, 1 L.	7
			Derby, 12 E.	5
			Atholl, 4 D. (S) (Strange, 1 E. (GB))	3
			Fitzwilliam, 4 E.	3
			Lauderdale, 8 E.	3
			Macclesfield, 3 E.	3
			Stormont, 7 V.	3
			16 Others	20
	Total	**62**	**Total**	**181**
1792–3	Cathcart, 10 L.	42	Bangor, Bp	102
	Bangor, Bp	9	Cathcart, 10 L.	58
	Exeter, Bp	8	Sydney, 1 V.	8
	Chedworth, 4 L.	3	Fitzwilliam, 4 E.	6
	Walsingham, 2 L.	3	Gloucester, Bp	6
	8 Others	10	Ferrers, 7 E.	5
			Suffield, 1 L.	5
			Derby, 12 E.	4
			Lauderdale, 8 E.	4
			Strafford, 3 E.	4
			Coventry, 6 E.	3
			Grey de Wilton, 1 V.	3
			Hawke, 2 L.	3
			Somers, 1 L.	3
			18 Others	20
	Total	**75**	**Total**	**234**

Session	Whole House		Select	
1794	Bangor, Bp	57	Bangor, Bp	150
	Auckland, 1 L.	7	Derby, 12 E.	5
	Walsingham, 2 L.	4	Leeds, 5 D.	5
	Suffolk, 15 E.	3	Brownlow, 1 L.	3
	2 Others	3	Hawke, 2 L.	3
			Sydney, 1 V.	3
			15 Others	19
	Total	**74**	**Total**	**188**
1794–5	Walsingham, 2 L.	87	Walsingham, 2 L.	148
	2 Others	2	Bangor, Bp	37
			5 Others	5
	Total	**89**	**Total**	**190**
1795–6	Walsingham, 2 L.	88	Walsingham, 2 L.	173
			Bangor, Bp	8
			3 Others	3
	Total	**88**	**Total**	**184**
1796–7	Walsingham, 2 L.	89	Walsingham, 2 L.	222
			6 Others	8
	Total	**89**	**Total**	**230**
1797–8	Walsingham, 2 L.	93	Walsingham, 2 L.	160
			3 Others	3
	Total	**93**	**Total**	**163**
1798–9	Walsingham, 2 L.	118	Walsingham, 2 L.	199
			2 Others	3
	Total	**118**	**Total**	**202**
1799–1800	Walsingham, 2 L.	100	Walsingham, 2 L.	220
			2 Others	2
	Total	**100**	**Total**	**222**

Chapter 5. The Parliament Office in the Seventeenth and Eighteenth Centuries: Biographical Notes on Clerks in the House of Lords 1600 to 1800

Note on Sources

In 1958 Mr M.F. Bond published in the *English Historical Review* an article entitled 'Clerks of the Parliaments, 1509–1953'. This provides a definitive account of the succession to the office during the period covered by these notes, derived from the letters patent of appointment and records of salary payments at The National Archives, supplemented by information from biographical sources.

There is no distinct class of document dealing with the clerical organisation of the parliament office amongst the records of the House of Lords which is earlier in date than 1800. References to clerks in the Journals and manuscripts are largely of an incidental character. Perhaps the most useful documents are the petitions presented by clerks to the House which are recorded in the Journals. Where the manuscript originals of such petitions survive they often contain additional material of value. From 1724 appointments to the offices of clerk assistant and reading clerk were, as a general rule, reported to the House and recorded in the Journals. A few deeds of appointment to various posts in the parliament office, executed by the clerk of the parliaments, survive amongst the manuscripts of the House. Also preserved in the Parliamentary Archives are photocopies of two documents from the Braye Papers which have a special significance: the agreement between Robert Bowyer and Owen Reynolds 1610 and the list of fees compiled by John Throckmorton about 1624. In the same repository are four printed circulars drawn up by Ashley Cowper in 1753 and 1763 in defence of his rights of appointment.

A certain amount of material survives in other repositories. Amongst the Stowe MSS at the British Library is a valuable memorandum dealing with the case of James Merest c. 1724. The Rose Papers contain some material relating to the periods of office of George Rose (1788–1818) and of his two predecessors, William and Ashley Cowper (1716–40 and 1740–88) which is photocopied in the Parliamentary Archives. At The National Archives a certain amount of material survives amongst the treasury books and papers. This includes petitions of clerks seeking remuneration and also records of payment of salaries or bounties.

From 1742 the various annual directories such as the *Court and City Register* and *Royal Kalendar* regularly list the staff of the House of Lords. When the information provided by these directories can be checked against other evidence it is found to be generally accurate.

Introduction

In 1960 the House of Lords Record Office published memorandum No. 22 entitled *Clerks in the Parliament Office 1600–1900*. In 1971 this was replaced by memorandum No. 45 entitled *Officers of the House of Lords, 1485–1971*. Neither of these memoranda aimed to do more than provide handlists of those who served House during the relevant periods. In the course of compiling these lists a considerable amount of biographical material was assembled from a variety of sources. Of this that which relates to clerks who served in the parliament office between 1600 and 1800 is presented here.

While it is outside the scope of this introduction to provide a full account of the development of the parliament office during the two centuries in question, something must be said on the subject so that the careers of individual clerks may be related to a general framework. The office was presided over by the clerk of the parliaments from whom it took its name. The clerk of the parliaments was the only clerk appointed by the crown for the service of the House of Lords. There was probably never a time when he could have carried out his duties single-handed, at least while parliament was in session. In the earliest period he doubtless obtained such assistance as he required from individuals employed at his pleasure on a temporary basis. In the course of time his freedom of action in this area came to be limited by the emergence of certain subordinate posts whose existence received a kind of prescriptive sanction.[1]

The first two such posts to emerge were those which subsequently acquired the titles of clerk assistant and reading clerk, whose holders sat at the table of the House beside the clerk of the parliaments. The clerk assistant, in addition to assisting the clerk of the parliaments in the general direction of the office, had a special responsibility for writing the minutes of proceedings of the House. The reading clerk's title referred to his function of reading documents publicly in the House. His most substantial duty was, however, reflected in his subsidiary designation, that of clerk of 'private' or 'outdoor' committees – that is to say, committees which sat outside the chamber.[2] The evolution of these two posts is difficult to trace because it was not originally the practice to use distinctive terms to identify them. Terms such as 'deputy', 'clerk', 'under clerk' and 'clerk assistant' tended at first to be used in a general rather than a specific sense to describe clerks in the parliament office. Nevertheless it seems reasonable to regard the expression 'the Clerk's Two Men' which occurs in 1626 as a reference to the holders of the posts in question.[3]

The first identifiable holder of the senior of the two posts is Owen Reynolds who was appointed by Sir Thomas Smith, clerk of the parliaments 1597–1609. Smith referred to Reynolds indifferently as his 'deputy' or 'under clerk'.[4] Reynolds was retained in office by the next clerk of the parliaments, Robert Bowyer, and served until his death

---

[1] For the office of clerk of the parliaments during the period, see Bond, 'Clerks of the Parliaments'; M.F. Bond, 'The Formation of the Archives of Parliament', *Journal of the Society of Archivists*, i (1957), 151–8; C. Ryscamp, *William Cowper of the Inner Temple, Esq.* (Cambridge, 1959), 148–53.

[2] The duties of the clerk assistant and the reading clerk were described to a House of Lords Committee by the then clerk assistant, Joseph Wight, in 1763 (PA, MS Committee Books, 13 Dec. 1763).

[3] *LJ*, iii, 682. See also E.R. Foster, 'The Painful Labour of Mr Elsyng', *Transactions of the American Philosophical Society*, lxii, (1972), 12.

[4] PA, Braye MS 54/37: draft agreement between Robert Bowyer and Owen Reynolds, Mar. 1610.

in 1610. Reynolds' successor, Henry Elsyng, was probably appointed in the same year and served until 1621 when he himself became clerk of the parliaments.[5] Elsyng appointed John Throckmorton to the post, probably in the same year. Throckmorton served in this capacity until his death in 1664 except for the period when the House of Lords was abolished 1649–60. Throckmorton kept the minutes of the House.[6] This, as already noted, was regarded as the distinctive function of the clerk assistant and it therefore seems reasonable to regard Reynolds, Elsyng and Throckmorton and their successors, the elder and younger John Walker (1664–82 and 1682–1715) as the earliest known holders of that post. The term 'clerk assistant' appears first to have been used in a specific sense to describe the office in 1663[7] but for some time after this it remained only an alternative to such designations as 'deputy clerk of the parliaments'. In all probability it was not until after the appointment of James Merest to the post in 1724 that it finally established itself as the usual title of the office.

The earlier history of the junior of the clerk of the parliaments' 'two men' is a good deal more obscure than that of his senior colleague. The title 'reading clerk' is first found used in 1661 when it was applied to the elder John Walker who had held the office since the Restoration in the previous year.[8] No predecessor of Walker can be identified with any certainty although it is conceivable that Thomas Ken, who is known to have been a clerk in the 1640s, occupied the post. Walker probably remained reading clerk until 1664 when he was made clerk assistant. The next known occupant of the post was John Relfe who first occurs in 1673. He may have been appointed to replace Walker in 1664 but there can be no certainty on the point. From the time of Relfe the succession to the office presents no problems.

Both the clerk assistant and the reading clerk enjoyed a recognised right to fees on business transacted in the House.[9] In addition, salaries of £100, payable at the treasury, were attached to the offices from 1724 and 1736 respectively.[10]

The next two offices to emerge within the parliament office were those of clerk of the journals and copying clerk. The clerk of the journals was, as his title implies, responsible for compiling the journals of the House. The copying clerk supervised the business of copying acts of parliament and other documents from the fees on which the clerk of the parliaments derived a substantial income. The first identifiable clerk of the journals is Jeremiah Sambrooke who was appointed at an unknown date before his resignation in 1709.[11] He was succeeded by James Merest who seems to have served until his appointment as reading clerk in 1715. In 1718 John Jenings was appointed. The first identifiable copying clerk was Gerald Fitzgerald who held the office at his death in 1718.[12] His successor may have been John Wheake who was probably replaced by Edmund Fitzgerald in 1724. From the time of John Jenings (1718–37) and Edmund

---

[5] Foster, 'Painful Labour of Elsyng', 11.

[6] Throckmorton's death is recorded in the manuscript minutes (PA, Manuscript Minutes 1660–4, f. following 2 May 1664).

[7] *LJ*, xi, 577.

[8] *LJ*, xi, 318.

[9] *LJ*, xxii, 627–9.

[10] TNA, T53/31, p. 93; T 53/39, p. 80.

[11] BL, Stowe MS 354, f. 233.

[12] PA, Main Papers, petition of Edmund Fitzgerald, 12 June 1733.

Fitzgerald (1724–35) respectively the succession to the offices of clerk of the journals and copying clerk is firmly established. That the two clerks regarded themselves as occupying positions of approximately equivalent rank is clear from the fact that they made a habit of presenting their claims for remuneration at the same time and in the same manner. Thus Merest and Gerald Fitzgerald petitioned the treasury together in 1714 and 1715 while Jenings and Gerald Fitzgerald did likewise in 1718. Jenings and Edmund Fitzgerald both petitioned the House in 1726 and 1733. As a result of the last application the clerk of the journals and the copying clerk were each accorded an annual bounty or salary of £50 payable at the treasury.[13]

One other post requires particular mention. When in 1742 a list of clerks in the parliament office appeared, seemingly for the first time, in a published directory, it contained the name of John Merest 'Engrossing Clerk' ranking between the reading clerk and the clerk of the journals. The same person was ranked in the same position until 1755 when the office disappears from directories.[14] There is no other evidence of the existence of the clerkship of engrossments as a distinct office until 1820 although John Croft was at his death in 1797 described as 'Clerk of the Journals and Engrossments to the House of Lords'.[15] Possibly the two posts were combined in 1755.[16]

Apart from the five offices just described no other posts of special responsibility emerged within the parliament office before 1800. However, it is clear from the evidence given to the Lords committee on the appointment of the reading clerk in 1763 and from other sources that it had long been the practice for clerks or writers to be employed by the holders of these offices at their own expense to assist them in their duties.[17] Such clerks appear to have varied in number and technically did not form part of the parliament office in the strict sense. In certain cases, however, their abilities were such that they themselves obtained one of the offices in question. The most noteworthy examples were James Merest, Joseph Wight and Samuel Strutt, all of whom rose to become clerk assistant.

In 1781 published directories list for the first time four 'other clerks in the office' while in 1784 there is a reference to 'Four Writing Clerks in the Office'. The fact that the number of such clerks remained constant until 1812 suggests that this was in some sense understood to be an established complement. By 1788 a sum of £200 a year had been made available, apparently by the clerk of the parliaments, out of which the remuneration of these clerks was found.[18] It is impossible to say with certainty what the origin of these arrangements was. It is noteworthy that no allusion is made to them in the evidence given to the committee of 1763. Such evidence as there is, therefore, points to the conclusion that, at an unknown date between then and 1781, a fluctuating group of clerks of indeterminate status was transformed into a fixed number of junior clerks who were fully embodied in the parliament office.

[13] TNA, T 1/173, no. 42; T 1/193, no. 2; T 1/219, no. 36; *LJ*, xxii, 619; xxiv, 298, 306; *CTBP 1731–4*, pp. 404, 514.

[14] *New Court Register: List of Lords and Commons* (1742), 45; *CCR* (1755), 2.

[15] *WAR*, 457.

[16] The engrossing account for 1774 was signed by John Croft (BL, Add. MS 42779, f. 75).

[17] PA, MS Committee Books, 13 Dec. 1763. See also PA, Main Papers, petitions of James Merest, 21 Jan. 1723/4; John Jenings, 12 Mar. 1725/6.

[18] RK (1781), 67; (1812), 48; BL, Add. MS 42779, f. 49; PA, PO 58/3.

No account of the office during the period covered by these notes would be complete without a brief description of the manner in which the clerk of the parliaments exercised his patronage. The clerk of the parliaments was appointed by letters patent under the great seal. By the time of Sir Thomas Smith, the first seventeenth century clerk, it was the established practice for the office to be granted for life with provision for its duties to be exercised by deputy. From 1597 it was common for the office to be granted in reversion. The clerkship of the parliaments had thus throughout the period all the characteristic features of a proprietary office. As such it had considerable attractions. It did not require personal attendance. Although the patent salary was only £40 the income from fees, which arose principally on private bill and judicial business, was very much more substantial.[19] Finally there was the patronage attached to the office which enabled the clerk of the parliaments to provide for his relatives and dependants. However, it was not until the office passed into the hands of the Cowper family in 1716 that its potentialities were to be exploited in an extreme form.

Before this date successive clerks of the parliaments had officiated at the Table of the House and taken an active part in the daily business of the office. Matthew Johnson, clerk of the parliaments from 1691 to 1716, regularly participated in the ceremony of royal assent until 1714. Only for the last two years of his period of office did he delegate this function to the clerk assistant – a not unreasonable step to take given that he had reached the advanced age of 76.[20] Until the time of Johnson, too, incoming clerks of the parliaments respected the appointments made by their predecessors. In 1691, for example, Johnson retained both the clerk assistant, John Walker, and the reading clerk, John Relfe, who had been appointed by John Browne. Furthermore, although the clerk of the parliaments frequently appointed his relations to posts in the office, there was originally no suggestion that the individuals in question would neglect to qualify themselves for these posts or fail to exercise their duties in person. However, in this respect Johnson's nomination of his son as reading clerk in 1711 initiated a new trend since the appointment was made with no other purpose than to provide him with an income on the understanding that all the duties would be carried out by a deputy.[21]

The real change came about, however, when William Cowper succeeded Johnson as clerk of the parliaments in 1716. From that year until the death of Sir George Henry Rose in 1855 the clerk of the parliaments took practically no part in the daily business of the House. He ceased entirely to officiate at the ceremony of royal assent while in 1763 Joseph Wight, the clerk assistant, stated that 'The Clerk of the Parliaments has the Superintendency over all the Clerks in the office and the Business thereof but as he has never interfered to give any Directions therein, the Business has been carried on under the Superintendency of Mr. Wight ever since he was Clerk Assistant'.[22] In the face of this circumstantial evidence the claim of a later clerk assistant, Henry Cowper, that his uncle, Ashley, 'attended regularly every day . . . till he was about seventy years of age' can probably be discounted. When George Rose became clerk of the parliaments in

---

[19] Bond, 'Clerks of Parliaments', 78–81.

[20] *LJ*, xix, 695, 758; xx, 13, 50, 68, 122, 128, 176, 189, 235. Previously Johnson had absented himself from the ceremony only during the session of 1696 (*LJ*, xv, 647, 668, 679, 697, 732, 742).

[21] BL, Stowe MS 354, f. 233.

[22] PA, MS Committee Books, 13 Dec. 1763.

1788 Lord Chancellor Thurlow attempted to oblige him to act in person but, in the event, succeeded only in requiring him to sign the orders of the House.[23]

There seems little doubt that, from the time of William Cowper, the clerk of the parliaments delegated virtually all his functions to the clerk assistant and confined himself to receiving the profits of the office and exercising his rights of patronage. On becoming clerk of the parliaments Cowper seems to have made an agreement with Johnson that he would retain the latter's son as clerk assistant as long as he (the elder Johnson) lived. Evidently no similar guarantee was given to the reading clerk, James Merest, who was summarily dismissed and replaced by Charles Reynell. Reynell later claimed that he had been promised the office of clerk assistant by the Cowper family when it became vacant. It was possibly the fear that this promise would be honoured that finally led Merest in 1724 to appeal to the House to consider his case. His petition seeking reinstatement in the office of reading clerk was referred to the committee for privileges but before the committee had had time to report Cowper informed the House that he had appointed Merest clerk assistant and John Wheake reading clerk. Reynell, deprived of all standing in the parliament office, pursued Cowper unavailingly through the courts seeking redress. As a result of this incident the House adopted a standing order which provided that no clerk was to be removed from office without its leave.[24] Thereafter it became the practice for the appointments to the offices of clerk assistant and reading clerk to be notified to the House and to be subject to its approval. However, if one of the objects of the House in establishing this procedure was to secure the personal attendance of the holders of these offices it was only partially successful. The House had to acquiesce in the tenure of the office of reading clerk by an absentee between 1724 and 1736.

The authority of the House was exerted in 1753 when, as a result of Merest's death, a vacancy occurred in the office of clerk assistant. The clerk of the parliaments, Ashley Cowper, thereupon appointed his niece's husband, William de Grey, a barrister with no previous experience of the parliament office, to fill the post. On receiving notification of this appointment the House at once referred it to a committee. This action was sufficient to induce Cowper to revoke his appointment of de Grey and to nominate in his stead Joseph Wight, a clerk of great experience who had acted as reading clerk since 1724. However, this was to some extent a compromise solution as the House, at the same time that it confirmed Wight's appointment, also approved that of de Grey as reading clerk although it was probably clear from the outset that he did not intend to exercise his duties in person.[25]

The House acted in a more forceful fashion in 1763. Ashley Cowper's original choice of his nephew, William Cowper the poet, to succeed de Grey as reading clerk was rendered abortive by William Cowper's refusal to undertake so public an appointment. Matthew Robert Arnott was then nominated and his appointment was referred to a committee which conducted a searching enquiry into the state of the parliament office.

[23] *First Report from the Select Committee on Sinecure Offices*, HC 362, pp. 10–11, 37–8, 41–2 (1810), ii, 600–1, 627–8, 631–2; BL, Add. MS 42779, f. 51.

[24] *LJ*, xxii, 243, 250, 253, 265; PA, Main Papers, petition of James Merest, 21 Jan. 1723/4; BL, Stowe MS 354, f. 233.

[25] *LJ*, xxviii, 6, 9, 10, 13. For Ashley Cowper's defence of his rights, see PA, PO 79/1, *Reasons upon which the Right of the Clerk of the Parliaments to appoint a Clerk Assistant is founded* (1753); PO 79/1A, *Reasons upon which the Right of the Clerk of the Parliaments to appoint the Clerks under him is founded* (1753).

This enquiry revealed that de Grey had held the office of copying clerk as well as that of reading clerk and that he had exercised both by deputy. His deputy as reading clerk was the clerk of the journals whose duties as such were carried out by yet another deputy. In the event the committee endorsed Cowper's appointment of Arnott as reading clerk but declined to approve his nomination of Arnott to the post of copying clerk or of Richard Blyke to that of clerk of the journals. The committee showed its determination to reward past service to the House and to require the personal attendance of those occupying posts in the parliament office by insisting that the two clerks who had actually undertaken the duties of clerk of the journals and copying clerk should be recognised as the holders of those posts.[26]

Nevertheless, the House was evidently reluctant to circumscribe the rights of patronage of the clerk of the parliaments too radically, since in 1765 it acquiesced in an arrangement whereby Samuel Strutt was appointed clerk assistant on condition that he would relinquish that office in the event of Ashley Cowper wishing to appoint one of his great nephews to the post on attaining the age of twenty-one – a condition that was in the event abrogated in 1771 when Strutt was appointed without restrictions.[27]

The potential conflict of interest between the clerk of the parliaments and the House over the manner in which he exercised the functions of his office and the patronage attached to it was not resolved until after the period covered by these notes. An enquiry undertaken into the parliament office in 1824 led to the passage of the clerk of the parliaments act which, prospectively, required the personal attendance of the clerk of the parliaments and reduced his powers of patronage by transferring to the Lord Chancellor the right of nominating the clerk assistant and the reading clerk.[28] It was not, however, until the death of Sir George Henry Rose in 1855 that the provisions of the act could be brought fully into effect and the parliament office assumed its modern character.

Lists of Appointments

Clerk of parliaments

1597	Smith, T.
1609	Bowyer, R.
1621	Elsyng, H.
c. 1635	Knyvett, T.
1637	Bedingfield, D.
1638	Browne, J.
	(House abolished 1649–60)
1660	Browne, J.
1691	Johnson, M.
1716	Cowper, W.

[26] *LJ*, xxx, 420, 446, 514, 517–19; PA, MS Committee Books, 23 Nov., 1, 2, 5, 6, 13 Dec. 1763, 21 Mar. 1764. For Ashley Cowper's defence of his rights, see PA, PO 72/2, printed memorandum on clerks' bounties (1763); PO 72/3, printed memorandum on office of clerk of parliaments (1763).

[27] *LJ*, xxxi, 210; xxxiii, 77, 97, 690.

[28] *LJ*, lvi, 322–4, 441–2; Clerk of Parliaments Act 1824.

1740	Cowper, A.
1788	Rose, G.

Clerk assistant

By 1610	Reynolds, 0.
1610	Elsyng, H.
1621	Throckmorton, J.
	(House abolished 1649–60)
1660	Throckmorton, J.
1664	Walker, J.
1682	Walker, J.
1715	Johnson, M.
1724	Merest, J.
1752	de Grey, W.
1753	Wight, J.
1765	Strutt, S.
1785	Cowper, H.

Reading clerk

1660	Walker, J.
c. 1664	Relfe, J.
1711	Johnson, M.
1715	Merest, J.
1716	Reynell, C.
1724	Wheake, J.
1736	Wight, J.
1753	de Grey, W.
1763	Arnott, M.R.

Clerk of journals

By 1709	Sambrooke, J.
1709	Merest, J.
1718	Jenings, J.
1737	Macklay, F.
1763	Cowper, W.
1763	Blyke, R.
1764	Macklay, W.
1771	Croft, J.
1797	Parratt, E.

Copying clerk

By 1718	Fitzgerald, E.
(?) By 1724	Wheake, J.
1724	Fitzgerald, G.

1735	Wight, J.
1753	de Grey, W.
1763	Arnott, M.R.
1764	Strutt, S.
1765	Blackstock, E.
1799	Walmisley, W.

Clerks

By 1642	Ken, T.
1660	Relfe, J.
1689	Sambrooke. J.
1700	Merest, J.
1706	Jenings, J.
1715	Fitzgerald, E.
1716	Wight, J.
By 1718	Wheake, J.
By 1725	Merest, J.
1725	Price. J.
By 1733	Fitzgerald, G.
1753	Macklay. W.
1753	Strutt, S.
c. 1757	Croft, J.
1777	Walmisley, W.
By 1781	Parratt, E., Hamilton, J., Feary, F.W.
1793	Payne, W.C.
1797	Walmisley, W.
1799	Walmisley, E.G.

Alphabetical List of Clerks

Arnott, Matthew Robert *Reading clerk* 1763–1800. *Copying clerk* 1763–4.

Son of George Arnott (died 1750), vicar successively of Holbeach, Lincolnshire, and (1729–50) of Wakefield, Yorkshire (*Al. Cantab.*, i, 41). Died between 25 March 1800 when his will was made (TNA, Prob. 11/1341, f. 335) and 25 April 1800 when his successor as reading clerk, William Stewart Rose, was appointed (PA, PO 51/10).

Educated at Wakefield School. Admitted sizar Clare College, Cambridge 13 January 1741. Later pensioner at same college. Matriculated 1741. BA 1745. MA 1748. Fellow of Clare College 1748–52. Governor of Wakefield School 1787–1800 (*Al. Cantab.*, i, 41). Usher of order of Thistle 1787–1800 (*Al. Cantab.*, i, 41; TNA, HO 38/3, pp. 78–81, warrant 26 June 1787).

Appointed reading clerk and copying clerk 9 May 1763 (PA, MS Committee Books, 13 Dec. 1763). Appointment as reading clerk communicated to House 17 November 1763 and referred to a committee. Committee's report recommending that appointment as reading clerk, but not as copying clerk, should be confirmed agreed to by House 21 March 1764 (*LJ*, xxx, 420, 517–19). Remained reading clerk until death (*LJ*, xlii, 519).

Bedingfield, Daniel *Clerk of parliaments* 1637–8.

Belonged to younger branch of family of Bedingfield of Oxburgh, Norfolk. Fifth son of Christopher Bedingfield (1560–1627), of Wighton, Norfolk by Frances (died 1629), daughter of Humphrey Chambers, of Sturston, Suffolk (F. Blomefield, *An Essay towards a Topographical History of the County of Norfolk* (1739–75), v, 785–6; *Visitation of London* (Harleian Soc., xv, 1880), 62). Died 7 February 1638 (1637–8) (*Musgrave's Obituary* (Harleian Soc., xliv, 1899), 143).

Student Gray's Inn 9 February 1624 (*Register of Admissions to Gray' Inn, 1695–1889*, ed. J. Foster (1889), 171).

Clerk of parliaments December 1637–7 February 1638 (Bond, 'Clerks of Parliaments', 83).

Blackstock, Edward *Copying clerk* 1765–99

Parentage unknown. Born about 1733, being 66 at death 15 July 1799. His widow, Harriet, died 18 December 1831 (*WAR*, 460, 505).

Probably appointed copying clerk May 1765 in place of Samuel Strutt, promoted clerk assistant. First occurs as such 1766 (*CCR* (1766), ii). On 14 June 1793 Blackstock and John Croft, clerk of journals, presented memorial to House seeking recompense for diminution in income caused by Irish Judicature Act and other factors (*LJ*, xxxix, 764). Following address to crown received compensation of £100 from Treasury (TNA, T 53/61, pp. 122–3). Remained in office until death when described as 'Clerk of the Papers to the House of Lords for upwards of thirty years' (*WAR*, 460).

Blyke, Richard *Clerk of journals* 1763–4.

Elder son of Theophilus Blyke (died 1719), deputy secretary at war (*DNB;* TNA, Prob. 11/568, f. 60, will of Theophilus Blyke). Died 1775 (D. Lysons, *The Environs of London* (1796), iii, 105).

By 1748 a clerk in office of one of auditors of imprests (*CCR* (1748), 110). Deputy auditor of imprests 1767–75 (TNA, E 403/2480, f. 318, deed 4 July 1767). Employed by House of Lords 1767–8 to transcribe and collate rolls of parliament for publication (PA, MS Committee Books, 10 Apr., 6, 20, 27 May, 1 June 1767, 5 Feb. 1768). Fellow Royal Society 29 April 1773 (*Record of the Royal Society* (3rd edn, 1912), 357).

On 15 December 1763 Blyke's appointment as clerk of journals communicated to House and referred to committee on office of reading clerk. Appointment not favoured by committee which recommended that William Macklay should be recognised as clerk of journals. Recommendation agreed to by House 21 March 1764 (*LJ*, xxx, 446, 517–19).

Bowyer, Robert *Clerk of parliaments* 1609–21.

Belonged to Sussex family. Second son of William Bowyer (died 1569), keeper of records in Tower, by Agnes (died 1579), daughter of Sir Simon Harcourt, of Stanton Harcourt, Oxfordshire, and widow of John Knyvett, of Ashwellthorpe, Norfolk

(J.H. Cooper, 'Cuckfield Families', *Sussex Archaeological Collections*, xlii (1899), 32: *Le Neve's Pedigrees of Knights* (Harleian Soc., viii, 1873), 22; TNA, Prob. 11/52, f. 20, will of William Bowyer). Died by 22 November 1622 (Bond, 'Clerks of Parliaments', 83).

BA Oxford 17 March 1579 (*Al. Oxon. 1500–1714*, p. 162). Student Middle Temple 9 November 1580. Bar 17 October 1589 (*RAMT*, i, 47). Secretary to Lord Buckhurst, later Earl of Dorset, Lord Treasurer 1599–1608. MP Steyning 1601, Evesham 1605 (*The Parliamentary Diary of Robert Bowyer*, ed. D.H. Willson (Minneapolis, 1931), ix–xi). Joint keeper of records in Tower with Henry Elsyng 1604–12 (TNA, C 66/1649, letters patent to Bowyer and Elsyg; C 66/1956, letters patent to John Borough and Nicholas Parker).

Clerk of parliaments 27 November 1609–March 1621 (Bond, 'Clerks of Parliaments', 83).

Browne, John *Clerk of parliaments* 1638–49; 1660–91.

Son of Thomas Browne (1567–1621), citizen and grocer of London by Joan (? Wilson). Possibly related to Henry Elsyng and Thomas Knyvett, successively clerk of the parliaments, whose mother was Frances Browne. Born 1608. Buried 8 June 1691. Married (1) Temperance, third daughter of Sir Thomas Crewe of Steane, Northamptonshire. She died 22 September 1634 aged 25; (2) 28 January 1636 Elizabeth, daughter of John Packer of Shillingford, Berkshire. She died 13 June 1691. (PA, MS Pedigree of John Browne by M. Edmond).

Belonged to Middle Temple. Was either the John Browne, son of Thomas Browne of London, gent., deceased, admitted student 28 October 1628 or the John Browne, son and heir of Thomas Browne of St Antholin's, London, gent., admitted student 26 January 1631 and called to Bar 6 June 1638 (*RAMT*, i, 121, 124).

Clerk of parliaments 13 March 1638–1649; 1660–June 1691 (Bond, 'Clerks of Parliaments', 83).

Cowper, Ashley *Clerk of parliaments* 1740–88.

Third son of Spencer Cowper (c. 1670–1728) and brother of William Cowper, clerk of parliaments 1716–40. Born about 1701, being aged 87 at death 6 June 1788. Married Dorothy, daughter of John Oakes and widow of one Bedel. She died 10 May 1788 (VCH *Hertfordshire*, genealogical volume, 146).

Student Middle Temple 24 February 1717. Bar 10 February 1727 (*RAMT*, i, 281). Matriculated Merton College, Oxford 5 May 1718 (*Al. Oxon. 1715–1886*, p. 307). Chafewax in chancery 1755–88 (TNA, C 66/3649, letters patent 19 Dec. 1755).

Clerk of parliaments 14 February 1740–6 June 1788 (Bond, 'Clerks of Parliaments', 84).

Cowper, Henry *Clerk assistant* 1785–1826.

Third son of Spencer Cowper (died 1779) and grandson of William Cowper, clerk of parliaments 1716–40. Born about 1753, being aged 87 at death 28 November 1840. Married first cousin, Maria Judith, daughter of William Cowper (1721–69), elder son of William Cowper, clerk of parliaments. She died 22 March 1815 (VCH *Hertfordshire*, genealogical volume, 148).

Student Middle Temple 7 February 1770. Bar 26 May 1775. Bencher 25 January 1811. Lent reader 1813 (*RAMT*, i, 167). Matriculated Exeter College, Oxford 4 January 1771 (*Al. Oxon. 1715–1886*, 307). Commissioner of bankrupts 1777–85 (*RK* (1777), 171; *RK* (1785), 99).

Appointment as clerk assistant communicated to House and approved 25 January 1785. Resigned February 1826 when recommended by House to crown for pension (*LJ*, xxxvii, 177; lviii, 18, 24, 31, 36).

Cowper, William *Clerk of Parliaments* 1716–40.

Eldest son of Spencer Cowper (c. 1670–1728) and nephew of William Lord Cowper, Lord Keeper 1705–7; Lord Chancellor 1707–10, 1714–18. Born about 1689, being aged 51 at death 14 February 1740. Married 19 July 1716 Joan, daughter of John Budget. She died 3 June 1771 (VCH *Hertfordshire*, genealogical volume, 147).

Student Middle Temple 5 November 1705. Bar 8 February 1712 (*RAMT*, i, 258). Joint officer for making out commissions in bankruptcy 1731–40 (TNA, C 66/3466, letters patent 6 Nov. 1708 to William and John Cowper; *GM* (1731), i, 175).

Clerk of parliaments 5 January 1716–14 February 1740 (Bond, 'Clerks of Parliaments', 84).

Cowper, William *Clerk of journals* 1763.

The career of the poet William Cowper (1731–1800) is in general sufficiently recorded elsewhere (*DNB*; and most recently C. Ryscamp, *William Cowper of the Inner Temple, Esq.* (Cambridge, 1959). His association with parliament office arose from the fact that he was nephew of Ashley Cowper, clerk of parliaments 1740–88. In April 1763 the absentee reading clerk, William de Grey, resigned office following death of his deputy, Francis Macklay, who was also clerk of journals. Both the office of reading clerk and that of clerk of journals thus became vacant.

According to Cowper's own account ('Memoir of William Cowper', ed. M.J. Quinlan, *Proceedings of American Philosophical Society*, xc (1953), 369–72), Ashley Cowper's original intention was to appoint him reading clerk and Matthew Robert Arnott clerk of journals. However, Cowper declined office of reading clerk on ground that it involved duties of too public a nature. Ashley Cowper thereupon appointed Arnott reading clerk and Cowper clerk of journals. Arnott's appointment was dated 9 May 1763 and it is probable that Cowper's was of same date. This was at a time when parliament was prorogued. During recess Cowper made fruitless attempts to qualify himself for his post.

At opening of new session on 17 November 1763 Arnott's appointment as reading clerk was communicated to House and referred to a committee. Cowper resigned at some point between this date and 15 December 1763 when Ashley Cowper's appointment of Richard Blyke in his place was communicated to House and referred to same committee (*LJ*, xxx, 420, 446).

Croft, John *Clerk* c. 1757–71. *Clerk of journals* 1771–97.

Parentage unknown. Born about 1727, being aged 70 at death 28 January 1797. His widow, Sarah, died 1 November 1798 (*WAR*, 457, 461).

Entered parliament office by 1757, being said to have served for more than 40 years at death (*WAR*, 457). First named as clerk 18 December 1769 (TNA, Prob.

11/457, f. 418. will of Joseph Wight). Probably appointed clerk of journals 1771 in place of William Macklay. First occurs as such in directories 1772 (*RK* (1772), vi). First received salary of office 24 June 1772 for session 21 January–9 June 1772 (TNA, T 53/52, p. 300). On 14 June 1793 Croft and Edward Blackstock, copying clerk, presented memorial to House seeking recompense for diminution in income caused by Irish Judicature Act and other factors (*LJ*, xxxix, 176). Following address to crown received £120 from treasury (TNA, T 53/61, pp. 122–3). Remained in office until death when described as 'Clerk of the Journals and Engrossments to the House of Lords' (*WAR*, 457).

de Grey, William *Clerk assistant 1752–3. Reading clerk 1753–63. Copying clerk 1753–63.*
    The career of William de Grey (1719–81) is recorded in standard biographical sources. His association with the parliament office arose from his marriage in 1743 to Mary, daughter of William Cowper, clerk of parliaments 1716–40. (*DNB; Complete Peerage*, ed. G.E.C. (2nd edn, 1910–59), xii, 333–4; L.B. Namier and J. Brooke, *The History of Parliament: The Commons 1754–90* (1964), ii, 308–9).
    Appointed clerk assistant by clerk of parliaments, Ashley Cowper, 31 December 1752. Appointment communicated to House and referred to committee 11 January 1753. On 31 January 1753 House informed that Cowper had revoked this appointment and nominated de Grey reading clerk instead. This appointment approved by House. At same time de Grey appointed copying clerk. Did not exercise either office in person but appointed Francis Macklay and Samuel Strutt as his deputies as reading clerk and copying clerk respectively (*LJ*, xxviii, 6, 9, 10, 13; xxx, 518–19; BL, Add. MS 42779, f. 23).
    Resigned both offices between end of session 19 April 1763 and appointment of Matthew Robert Arnott as reading clerk 9 May 1763 (BL, Add. MS 42779, f. 27; PA, MS Committee Books, 13 Dec. 1763). Decision to resign probably occasioned by death of deputy, Francis Macklay, 22 April 1763.

Elsyng, Henry *Clerk assistant 1610–21. Clerk of parliaments 1621–c. 1635.*
    Belonged to family originally from Duxworth, Cambridgeshire. Eldest son of Henry Elsyng (died 1582), citizen and merchant tailor of St Dunstan's in the West, London, by Frances Browne (died 1602) who subsequently remarried Henry Knyvett (died 1603), an elder half-brother of Robert Bowyer, clerk of parliaments 1609–21 (*MGH*, 4th ser., v, 142; *Inquisitions Post Mortem of the Tudor Period for the City of London*, ed. E.A. Fry (Index Soc., xxxvi, 1908), 64; *CTH*, iv, 123 n. x; *Register of St Antholin's Budge Row* (Harleian Soc. Registers, viii, 1883), 30). Baptised 21 August 1577 (*CTG*, iv, 103 n. d). Died before 7 March 1636 when will proved (TNA, Prob. 11/170, f. 28). Married (1) 12 July 1600 Blanche (sometimes called Alse), daughter and heiress of Richard Hyett, of Cornwell, Oxfordshire (*MGH*, 4th ser., v, 142; J.G. Taylor, *Our Lady of Battersea* (1925), 212). She was buried 23 October 1612 (*CTG*, iv, 103 n. d); (2) by 29 June 1615 Jane, daughter of Richard Hardy, of Dorset (*MGH*, 4th ser., v, 142; *Memorials of St Margaret's*, 90). She died by 7 October 1634 when Elsyng made his will (TNA, Prob. 11/170, f. 28).
    Educated St Albans School. Pensioner Gaius College, Cambridge 14 October 1595 (*Al. Cantab.*, ii, 100). Student Middle Temple 19 February 1597. Bar 19 April 1605

(*RAMT*, i, 71). Joint keeper of records in Tower with Robert Bowyer 1604–12 (TNA, C 66/1649, letters patent to Bowyer and Elsyng; C 66/1956, letters patent to John Borough and Nicholas Parker).

Appointed deputy or assistant by Robert Bowyer, probably to replace Owen Reynolds who died 18 April 1610. Certainly in office by 1614 (E.R. Foster, 'The Painful Labour of Mr. Elsyng', *Transactions of the American Philosophical Society*, lxii, 8 (1972), 7). Clerk of parliaments March 1621–c. September 1635 (Bond, 'Clerks of Parliaments', 83).

Feary, Fenwick William *Clerk* c. 1781–1802.

Parentage unknown. Died between 4 July 1802 when he made his will and 13 August following when will was proved (TNA, Prob. 11/1379, f. 615).

Occurs second amongst the four 'other clerks' in parliament office when first listed 1781. Remained in office until death (*RK* (1781), 67; (1802), 38).

Fitzgerald, Edmund *Clerk* 1715–24. *Copying clerk* 1724–35.

Son of Gerald Fitzgerald (died 1718), copying clerk. Born about 1698, being aged 37 at death 25 May 1735. Married Anne, daughter of Michael Brandreth, of Shenstone, Staffordshire. She died 2 May 1727 (MI, St Margaret's, Westminster; TNA, Prob. 11/671, f. 120, will of Edmund Fitzgerald).

Entered parliament office 1715. Appointed copying clerk 1724 (1723/4), probably succeeding John Wheake in February of that year (PA, Main Papers, petition of Edmund Fitzgerald, 12 June 1733). On 12 March 1726 his petition seeking provision referred to committee appointed to examine fees of officers of House which made no recommendation in his favour (*LJ*, xxii, 619). On 12 June 1733 again petitioned House which recommended him to crown with the result that he received £50 from treasury (*LJ*, xxiv, 306; *CTBP 1731–4*, p. 514). Thereafter a like sum paid annually to Fitzgerald and his successors as copying clerk.

Fitzgerald, Gerald *Copying clerk* (?)–1718.

Parentage unknown. Born about 1666, being aged 52 at death 14 September 1718. His widow, Anne, died 15 June 1740 (MI, St Margaret's, Westminster).

Entered parliament office by 1706 when described as clerk of then clerk assistant, John Walker, junior (PA, Main Papers petition of John Jenings, 12 Mar. 1725/6). At an unknown date appointed to the office of copying clerk which he held at his death (PA, Main Papers petition of Edmund Fitzgerald, 12 June 1733). In March 1714, together with James Merest, petitioned treasury for provision. Granted £50 each (TNA, T 1/173, no. 42; *CTB*, xxvii, 552). Similar application refused November 1715 (TNA, T 1/193, no. 2). In April 1718 Fitzgerald again petitioned treasury for provision, jointly with John Jenings, but was unsuccessful (TNA, T 1/219, no. 36; *CTB*, xxxii, 39).

Fitzgerald, Gerald *Clerk* (?)–1733.

Youngest son of Gerald Fitzgerald (1666–1718), copying clerk. Born about 1702, being aged 31 at death on 5 December 1733 (MI, St Margaret's, Westminster).

Entered parliament office at unknown date. In office at death (MI, St Margaret's, Westminster).

Hamilton, James *Clerk* c. 1781–93.

Parentage unknown.

Occurs second amongst the four 'other clerks' in parliament office when first listed 1781. Last occurs as such 1793 (*RK* (1781), 67; (1793), 68). On 5 February 1788 reprimanded for misconduct by clerk of parliaments who reduced salary from £50 to £40 (PA, PO 58/3).

Jenings, John *Clerk* 1706–18. *Clerk of journals* 1718–37.

Eldest son of Thomas Jenings (died 1734), gentleman of Chapel Royal by first wife, Elizabeth Loton (died 1720). Baptised 12 February 1691. Died 11 January 1737 (*WAR*, 75, 300 n. 2, 341 n. 1; TNA, Prob. 11/681, f. 31, will of John Jenings).

Brought into parliament office 1706 by clerk assistant, John Walker, junior, and Gerald Fitzgerald. In 1717 directed to assist in providing index and marginal notes for the Journals. In 1718 appointed clerk of journals (PA, Main Papers, petition of John Jenings, 12 Mar. 1725/6). In July 1717 received £2 3s. for searching and attending with Journals at trial of Earl of Oxford (*CTB*, xxxii, 153). In April 1718, jointly with Gerald Fitzgerald, petitioned treasury seeking provision but was unsuccessful (TNA, T 1/219, no. 36; *CTB*, xxxii, 39). On 12 March 1726 his petition seeking provision referred to committee appointed to examine fees of officers of House which made no recommendation in his favour (*LJ*, xxii, 619). On 5 June 1733 again petitioned House which recommended him to crown with the result that he received £50 from treasury (PA, Main Papers, petition of John Jenings, 5 June 1733; *LJ*, xxiv, 298; *CTBP 1731–4*, pp. 404, 514). Thereafter a like sum was paid annually to Jenings and his successors as clerk of journals.

Johnson, Matthew *Clerk of parliaments* 1691–1716.

Eldest son of Templer Johnson (1609–61), of Gretton, Northamptonshire, by his wife, Mary. Baptised 8 September 1637 (Gretton Parish Register). Died 13 December 1723. Married 1676 Margaret, daughter of Edward Palmer by his wife, Elizabeth, daughter of Sir Geoffrey Palmer, attorney general. She died 19 September 1725 (J. Nichols, *The History and Antiquities of the County of Leicester* (1795–1811), ii, 393–4; *Marriage Licences Westminster and Vicar General* (Harleian Soc., xxiii, 1886), 257).

Student Middle Temple 29 July 1662. Bar 2 June 1671. Bencher 27 November 1691. Associate bencher 29 January 1692 (*RAMT*, i, 167). Received legal education from Sir Geoffrey Palmer, attorney general 1660–70 (Nichols, *Leicester*, ii, 393). In Palmer's office by 31 October 1662 (*CSPD 1661–2*, p. 524). Clerk of patents to attorney general by 28 October 1668. Retained office until Palmer's death May 1670 (*CSPD 1668–9*, p. 39; *CTB*, iii, 566). In February 1672 Johnson, together with John Markham, obtained reversionary grant of office of head searcher of customs in London which he surrendered June 1674 (*CSPD 1671–2*, p. 139; *CTB*, iii, 1185; iv, 539).

Clerk of parliaments June 1691–5 January 1716 (Bond, 84).

Johnson, Matthew *Reading clerk* 1711–15. *Clerk assistant* 1715–24.

Younger son of Matthew Johnson, clerk of parliaments 1691–1716. Born about 1683, being in his forty-third year at death 22 May 1725 (*WAR*, 313 n. 6).

Probably educated at Eton (*Eton College Register 1441–1698*, ed. W. Sterry (Eton, 1943), 191–2). Student Middle Temple 4 December 1695 (*RAMT*, i, 238). Matriculated Trinity College, Oxford 5 November 1698 (*Al. Oxon. 1500–1714*, p. 815).

Appointed reading clerk April 1711, the duties being carried out by James Merest as his deputy. Promoted clerk assistant April 1715 (BL, Stowe MS 354, f. 233; PA, Main Papers, petition of James Merest, 21 Jan. 1723/4). Vacated office by 6 February 1724 (*LJ*, xxii, 253).

Ken, Thomas *Clerk* c. 1642–4.

Name of father unknown. Mother, Elizabeth Ken, died by 23 February 1631 when will proved. He died by 18 May 1653 when will proved. Married (1) Jane, daughter of Rowland Hughes, rector of Essendon and Little Berkhamstead, Hertfordshire; (2) December 1624 Martha, daughter of Ion or Ivon Chalkhill, of Kingsbury, Middlesex, and widow of one Carpenter. Her mother was Martha, sister of Thomas Browne, father of John Browne, clerk of parliaments 1638–49; 1660–91. She was buried 19 March 1641 (L.H. Chambers, 'Thomas Ken of Furnival's Inn, Holborn' (*Transactions of the East Herts Archaeological Society*, ix (1934–6), 226–7; P.J. Croft, 'Izaak Walton's John Chalkhill', *Times Literary Supplement* (1958), 365).

Clerk of great sessions in Glamorgan, Brecon and Radnor.

Presumably owed appointment to his second wife's first cousin, John Browne, clerk of parliaments. On 25 November 1642 petitioned House as 'One of the Clerks attending this Honourable House of Peers' in connection with his Welsh office (*LJ*, 459). On 20 February 1644 described as 'an Attendant' and discharged from paying his twentieth part 'in regard of his Attendance on this House, and his great Losses' (*LJ*, vi, 444). Possibly occupied post of junior of clerk of parliaments' 'Two Men', or reading clerk.

Knyvett, Thomas *Clerk of parliaments* c. 1635–7.

Belonged to younger branch of family of Knyvett of Buckenham, Norfolk. Son of Henry Knyvett (died 1603) by Frances Browne (died 1602). Henry Knyvett was third son of John Knyvett of Ashwellthorpe, Norfolk, first husband of Agnes Harcourt (died 1579), whose second husband was William Bowyer (died 1569), keeper of records in Tower. Frances Browne's first husband was Henry Elsyng (died 1582). Knyvett was thus nephew of one clerk of parliaments, Robert Bowyer and half-brother of another, Henry Elsyng (*The Knyvett Letters 1620–1644*, ed. B. Schofield (Norfolk Record Soc., 1949), 54–5; *CTG*, iv, 123 n. x; *Register of St Antholin's Budge Row* (Harleian Soc. Registers, viii, 1883), 30). Born about 1585, being aged 17 at his matriculation 1602 (*Al. Oxon. 1500–1714*, p. 866). Died between 1 and 7 December 1637, the dates respectively of his will and his burial (TNA, Prob. 11/175, f. 165; *The Parish Register of Putney, Surrey*, ed. W.B. Bannerman (Croydon, 1913–16), i, 102). Married Mary, second daughter of George Scott, of Stapleford Tauney, Essex, and widow of Richard Lusher (died 1615), of Putney, Surrey. She died 27 August 1623 (*History of Surrey*, ii, 293–4).

Matriculated Christ Church, Oxford 10 December 1602. BA 27 June 1605. MA 30 May 1608 (*Al. Oxon. 1500–1714*, p. 866). Student Middle Temple 15 June 1608. Bar 27 October 1615 (*RAMT*, i, 91). MA Cambridge 1627 (*Al. Cantab.*, iii, 28). Clerk of parliaments c. 1635–December 1637 (Bond, 'Clerks of Parliaments', 83).

Macklay, Francis *Clerk of journals* 1737–63. *Deputy reading clerk* 1753–63.

Parentage unknown. Died 22 April 1763 (*GM* (1763), xxxiii, 202). Married Helen, daughter of Christopher Shrider, organ maker to king, by Helen, sister of John Jenings, clerk of journals 1718–37 (*Old Westminsters*, ii, 607; *WAR*, 383 n. 4; TNA, Prob. 11/681, f. 31, will of John Jenings). She died 24 June 1788 (*GM* (1788), lviii, 660). Father of William Macklay, clerk of journals 1764–71, to whom he left manuscript journals and other material lodged in parliament office and of Francis Macklay, probably identical with person of same name who was deputy serjeant at arms to Lord Chancellor and who died 7 January 1799 (TNA, Prob. 11/887, f. 241, will of Francis Macklay; *GM* (1799), lxix, 82).

Brought into parliament office by clerk of journals, John Jenings. Appointed clerk of journals 29 January 1737, having purchased office from William Cowper, clerk of parliaments for £300. Appointed deputy reading clerk by William de Grey 29 January 1753. Held both posts until death (PA, MS Committee Books, 13 Dec. 1763; BL, Add. MS 42779, f. 21).

Macklay, William *Deputy clerk of journals* 1753–64. *Clerk of journals* 1764–71.

Elder son of Francis Macklay, clerk of journals 1737–63. Born about 1748, being aged 10 in April 1748 when admitted to Westminster School (*Old Westminsters*, ii, 607; PRO, Prob. 11/887, f. 241, will of Francis Macklay). Date of death unknown.

Brought into parliament office by father on latter's appointment as deputy reading clerk January 1753 to serve as deputy clerk of journals (PA, MS Committee Books, 13 Dec. 1763). Recognised by House as clerk of journals 21 March 1764 (*LJ*, xxx, 518–19). Remained in office until 1771, last receiving salary on 16 May 1771 for session 13 November 1770–8 May 1771 (TNA, T 53/52, p. 123).

Merest, James *Clerk* 1700–9. *Clerk of journals* 1709–(?)1715. *Deputy reading clerk* 1711–15, 1716–24. *Reading clerk* 1715–16. *Clerk assistant* 1724–52.

Possibly belonged to Surrey family of Merehurst (*Visitation of Surrey* (Harleian Soc., xliii, 1899), 159). Fifth son of John Merest (died 1699), vicar of Woking, Surrey, 1674–99, by his wife, Mary. Born 2 May 1683. Died 27 December 1752. Married (1) 13 July 1725 Frances, elder daughter of Matthew Johnson, clerk of parliaments 1691–1716. She died 14 November 1727; (2) 13 April 1728 Jane, sixth daughter of Charles Battely, secondary in office of Lord Treasurer's remembrancer and receiver of rents of Westminster Abbey. She died 15 February 1780 (*History of Surrey*, i, 139, 144; *WAR*, 78 n. 11, 321 n. 6; Woking Parish Register).

Brought into parliament office 1700 by Matthew Johnson, clerk of parliaments. Appointed clerk of journals 1709. Appointed deputy to Matthew Johnson, junior, as reading clerk April 1711. Appointed reading clerk April 1715. Removed from this office January 1716 but apparently continued to carry out duties for his successor, Charles Reynell 1716–24 (*History of Surrey* i, 139; BL, Stowe MS 354, f. 233; PA, Main Papers, petition of James Merest, 21 Jan. 1723/4).

In March 1714 Merest and Gerald Fitzgerald petitioned treasury for provision. Granted £50 each (TNA, T 1/173, no. 42; *CTB*, xxvii, 552). Similar application refused November 1715 (TNA, T 1/193, no. 2). In August 1716 Merest received £30 'as a reward for making several copies and other services for the public' (*CTB*, xxx,

389). From 1717 to 1720 received £50 a year for same service (*CTB*, xxxi, 579; xxxii, 31, 291; TNA, T 53/27, p. 247; T 53/28, p. 199). In September 1721 petitioned treasury alleging that he attended all committees of House but received no recompense for those of a public nature. As a result allowance raised to £100 a year (TNA, T 1/238, no. 72; T 53/29, p. 144). Continued to receive this allowance up to and after appointment as clerk assistant. It was paid as a matter of course to subsequent holders of that office.

On 21 January 1724 Merest petitioned House drawing attention to circumstances in which he had been deprived of office of reading clerk and seeking relief. However, on 31 January House was informed that Merest had received satisfaction from clerk of parliaments while on 6 February his appointment as clerk assistant was communicated to House and approved. Remained in office until death (*LJ*, xxii, 243, 250, 253; xxviii, 6).

Merest, John *Clerk* c. 1725–55.

Probably son of John Merest (died 1699), vicar of Woking, Surrey, 1674–99 and brother of James Merest, clerk 1700–52 and identical with John Merest baptised 3 December 1683 (Woking Parish Register).

Had entered parliament office by June 1725 when he and his fellow 'under clerk', Joseph Wight, petitioned treasury stating that they received no allowance for public business, in particular for their work in sorting and digesting records and papers in parliament office, and seeking compensation for their services. Petition refused (TNA, T 1/253, no. 8). Nothing further heard of Merest until 1742 when listed immediately after reading clerk as 'Engrossing Clerk'. Continued to be so listed until 1755 (*New Court Register: List of Lords and Commons* (1742), 45; *CCR* (1755), 2).

Parratt, Edward *Clerk* c. 1781–97. *Clerk of journals* 1797–1819.

Parentage unknown. Born about 1748, being aged 71 at death 18 March 1819. His wife, Elizabeth, died 1 April 1815 (MI, St Margaret's Westminster; *GM* (1819), lxxxix, 378; TNA, Prob. 11/1614, f. 140, will of Edward Parratt).

Occurs first amongst the four 'other clerks' in parliament office when first listed 1781. Promoted clerk of journals 1797 on death of John Croft. Remained in office until death (*RK* (1781), 67; (1797), 68; (1798), 68; (1819), 44).

Payne, William Charles *Clerk* 1793–1819. *Copying clerk* 1819–22.

Parentage unknown. Born about 1757, being aged 65 at death 22 May 1822 (*GM* (1822), xcii, 572).

Appointed one of the four 'other clerks' in parliament office 1793, first occurring as such in following year. Promoted copying clerk 1819 on death of William Walmisley. Remained in office until death (*RK* (1794), 68; (1819), 44; (1820), 44; (1822), 46).

Price, James *Clerk* 1725–c. 1739.

Parentage unknown. Entered parliament office about 1725, having served for 14 years when he petitioned House in 1739 (*LJ*, xxv, 404, 414). No further mention.

Relfe, John *Clerk* 1660–4. *Reading clerk* (?) 1664–1711.

Parentage unknown. Born 1643 at Newbiggin, Cumberland. Died 11 April 1711 (G. Baker, *The History and Antiquities of the County of Northampton* (1822–30), i, 331). Married after 7 August 1701 Lettice, daughter of John Ramsden (TNA, Prob. 11/520, f. 88, will of John Relfe). Received grant of arms 28 January 1693 (*Grantees of Arms* (Harleian Soc., lxvi, 1915), 212).

Brought into parliament office 1660 by John Browne, clerk of parliaments 1638–49; 1660–91. Appointed reading clerk a few years later (Baker, *Northampton*, i, 331). Precise date of appointment to this office unknown. It became vacant 1664 when its holder, John Walker, senior, was promoted to office of clerk assistant or deputy clerk of parliaments. Relfe first described as reading clerk April 1673 when awarded £100 as royal bounty for his service (*CTB*, iv, 105; v, 123). No other individual is known to have held the office 1664–73. Relfe possibly appointed 1664 although only 21 at the time.

In April 1679 Relfe received £100 from treasury for services to committee on Popish plot (*CTB*, vi, 13–14, 18). In February 1690 Relfe and the younger John Walker, described as deputies to John Browne, clerk of the parliaments, paid £50 for services in connection with money bills (*CTB*, xvii, 555). On 7 February 1696 Relfe given leave to officiate for clerk of crown in House (*LJ*, xv, 663). On 31 March 1704, following enquiry into Scottish conspiracy, Relfe and Walker ordered to be recommended to queen for services. Received £100 between them from treasury (*CTB*, xvii, 558; TNA, T 1/94, no. 40; *CTB*, xx, 122, 256). Compiled 'Relfe's Journals', now in PA (Baker, *Northampton*, i, 331; M.F. Bond, *Guide to the Records of Parliament* (1971), 191, 280). Held office of reading clerk until death (PA, Main Papers, petition of James Merest, 21 Jan. 1723/4).

Reynell, Charles *Reading clerk* 1716–24.

Belonged to younger branch of Devonshire family of Reynell. Second son of Carew Reynell (died 1690), of Binstead Popham, Hampshire (*Transactions of the Devonshire Association*, xxxii (1900), 248; TNA, Prob. 11/399, f. 61, will of Carew Reynell 1690; BL, Add. MS 36154, ff. 16–19; *RAMT*, i, 291). Died October 1741 (*London Magazine* (1741), 517 – 'Mr Reynolds').

Possibly identical with Charles Reynell, appointed clerk of patents to attorney general September 1709 (*Post Boy*, nos 2238, 2239, 17 and 20 Sept. 1709). Student Middle Temple 7 May 1722 (*RAMT*, i, 291).

Appointed reading clerk January 1716 by William Cowper. Removed from office by Cowper by 6 February 1724 when he petitioned House asking for his case to be considered. Petition referred to committee for privileges but no further action taken (*LJ*, xxii, 253). Brought actions in courts against Cowper and his father, Spencer Cowper, for performance of promise alleged to have been made by the latter in 1714 that he would procure his appointment as deputy clerk of parliaments or clerk assistant. On 25 January 1726 William Cowper petitioned House seeking directions as to how he should conduct himself in relation to action in court of exchequer. On 18 February 1726 Reynell petitioned House seeking restitution to office of reading clerk or alternatively performance of terms on which he had abandoned his interest in the office. On 13 May 1726 Reynell's petition dismissed and Cowper given leave to make his defense in any action brought against him (*LJ*, xxii, 578, 599, 601, 602, 676, 681; PA, Main Papers, petition of William Cowper, 25 Jan. 1725/6). Nothing further heard of the matter.

Reynolds, Owen *Clerk assistant* (?)–1610.

Family associated with Southampton. Parentage unknown. Elder brother, Edward (died 1623), secretary to Earl of Essex 1588 and clerk of privy seal c. 1608–23 (TNA, Prob. 11/143, f. 1, will of Edward Reynolds 1623; *Visitation of Northamptonshire 1681* (Harleian Soc., lxxxvii, 1935), 178–80; HMC, Salisbury MSS, vii, 333; *CSPD 1598–1601*, p. 66; *CSPD 1603–10*, p. 436). Died 18 April 1610. Married but wife's name unknown (HMC, Downshire MSS, ii, 279, 280; *Memorials of St Margaret's*, 493; MI, Edward Reynolds, St Margaret's Westminster; *CSPD 1603–10*, p. 602).

Entered service of Thomas Smith who preceded Edward Reynolds as secretary to Earl of Essex. Probably under clerk to Smith as clerk of privy council. Appointed 1608 keeper of council chest or under keeper of council records, an office customarily held by one of under clerks of the council (*DNB*, under Smith, Sir Thomas; *CSPD 1603–10*, p. 602; HMC, Salisbury MSS, xx, 307; HMC, Downshire MSS, ii, 279, 280).

At unknown date appointed deputy by Smith as clerk of parliaments (1597–1609) (PA, Braye MS 54/37). First clear reference to him in parliamentary context dated 27 May 1606 (House of Lords MSS, new ser., xi, 107) but living near St Margaret's, Westminster March 1602 (*CSPD 1601–3*, p. 166). Continued as deputy by Robert Bowyer, Smith's successor as clerk of parliaments March 1610 (PA, Braye MS 54/37).

Rose, George *Clerk of parliaments* 1788–1818.

The career of George Rose (1744–1818) is recorded in standard biographical sources (*DNB*; L.B. Namier and J. Brooke, *The History of Parliament: The Commons 1754–90* (1964), iii, 375–6).

Clerk of parliaments 6 June 1788–13 January 1818 (Bond, 'Clerks of Parliaments', 84).

Sambrooke, Jeremiah *Clerk* 1689–(?). *Clerk of journals* (?)–1709.

Younger son of Francis Sambrooke, of The Close, Salisbury, who died before 5 December 1682 when his elder son, Francis, was admitted student at Middle Temple. The younger Francis, who subsequently occupied the offices of clerk of patents to attorney general and deputy clerk of crown in chancery, died about September 1709 whereupon his younger brother, Jeremiah, succeeded him as deputy clerk of crown (BL, Stowe MS 354, f. 233; *RAMT*, i, 208; *Post Boy*, nos 2238, 2239, 17 and 20 Sept. 1709). Died by 15 December 1722, leaving widow, Elizabeth (TNA, Prob. 6/98, f. 246). His son, Jeremiah, granted reversion of office of registrar of affidavits in chancery 1716 in recognition of his father's services (TNA, C 66/3515, letters patent 15 June 1716).

Entered parliament office about 1689, having served for almost 20 years before he moved to crown office (TNA, C66/3515, Letters Patent 15 June 1716). Probably identical with 'Mr Sambrooke' who occurs 10 May 1701 (House of Lords MSS, new ser., iv, 351). At unknown date entrusted with task of compiling the Journals and may be regarded as the first identifiable clerk of the journals. Resigned office September 1709 on becoming deputy clerk of crown (BL, Stowe MS 354, f. 233).

Smith, Thomas (knighted 20 May 1603) *Clerk of parliaments* 1597–1609.

For biographical details, see *DNB*.

Clerk of parliaments 5 October 1597–27 November 1609 (Bond, 'Clerks of Parliaments', 83).

Strutt, Samuel *Deputy copying clerk* 1753–64. *Copying clerk* 1764–5. *Clerk assistant* 1765–85.

Parentage unknown. Possibly son of Samuel Strutt, attorney and author, who died 9 February 1737 (*GM* (1737), vii, 124) who may have been brother of Carnaby Strutt (died 1769), of Wattisfield, Suffolk and of Isaac Strutt (died 1772), of Hampstead, Middlesex (TNA, Prob. 11/953, f. 434; Prob. 11/984, f. 34). Born about 1736, being aged 49 at death 22 January 1785. Married (1) Catharine Ruth (surname unknown). She died 17 July 1770; (2) 10 September 1771 Charlotte Locke. She died 11 May 1815 (*WAR*, 413, 439, 489). Received grant of arms 1772 (*Grantees of Arms 1687–1898* (Harleian Soc., lxviii, 1917), 352).

Brought into parliament office 1753 by Joseph Wight to become deputy to William de Grey as copying clerk. Recognised by House as copying clerk 21 March 1764 (PA, MS Committee Books, 13 Dec. 1763; *LJ*, xxx, 518–19). From same date authorised to officiate as clerk assistant during sickness of Wight (*LJ*, xxx, 514–19; xxxi, 10). Appointment as clerk assistant communicated to House and approved 20 May 1765. Terms of appointment provided that Strutt should hold the office until such time as one of the sons of Ashley Cowper's nephew, William, should attain age of 21 and be admitted to it, in which case such son was to pay Strutt annuity of £300 until death or appointment as reading clerk (*LJ*, xxxi, 210). In February 1771 William Cowper's eldest son given leave to attend at table with a view to qualifying himself as clerk assistant whereupon Strutt petitioned House stating that his financial and professional future was entirely dependent on the lives of the Cowpers and that, in the event of their deaths, he would be deprived of any provision. Strutt's petition referred to committee which recommended that crown should be invited to make provision for him in the event of his being removed from office of clerk assistant. Crown agreed to provide accordingly (*LJ*, xxxiii, 77, 97, 101). On 25 July 1773 House informed that Strutt had been appointed clerk assistant without conditions. Remained in office until death (*LJ*, 690; xxxiii, xxxvii, 177).

On 24 February 1783 granted reversion of office of clerk of parliaments but did not live to succeed to it (Bond, 'Clerks of Parliaments', 84).

Throckmorton, John *Clerk assistant* 1621–49; 1660–4.

Belonged to younger branch of family of Throckmorton of Coughton, Warwickshire. Son of George Throckmorton, of Great Rowlright, Oxfordshire, by Elizabeth, daughter of Robert Gynes (Guisnes), of Colchester, Essex. Gynes' wife, Ursula, was daughter of Sir Simon Harcourt, of Stanton Harcourt, Oxfordshire, and sister of Agnes, wife of William Bowyer, keeper of records in Tower and mother of Robert Bowyer, clerk of parliaments 1609–21 (T. Nash, *Collections for the History of Worcestershire* (1781–2), ii, 452 (pedigree); C.W. Throckmorton, *A Genealogical and Historical Account of the Family of Throckmorton* (Richmond, VA, 1930), 192; *The Harcourt Papers*, ed. E.W. Harcourt (Oxford, 1880–1905), i, 245–6; TNA, Prob. 11/52, f. 20, will of William Bowyer

1570). Throckmorton was thus first cousin once removed of Robert Bowyer. Died 10 May 1664 (PA, Manuscript Minutes 1660–4, f. following 2 May 1664; J Hatton, *New View of London* (1708), i, 342; TNA, Prob. 11/313, f. 37, will of John Throckmorton). Married (1) Dorothy, daughter of Richard Hardy, of Dorset, and sister of Jane, second wife of Henry Elsyng, clerk of parliaments 1621–c. 1635 (Nash, *History of Worcestershire*, i, 452 (pedigree); Throckmorton, *Family of Throckmorton*, 192; *MGH*, 4th ser., v, 142). Marriage took place between 7 October 1634 when Elsyng made his will (TNA, Prob. 11/170, f. 28) and 28 August 1640 when son baptised. She was buried 6 September 1647 (*Memorials of St Margaret's*, 167, 617); (2) Ursula, daughter of George Throckmorton, of Grove Ash, Great Tew, Oxfordshire, and widow of Edward Osborne (1603–54), of Piddington, Northamptonshire (Throckmorton, *Family of Throckmorton*, 192; *Visitation of Northamptonshire 1681* (Harleian Soc., lxxxvii, 1935), 158).

Probably appointed deputy or clerk assistant by Elsyng when he became clerk of parliaments March 1621. Contents of confused note on fees belonging to 'the Clerk of the Upper House his man', apparently compiled in 1624 and initialled 'J. Th.' suggest that Throckmorton occupied post at that date and that his immediate predecessor was Elsyng (PA, Braye MS 55/86). Described as deputy clerk of parliaments (DCP) 1629 (*LJ*, iv, 44). Occurs frequently in service of House during 1640s (HMC, *4th Report*, 27, 52, 75, 94; *6th Report*, 180, 184). On 25 March 1645 petitioned House stating that he was in danger of losing office in the customs which he had occupied for six years because of his daily attendance on House whereupon House ordered that he should be continued in his post. On 27 September of same year he petitioned House asking for protection against certain individuals who had seized some of his goods for debt whereupon House ordered accordingly (*LJ*, vii, 286, 605, 613).

Returned to service of House at Restoration 1660 (O.C. Williams, *The Clerical Organisation of the House of Commons 1660–1850* (Oxford, 1954), 313). Died in office (PA, Manuscript Minutes 1664, f. following 2 May 1664).

Walker, John *Reading clerk 1660–4. Clerk assistant 1664–82.*

Son of William Walker, of Wakefield, Yorkshire and of London, by Martha (died 1634), daughter of Robert Maunsell whose wife, Mary, was sister of Thomas Browne, father of John Browne, clerk of parliaments 1638–49; 1660–4 (*Visitation of London 1633–5* (Harleian Soc., xvi, 1883), 90; *Visitation of Middlesex*, ed J. Foster (1887), 13; PA, MS Pedigree of John Browne by M. Edmond; TNA, Prob. 11/166, f. 71, will of Martha Walker 1634). Walker was thus Browne's first cousin once removed. Probably identical with John Walker who matriculated University College, Oxford 24 May 1637 aged 18 in which case he would have been born about 1619 and have graduated BA 22 February 1641 (*Al. Oxon. 1500–1714*, p. 1557). Died 1682 (D. Lysons, *Historical Account of those parishes in the County of Middlesex which are not described in the Environs of London* (1800), 161; Parish Register, Hillingdon, Middlesex, burial 30 Aug. 1682; TNA, Prob. 6/57, f. 144, administration 3 Oct. 1682). Married by 1652 Mary, daughter of Peter Fountaine, a London merchant (*Visitation of Middlesex*, 13). Received grant of arms 1663 (*Grantees of Arms* (Harleian Soc., lxvi, 1915), 265).

Secretary to English commissioners for regulating trade between England and Scotland 1668–74 and to English commissioners for negotiating Union between England and Scotland 1670–4 (J. Bruce, *Report of the Events and Circumstances which Produced the*

Union of the Kingdoms of England and Scotland (1799), appendix, cclvii, cclxii, cclxxviii, cclxxxiv; HMC, *10th Report*, pt vi, 180–l; *CTB*, iii, 410, 588, 727, 728, 773; v, 123).

Probably appointed reading clerk 1660. On 23 July 1661 petitioned House as reading clerk and was awarded certain allowances in respect of his services 'in this and the former Parliament' (*LJ*, xi, 318). On 15 May 1662 House ordered him to be recommended to king with the result that he received £100 from the Treasury (*LJ*, xi, 461; *CTB*, i, 44. Last occurs as reading clerk 5 March 1663 (*LJ*, xi, 489). Probably appointed deputy clerk of parliaments or clerk assistant May 1664 in succession to John Throckmorton. First occurs as deputy clerk 20 August 1664 (*LJ*, xi, 662). In June 1673 received £200 from Treasury for services in House of Lords (TNA, T 1/94, no. 40; see also *CTB*, v, 123). Last occurs as deputy clerk of parliaments 12 November 1681 (*CTB*, vii, 301). Probably remained in office until death.

Walker, John *Clerk assistant* 1682–1715.

Elder son of John Walker, reading clerk 1660–4 and clerk assistant 1664–82. Born about 1652, being aged 11 in 1663 (*Visitation of Middlesex*, ed. J. Foster (1887), 13). Died 12 April 1715 (MI, Hillingdon, Middlesex; PΛ, Main Papers, Petition of James Merest 21 Jan. 1723/4; TNA, Prob. 11/546, f. 105, will of John Walker). Married 19 February 1691 Elizabeth, second daughter of Sir William Clerke, second baronet, of Shabbington, Buckinghamshire. She died 29 September 1731 (*Marriage Licences Faculty Office* (Harleian Soc., xxiv, 1886), 199; Parish Register, Hillingdon, Middlesex; MI, Hillingdon). His son, John, granted reversion of office of registrar of affidavits in chancery 1701 in recognition of his father's services to House of Lords (*CSPD 1701–2*, pp. 365–6).

Assisted father in duties as secretary to English commissioners for regulating trade and for negotiating a Union between England and Scotland 1668–74 (*CSPD 1703–4*, p. 350; *CTB*, xviii, 272).

Probably appointed deputy clerk of parliaments or clerk assistant 1682 in succession to father. First occurs in service of House 22 April 1687 (*House of Lords MSS 1678–1688*, p. 324). On 13 February 1690 Walker and the reading clerk, John Relfe, described as deputies to John Browne, clerk of the parliaments (*CTB*, xvii, 555). Described as clerk assistant 9 November 1696 (*LJ*, xvi, 10). On 31 March 1704, following enquiry into Scottish conspiracy, Walker and Relfe ordered to be recommended to queen for services. Received £100 between them from Treasury (*LJ*, xvii, 558; TNA, T 1/94, no. 40; *CTB*, xx, 122, 256). Remained in office until death (PA, Main Papers, petition of James Merest, 21 Jan. 1723/4).

Walmisley, Edward George *Clerk* 1799–1819. *Clerk of journals* 1819–35.

Eldest son of William Walmisley, copying clerk 1799–1819. Born 26 December 1778. Died 19 September 1835. Married (1) 9 November 1810 Amelia Matilda, widow of George Fox, of Westminster; (2) 29 August 1825 Mary Selina Sybella, daughter of Thomas Harris Bradshaw, senior clerk in post office. Educated Westminster School (*Old Westminsters*, ii, 960; *GM* (1835), cv, 442).

Appointed one of the four 'other clerks' in parliament office 1799, first occurring as such in directories 1800. Promoted clerk of journals 1819 on death of Edward Parratt. Remained in office until death (*RK* (1800), 32; (1819), 44; (1820), 44; (1835), 48).

Walmisley, William *Clerk* 1777–99. *Copying clerk* 1799–1819.

Parentage unknown. First cousin of Edward Blackstock, copying clerk 1765–99. Born about 1745, being in his seventy-fourth year at death 17 January 1819. Married Mary, daughter of Thomas Jackson, of Bewdley, Worcestershire. She died 4 April 1822 in her seventy-second year (*WAR*, 462 n. 5; *Old Westminsters*, ii, 960; *GM* (1819), lxxxix, 184; MI, Bromley, Kent; TNA, Prob. 11/1613, f. 99, will of William Walmisley).

Entered parliament office about 1777, being described at his death as having served there for 42 years (MI, Bromley, Kent). Occurs last of the four 'other clerks' in office when first listed 1781. Promoted copying clerk 1799 on death of Edward Blackstock. Remained in office until death (*RK* (1781), 67; (1799), 68; (1800), 32; (1819, 44).

Walmisley, William *Clerk* 1797–1822.

Younger son of William Walmisley, copying clerk 1799–1819. Born 9 May 1780. Died 16 April 1822. Married 26 April 1807 Eleanor, daughter of one Elyard, of London Stock Exchange. Educated Westminster School (*Old Westminsters*, ii, 960; *GM* (1822), xcii, 476).

Appointed one of the four 'other clerks' in parliament office 1797, first occurring as such in directories 1798. Remained in office until death, being described as clerk of enrolments from 1820 (*RK* (1798), 68; (1820), 44; (1822), 46).

Wheake, John *Clerk* c. 1718. (?)*Copying clerk* (?)–1724. *Reading clerk* 1724–36.

Probably identical with John Wheake, admitted student to Middle Temple 3 November 1709, as son and heir of Philip Wheake, a London merchant (*RAMT*, i, 266). Died 9 September 1736 (*GM* (1736), vi, 552 – 'John Weeks'; TNA, Prob. 6/112, f. 172, administration 27 Sept. 1736; Prob. 6/120, f. 141, administration 1 Mar. 1744).

Clerk of dispensations in chancery 1716–36 (TNA, C 66/3513, letters patent to Wheake; C 66/3596, letters patent to William Talbot).

First occurs in service of House 20 July 1718 when he received three guineas for writing copies of the minutes of the previous session for secretary of state, Lord Stanhope (Kent County Record Office, Stanhope Papers 76). Possibly copying clerk, succeeding Gerald Fitzgerald September 1718 and being succeeded by Edmund Fitzgerald February 1724 (1723/4) (PA, Main Papers, petition of Edmund Fitzgerald, 12 June 1733). Appointment as reading clerk communicated to House and approved 6 February 1724 (*LJ*, xxii, 253). Duties carried out by deputy, Joseph Wight (BL, Add. MS 42779, f. 23; *LJ*, xxiv, 147). Remained in office until death (BL, Add. MS 42779, f. 23).

Wight, Joseph *Clerk* 1716–24. *Deputy reading clerk* 1724–36. *Copying clerk* 1735–53. *Reading clerk* 1736–53. *Clerk assistant* 1753–65.

Parentage unknown. Possibly connected with family of Wight of Staffordshire and Worcestershire, some of whose members were called Joseph (*Al. Oxon. 1500–1714*, pp. 1627–8; *Al. Oxon. 1715–1886*, p. 1550). Born about 1696, being aged 74 at death 28 November 1770 (*History of Surrey*, iii, 355; TNA, Prob. 11/457, f. 418, will of Joseph Wight).

Brought into parliament office by Gerald Fitzgerald (died 1718), copying clerk (PA, MS Committee Books, 23 Nov. and 13 Dec. 1763). Appointed deputy to reading clerk,

John Wheake, February 1724 (1723/4) (BL, Add. MS 42779, f. 23). In June 1725 Wight and fellow 'under clerk', John Merest petitioned treasury stating that they received no allowance for public business, in particular for their work in sorting and digesting records and papers in parliament office, and seeking compensation for their services. Petition refused (TNA, T 1/253, no. 8). On 27 May 1732 Wight recommended by House to king on ground that his profits were not sufficient compensation for his pains and diligence in executing office of reading clerk with the result that he was granted £100 by Treasury for 'extraordinary services' (*LJ*, xxiv, 147; *CTBP 1731–4*, p. 332). Continued to receive this allowance up to and after appointment as reading clerk. It was paid as a matter of course to subsequent holders of that office.

Appointed copying clerk 2 December 1735 and reading clerk 22 October 1736 (BL, Add. MS 42779, f. 23; *LJ*, xxiv, 642). Held both offices until 31 January 1753 when appointed clerk assistant (*LJ*, xxviii, 13). On 21 March 1764 state of his health made it necessary for Samuel Strutt to be authorised to officiate as clerk assistant in his place. Retired 13 May 1765, whereupon House addressed crown asking for provision to be made for him (*LJ*, xxx, 514, 519; xxxi, 10, 200). On 5 July 1765 granted pension of £500 which was paid until death (TNA, T 52/37, p. 60; AO 1/1941/105).

Genealogical Table 1: *Bowyer – Elsyng – Knyvett – Throckmorton*

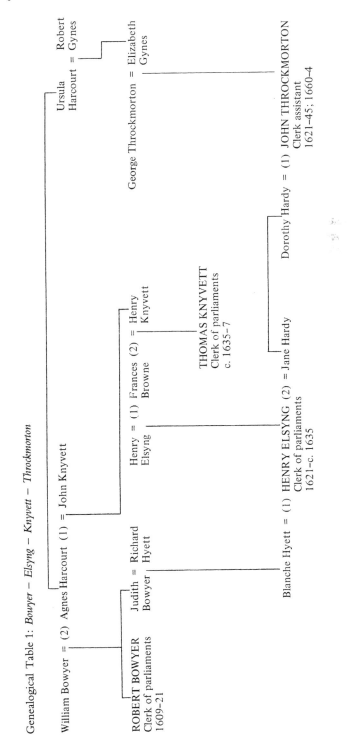

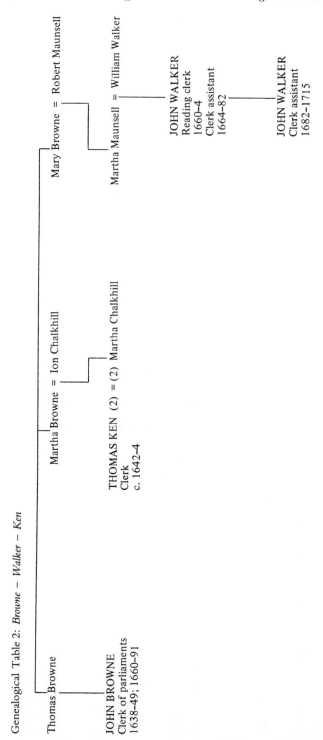

Genealogical Table 2: *Browne – Walker – Ken*

Thomas Browne

JOHN BROWNE
Clerk of parliaments
1638–49; 1660–91

Martha Browne = Ion Chalkhill

THOMAS KEN (2) = (2) Martha Chalkhill
Clerk
c. 1642–4

Mary Browne = Robert Maunsell

Martha Maunsell = William Walker

JOHN WALKER
Reading clerk
1660–4
Clerk assistant
1664–82

JOHN WALKER
Clerk assistant
1682–1715

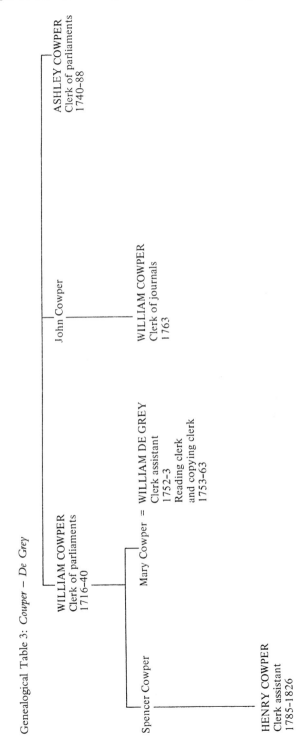

Genealogical Table 3: *Couper – De Grey*

ASHLEY COWPER
Clerk of parliaments
1740–88

John Cowper

WILLIAM COWPER
Clerk of journals
1763

WILLIAM DE GREY
Clerk assistant
1752–3
Reading clerk
and copying clerk
1753–63

Mary Cowper =

WILLIAM COWPER
Clerk of parliaments
1716–40

Spencer Cowper

HENRY COWPER
Clerk assistant
1785–1826

Chapter 6. Parliamentary Functions of the Sovereign since 1509

Introduction

The role which the Sovereign has played in Parliament is one of considerable signifi-cance in the constitutional history of the country. Yet it is not easy to discover, for any particular period, exactly what his parliamentary duties were nor how far he was expected to undertake them personally. A considerable amount of research will be necessary before a definitive picture emerges. In the meantime this chapter is offered, not as a scholarly treatment of the subject, but simply as a general framework which it is hoped will encourage further work on its more obscure aspects. The chapter will survey the broad lines of development from the accession of Henry VIII in 1509. This date has been selected as the point of departure because it is only during the sixteenth century that the relevant evidence becomes sufficiently abundant to enable firm con-clusions to be drawn.

The occasions on which the Sovereign's functions fall to be performed may be conveniently summarised as follows: the opening of the session; the arrangements for the approval of the Speaker of the Commons; the close of the session; and the giving of royal assent to bills.[1] Generally speaking the relevant functions have been performed in the presence of both Houses of Parliament either by or in the presence of the Sovereign or, in his absence, by commissioners authorised to act on his behalf. There are, however, two exceptions to this rule. Since 1922 the final session of a Parliament has, on occasion, been brought to a close by a proclamation of dissolution which involves no proceedings in Parliament[2] while in 1967 provision was made for royal assent to bills to be notified to the two Houses sitting separately by their respective Speakers[3] and this is now the normal practice.

Subsequent developments may perhaps be best understood if the arrangements cus-tomary during the sixteenth century are first described. At this period the Sovereign or his authorised representatives made three appearances in the first session of a parliament: on the opening day when the causes of summons were declared and the Commons were directed to choose a Speaker; on a day shortly thereafter when the Commons' choice was approved; and on the final day when, following an interchange of speeches between

---

[1] Unless otherwise noted the information in this chapter is derived from the *Lords Journals*. The *Journals* do not invariably contain full accounts of the proceedings until after the Restoration in 1660. The ceremonial observed during the Tudor period is described in S.E. Lehmberg, *The Later Parliaments of Henry VIII 1536–1547* (Cambridge, 1977), 251–2, 264–5; J.E. Neale, *The Elizabethan House of Commons* (2nd edn, 1963), 336–50, 403–15. Except where the context requires otherwise the term 'royal assent' means royal assent given at times other than the close of the session.

[2] 26 Oct. 1922, 12 Sept. 1964, 22 Sept. 1974, 7 Apr. 1979.

[3] 1967 c. 23.

the Speaker and the Crown, royal assent was given to or withheld from such bills as had been agreed upon by the two Houses and Parliament was either prorogued or dissolved. The declaration of the causes of summons and the election of the Speaker were distinctive features of the first session of a Parliament and were not repeated in any subsequent sessions. In the case of such sessions, therefore, the final day was the only occasion on which the Sovereign or his representatives were required to be present.

The Opening of Parliament and Choice of a Speaker

During the Tudor period it was not the usual practice for the Sovereign, if present, to participate actively in the proceedings. The necessary functions were carried out by the Lord Chancellor or some other spokesman in obedience to his directions. It was the spokesman who delivered the speeches and, while these were understood to reflect the royal views, they were phrased as the speeches of the spokesman not of the Sovereign. Royal interventions were not unknown but they appear not to have been regarded as part of the regular procedure. With the accession of James I the situation changed. James often delivered long speeches himself, sometimes dispensing entirely with the services of a spokesman. Initially Charles I reverted to the traditional practice as a matter of conscious policy and generally remained silent while the speeches were delivered by the Lord Chancellor or Lord Keeper. Later in his reign, however, he intervened himself with increasing frequency. Until 1679 Charles II as a general rule made short introductory speeches which were expanded by his spokesman. In that year the spokesman's speech was discontinued and thereafter the only speech delivered when the Sovereign was present was his own. Normally he delivered this himself. However, the practice was varied in the case of two monarchs. All George I's speeches were read for him by the Lord Chancellor. Victoria read her speeches herself until the death of the Prince Consort in 1861. Whenever she attended Parliament thereafter her speech was read by the Lord Chancellor. Originally, when the Sovereign's functions were delegated to Commissioners any speech that they made on his behalf was framed as proceeding from themselves. Since 1867 such speeches have been phrased as if they were the speeches of the Sovereign himself.

It is apparent from the Rolls of Parliament, where the opening ceremonies are regularly described from the fourteenth century, that it had long been the practice for the causes of summons to be declared and for the Commons to be directed to choose a Speaker on the first day and for the Speaker to be presented for approval on the second day of a new Parliament. This practice remained unchanged until the Parliament of James II in 1685. On this occasion the Sovereign's direction to the Commons and his approval of their choice both took place on the first day and the King's speech declaring the causes of summons was delayed until a subsequent day. Thereafter it was invariable for the proceedings in relation to the election of the Speaker to be completed before the delivery of the speech. Until 1790 it was usual for the direction to choose a Speaker to be given on the first day and for the Speaker to be approved and the speech delivered on the second day. However, on two occasions, in 1707 and 1714, two separate days were set aside for the proceedings in relation to the election of the Speaker, the delivery of the speech being delayed to a subsequent day. Since 1796 this has been the invariable practice.

A special procedure has evolved in connection with the election of a Speaker to fill a vacancy which occurs during the course of a Parliament. This differs from the procedure observed at the beginning of a Parliament in that the direction to elect has almost invariably been conveyed to the Commons by a minister in that House and the presence of the Sovereign or his representatives has only been required to approve the choice made by the Commons. However, in two cases, in February 1533[4] and February 1673, when the vacancy had occurred during a period of prorogation, the Sovereign appeared in Parliament at the beginning of the new session both to direct the Commons and to approve their choice.

Royal Speeches at the Beginning of the Session

As already noted it was not the practice during the Tudor period for a speech declaring the causes of summons to be delivered at the beginning of any session other than the first of a Parliament. James I broke this convention by delivering speeches at the beginning of both the second and the third sessions of his first Parliament of 1604–11, on 5 November 1605 and 18 November 1606 respectively. In only two instances between then and the Restoration were Parliaments extended to include a second session. In neither case were the opening days, 16 October 1610 and 29 January 1629, marked by the delivery of a speech. However, from the Restoration in 1660 it has been the invariable practice for every session of Parliament to be opened with a speech.

Royal Speeches during the Course of the Session

James I also frequently made speeches to Parliament during the course of the session. During his reign these speeches were usually differentiated from those made at the opening and close of the session by being delivered, not in the Parliament Chamber, but in the Banqueting House at Whitehall.[5] In the course of time such speeches were increasingly delivered in Parliament in the same manner as other speeches. This development was no doubt influenced by the fact that, as will be seen, the Sovereign was from the time of the Long Parliament frequently present in Parliament during the course of the session for the purpose of giving royal assent. In these circumstances it was natural that he should take advantage of the fact that the two Houses were assembled together to address them. Charles II, who made a habit of attending the House of Lords 'incognito' almost on a daily basis after 1670,[6] frequently addressed the two Houses both when giving royal assent and at other times. After the reign of Charles II additional

---

[4] S.E. Lehmberg, *The Reformation Parliament 1529–1536* (Cambridge, 1970), 171.

[5] There were precedents for James's practice. Elizabeth I addressed the two Houses during the course of the session at Whitehall in 1563, 1566, 1567 and 1601 and at Richmond in 1586 and 1589 (J.E. Neale, *Elizabeth I and Her Parliaments 1559–81* (1953), 106–10, 145–50, 273–6; *Elizabeth I and Her Parliaments 1584–1601* (1957), 116–21, 126–9, 213–14, 388–91).

[6] James II followed his brother's example in attending the House daily 'incognito'. William III did so only twice while Anne did so on thirty-three occasions. The practice was discontinued after Anne's death in 1714. For the Sovereign's 'incognito' attendances, see G.S. Holmes, *British Politics in the Reign of Anne* (1967), 390–1.

speeches became less frequent. However, after the accession of James II in 1685 forty-nine such speeches were delivered. In only ten of these cases were they not delivered at the same time that royal assent was given. The last additional speech was that made by George III on 19 June 1780.

The End of the Session

The ceremonial observed on the final day of the session originally consisted of four principal elements. First the Speaker made his speech which usually covered a variety of topics but which was mainly directed to the subsidy bill which he brought up with him from the Commons. This was followed by a speech from the Sovereign's spokesman which rehearsed the points made by the Speaker and expressed thanks for the subsidy bill. The titles of the bills to which the two Houses had agreed were then read and the bills either assented to or vetoed. Finally the spokesman, in obedience to the instructions of the Sovereign, either prorogued or dissolved Parliament.

Later Developments in the Manner of Giving Royal Assent to Bills

Originally the final day was the only occasion during the session on which royal assent was given. The reason for this was that it was held that the giving of assent had in itself the effect of terminating the session. However, this doctrine caused obvious inconvenience when statutory authority was required for some urgent action. Either such action had to be postponed until the other business of Parliament was complete or that business had to be jeopardised to enable the necessary authority to be given without delay. In fact, even as early as the reign of Henry VIII there were two exceptions to the rule. Both were concerned with attainders. On 11 February 1542 royal assent was given to a bill of attainder against Queen Katharine Howard and to a related bill on the subject of treason. Section 3 of the Act of Attainder specifically provided that the giving of royal assent should not affect the existence of the session which was in fact continued until 1 April when Parliament was prorogued and the remaining bills received the royal assent. On 27 January 1547 royal assent was given to an Act of Attainder against the Duke of Norfolk and the Earl of Surrey. The continuation of the session was not affected by this event although in the result it was brought to a close the following day when Parliament was automatically dissolved by the death of the King.

Between 1547 and 1621 the customary arrangement was invariably followed and royal assent only given on the final day of the session. However, on 22 March 1621 James I gave assent to two subsidy bills. The session continued until 19 December 1621 when Parliament was prorogued without any further bills receiving the royal assent. The next occasion on which the customary practice was varied was on 11 July 1625 when royal assent was given to six bills one of which was designed to remove any doubt about the effect which this action might have on the life of the session.[7] A similar bill had been introduced in the 1621 session but had not been passed. The 1625 session came to an

---

[7] 1 Cha. 1 c. 7.

end on 12 August when Parliament was dissolved. No further bills received the royal assent. On 7 June 1628 Charles I gave royal assent to the petition of right. The session ended on 26 June when upon prorogation the King gave assent to the remaining bills.

These five cases are the only occasions before the beginning of the Long Parliament on which the traditional practice of giving royal assent only on the last day of the session was departed from. It was during that Parliament that the practice was finally abandoned. Between the opening in November 1640 and the final breakdown of relations between the King and Parliament in June 1642 royal assent was given twenty-four times. The frequency is to some extent explained by the fact that the financial provision made for the Crown was of only limited duration and had to be periodically renewed by statute. More generally, of course, it was obviously impractical to await the end of a session which was of indefinite length before enacting important legislation. However, the uncertainty of the effect which the giving of royal assent might have on the life of the session remained. The first three Acts to be passed during the Long Parliament all contain special provisions to the effect that the giving of assent should not terminate the session and the fourth contains a general provision to regularise the position for the remainder of the session.[8] Provisions similar to these are also included in the first three acts to be passed after the Restoration[9] but this is the last indication that the old convention had any force and since 1660 it has been the established practice for royal assent to be given at regular intervals during the session.

Later Developments in the Ceremonial at the End of the Session

These developments, coupled with the difficulties which the early Stuarts encountered in dealing with their parliaments, inevitably affected the ceremonial observed at the end of the session. The first four sessions of the reign of James I were all brought to a close in the presence of the King in the traditional fashion with the giving of royal assent and the customary speeches. However, in the case of only two of the next nine sessions preceding the Long Parliament, those of 1624 and 1628, was this pattern followed. In none of the remaining cases was royal assent given on the final day. At the end of sessions 1629 and 1640 the King came personally to make brief speeches before dissolving Parliament. Otherwise Parliament was either prorogued or dissolved by commission without any other ceremony.

When, after the Restoration in 1660, royal assent began to be given several times during the session as a matter of course it became the usual practice for the Speaker, when such assent was given in person, to make a short speech in relation to any supply bills there might be. The Speaker's speech at the close of the session thus lost its uniqueness. This in turn had an effect on the speech made by or on behalf of the Sovereign on the final day. It ceased to be specifically related to that of the Speaker and became more general in character. The distinction was underlined by the fact that, from the beginning of the reign of Charles II, it was delivered, not immediately after the Speaker's as had been the case previously, but after royal assent had been given.

[8] 16 Cha.1 cc. 1–4.
[9] 12 Cha. 2 cc. 1–3.

The irregular structure of the sessions of Charles II's Parliaments makes it difficult to generalise about the practice during that reign. Until 1673 the closing day was marked by speeches and royal assent except on three occasions when Parliament was prorogued by commission without further formality. For the rest of the reign the King was invariably present on the final day but the session was frequently brought to a close without royal assent or speeches. With the advent of regular annual sessions during the reign of William III convention hardened. Thereafter whenever the Sovereign was present the proceedings began with the Speaker's speech in relation to the Supply Bill or Bills, followed by royal assent, the Sovereign's Speech and Prorogation or Dissolution. In the absence of the Sovereign the Speaker's Speech was dispensed with.

The Presence of the Sovereign in Parliament and the Development of Royal Commissions

For well over a hundred years the only one of the functions just described which the Sovereign has carried out in person has been to open the session, the remaining duties having been delegated to commissioners or to the Speakers of the two Houses. However, it was originally the expectation that these other duties would be performed in person as well. The purpose of this part of the chapter is to examine the record of successive monarchs from the accession of Henry VIII in 1509 in order to elucidate the process whereby their personal attendance has come to be confined to the opening of the session.[10]

On only three out of a possible forty-three occasions did Henry VIII delegate his parliamentary functions to commissioners. Commissioners gave royal assent on 11 February 1542 and 22 January 1547 and dissolved Parliament on 29 March 1544. Edward VI and Mary I carried out all their parliamentary functions in person, attending on nine and sixteen occasions respectively for this purpose. Elizabeth I was present on thirty-two out of a possible thirty-five occasions. Her three absences are accounted for by her refusal to attend the Parliament of 1586–87 when commissioners delivered the Opening Speech, approved the Speaker and dissolved Parliament on her behalf.

During the reign of James I royal functions were delegated to Commissioners on four out of a possible nineteen occasions. Commissioners brought sessions to a close by prorogation on 6 December 1610 and by dissolution on 7 June 1614 and 8 February 1622. Royal assent was given by Commission on 22 March 1621.

Charles I delegated his parliamentary functions to Commissioners on seventeen out of forty occasions. Only three of these pre-dated the Long Parliament. Commissioners gave royal assent on 11 July 1625 and terminated sessions by dissolution on 12 August 1625 and 15 June 1626. During the Long Parliament royal assent was given by Commission on fourteen out of twenty-four occasions. The King last gave royal assent in person on 2 December 1641; the last royal assent by Commission was given on 22 June 1642, immediately before the final rupture between the King and Parliament. During the reign of Charles II Commissioners carried out royal functions on six out of a possible

[10] See also Appendix.

seventy-four occasions. They gave royal assent on 2 May 1662, 3 June 1663 and 19 December 1667 and prorogued Parliament on 1 March and 11 December 1669 and 20 October 1673. James II was present in person on each of the six occasions on which he was called upon to carry out Parliamentary duties.

William III delegated his functions to Commissioners on only four out of a possible ninety-one occasions. All of these can be explained by special circumstances. In two cases, 26 May 1691 and 12 April 1692, Parliament was prorogued by Commission, the session having in each case already been effectively terminated by an earlier adjournment when the King made what amounted to a close of session speech. In the remaining two cases royal assent was given by Commission in March 1702 only days before the King's death when he was already suffering from his fatal illness.

Queen Anne's Parliamentary attendance was naturally affected by her poor health. Nevertheless she only delegated her functions to Commissioners on twenty-three out of a possible eighty-seven occasions. She was present in person on every occasion until 13 February 1708 when royal assent was given by Commission. She was absent for the whole of session 1708–9 and, as a result, her functions were carried out by Commissioners on seven occasions. She attended all the other twelve Openings of her reign and all but one of the remaining thirteen prorogations. The exception was July 1712 when Parliament was prorogued by Commission without either a speech or royal assent, the session having already been effectively terminated by an earlier adjournment as in 1691 and 1692. Otherwise Queen Anne was absent on thirteen occasions when royal assent was given and on two days when proceedings in relation to the election of the Speaker took place. It is noteworthy that in the last two sessions of her reign she attended only the opening and closing ceremonies.

On the death of Queen Anne both Houses met pursuant to the Succession to the Crown Act 1707 and remained in session from 1 to 25 August 1714. During this period the royal functions were, in accordance with the same Act, performed by Lords Justices who delivered speeches on 5 and 15 August, gave royal assent on 21 August and prorogued Parliament on 25 August.

George I arrived in England from Hanover on 18 September 1714. From then until his death he performed all his parliamentary duties in person. This involved him in seventy-six attendances during the thirteen years of his reign. His successor, George II, was almost equally assiduous between his accession in 1727 and 1756. There was one session during this period in which he delegated his functions entirely to commissioners. This was the short session at the beginning of the Parliament of 1754 when commissioners directed the Commons to choose a Speaker, approved their choice, delivered the opening speech and prorogued Parliament. Apart from this special case George II was absent only from the opening of the session on 1 February 1737 and when royal assent was given on 26 May 1749 and 22 March 1751.[11] After 1756 a change of practice is discernible. During session 1755–56 George II was absent when royal assent was given on 15 April 1756 and again when Parliament was prorogued on 15 July 1756. In the following session his absences were more frequent and he did not attend Parliament at

---

[11] This leaves out of account the prorogation by commission on 15 June 1727 when both Houses met pursuant to the Succession to the Crown Act 1707.

all after giving royal assent on 23 December 1757. However, he had then reached the relatively advanced age of seventy-four.

At the accession of George III in 1760 it was evidently still the expectation that the sovereign would, age and health permitting, carry out all his parliamentary functions in person. At the beginning of the Parliament of 1768 the precedent of 1754 was followed and a special short session held when all the royal functions were executed by commissioners. Apart from this George III was, in the early years of his reign, almost as assiduous in attending to his parliamentary duties as his grandfather had been.[12] As the reign progressed, however, the situation changed. Different considerations came to apply to the various functions. It remained the expectation that the King would be present at the opening of the session and at prorogation. Between his accession and 1805 George III was absent both from the opening and from prorogation only in the short session of 1768 and in the session of 1788–89 when he was recovering from his insanity. Apart from these instances his only absences were from the prorogations on 27 October 1785 and 2 July 1801. George III last appeared in Parliament at the opening of the session on 15 January 1805 and for the remaining six years during which he exercised royal authority all his parliamentary duties were carried out by commissioners.

As far as the election of the Speaker was concerned George III was present on all occasions except the election of 1768 down to 1790,[13] the last occasion on which a monarch participated personally in these proceedings.

George III invariably gave royal assent in person until the end of session 1763–64. Thereafter he increasingly delegated this function to commissioners. One reason for this was no doubt the fact that the number of occasions when royal assent was given was continuously growing. Before 1760 it was only very rarely given more than five times a session. By 1800 the average was about twenty times a session. The last session during which George III gave royal assent in person on every possible occasion was that of 1770. Session 1775–76 was the last in which royal assent was given more frequently in person than by commission. George III usually came to Parliament to give royal assent on at least one occasion during the session down to and including the session of 1793. From session 1780–81 he confined his attendances to those occasions when the more important supply bills were due to be enacted. After 1793 it seems to have been understood that the King would give royal assent in person only in exceptional circumstances. In fact George III did so on only one further occasion – on 2 July 1800 – when, at the special request of his ministers,[14] he gave his assent to the highly important Union with Ireland Bill.

George IV exercised royal authority as Regent 1811–20 and as King 1820–30. He opened the session in person on nine out of a possible twenty occasions.[15] His record for

---

[12] On 26 Oct. 1760 both Houses met pursuant to the Succession to the Crown Act 1707 and remained in session until 29 Oct. when Parliament was prorogued by commission. This prorogation has been ignored for the purposes of this chapter.

[13] This leaves out of account the election of Grenville on 5 Jan. 1789. Because of the King's indisposition Grenville never received the approval of the Crown.

[14] *The Later Correspondence of George III*, ed. A. Aspinall (1962–70), iii, 369.

[15] He opened the session in person on the following occasions: 30 Nov. 1812, 4 Nov. 1813, 8 Nov. 1814, 28 Jan. 1817, 23 Nov. 1819, 27 Apr. 1820, 23 Jan. 1821, 5 Feb. 1822, 21 Nov. 1826.

prorogations, including one dissolution, was precisely the same.[16] He did not attend Parliament after the opening of the session on 21 November 1826. He gave royal assent in person on one occasion – on 6 June 1820 – when the Civil List Bill was enacted, thus setting a precedent which was followed by his two successors, each of whom came specially to Parliament to give assent to bills making financial provision for the royal family.

William IV was more assiduous than his brother. He was present at every opening and every prorogation except the opening of the final session of his reign on 31 January 1837. He gave royal assent in person on one occasion – on 2 August 1831 – when the Queen's Annuity Bill was enacted.[17]

At the accession of Queen Victoria in 1837 it evidently remained the expectation that the sovereign would open and prorogue Parliament in person. The only occasion on which she gave royal assent in person, apart from prorogation, was on 23 December 1837 when the Civil List Bill was enacted. She ceased to attend prorogations after 1854. Between her accession and this date she was present on fourteen out of a possible nineteen occasions.[18] The ceremony on 12 August 1854 was both the last occasion when Parliament was prorogued in person and also the last on which royal assent was given in person.[19] Queen Victoria's last appearance in Parliament was at the opening of the session on 21 January 1886. Between her accession and this date she was present at openings on twenty-eight out of a possible fifty-three occasions.[20]

At the accession of Edward VII in 1901 more than fourteen years had elapsed since the sovereign had performed any of his parliamentary functions in person. However, the new King immediately decided to revive the practice of opening the session in person.[21] With only six exceptions[22] his example has been followed to the present day.

---

[16] He prorogued Parliament in person on the following occasions: 22 July 1813, 30 July 1814, 12 July 1815, 2 July 1816, 12 July 1817, 13 July 1819, 6 Aug. 1822 and 25 June 1824 and dissolved it in person on 10 June 1818.

[17] On this occasion Queen Adelaide expressed her gratitude to Parliament by curtseying to the King, Lords and Commons (*LJ*, lxiii (Index), 1157), thus following the example of Queen Charlotte in 1762 (PA, Manuscript Minutes, 2 Dec. 1762). There was no necessity for William IV to come specially to Parliament in connection with the Civil List Bill because it was given royal assent at the prorogation on 22 Apr. 1831.

[18] Queen Victoria prorogued Parliament in person on the following occasions: 17 July 1837, 16 Aug. 1838, 27 Aug. 1839, 11 Aug. 1840, 22 June 1841, 12 Aug. 1842, 24 Aug. 1843, 9 Aug. 1845, 23 July 1847, 5 Sept. 1848, 15 Aug. 1850, 8 Aug. 1851, 1 July 1852 and 12 Aug. 1854.

[19] It was also the last occasion when the Speaker of the Commons made a speech at prorogation.

[20] Queen Victoria opened the session in person on the following occasions: 20 Nov. 1837, 5 Feb. 1839, 16 Jan. 1840, 26 Jan. 1841, 3 Feb. 1842, 1 Feb. 1844, 4 Feb. 1845, 22 Jan. 1846, 19 Jan. 1847, 1 Feb. 1849, 4 Feb. 1851, 3 Feb. and 11 Nov. 1852, 31 Jan. and 12 Dec. 1854, 31 Jan. 1856, 3 Dec. 1857, 3 Feb. and 7 June 1859, 24 Jan. 1860, 5 Feb. 1861, 6 Feb. 1866, 5 Feb. 1867, 9 Feb. 1871, 8 Feb. 1876, 8 Feb. 1877, 5 Feb. 1880 and 21 Jan. 1886.

[21] S. Lee, *King Edward VII: A Biography* (1925–7), ii, 21–2. The problems which arose when Edward VII first opened the session on 14 Feb. 1901 occasioned the appointment of the Joint Committee on the Presence of the Sovereign in Parliament whose report *(Lords Papers* (1901), viii, 205–95) contains a considerable amount of information about the ceremony and its history.

[22] 15 Feb. 1916, 2 July 1929, 3 Dec. 1935, 6 Nov. 1951, 27 Oct. 1959 and 12 Nov. 1963.

Appendix: Exercise of Parliamentary Functions of the Sovereign 1509–1811

Occasion	In person	By Commission	Total
	HENRY VIII 1509–47		
Opening	9	0	9
Approval of Speaker	11	0	11
Close	20	1	21
Royal assent (excluding 21 at close)	0	2	2
	40	3	43
	EDWARD VI 1547–53		
Opening	2	0	2
Approval of Speaker	2	0	2
Close	5	0	5
Royal assent (excluding 5 at close)	0	0	0
	9	0	9
	MARY I 1553–8		
Opening	5	0	5
Approval of Speaker	5	0	5
Close	6	0	6
Royal assent (excluding 6 at close)	0	0	0
	16	0	16
	ELIZABETH I 1558–1603		
Opening	9	1	10
Approval of Speaker	11	1	12
Close	12	1	13
Royal assent (excluding 12 at close)	0	0	0
	32	3	35
	JAMES I 1603–25		
Opening	6	0	6
Approval of Speaker	4	0	4
Close	5	3	8
Royal assent (excluding 5 at close)	0	1	1
	15	4	19
	CHARLES I 1625–49		
Opening	5	0	5
Approval of Speaker	5	0	5
Close	2	2	4
Royal assent (excluding 1 at close)	11	15	26
	23	17	40
	CHARLES II 1660–85		
Opening	21	0	21
Approval of Speaker	9	0	9
Close	19	3	22
Royal assent (excluding 13 at close)	19	3	22
	68	6	74

Occasion	In person	By Commission	Total
	JAMES II 1685–9		
Opening	1	0	1
Approval of Speaker	1	0	1
Close	1	0	1
Royal assent	3	0	3
	6	0	6
	WILLIAM III 1689–1702		
Opening	14	0	14
Approval of Speaker	5★	0	5
Close	12	2	14
Royal assent (excluding 11 at close)	57	2	59
	87	4	91
	ANNE 1702–14		
Opening	12	1	13
Approval of Speaker	5	3	8
Close	12	2	14
Royal assent (excluding 12 at close)	35	17	52
	64	23	87
	GEORGE I 1714–27		
Opening	13	0	13
Approval of Speaker	2	0	2
Close	13	0	13
Royal assent (excluding 13 at close)	48	0	48
	76	0	76
	GEORGE II 1727–60		
Opening	31	4	35
Approval of Speaker	4	1	5
Close	30	5	35
Royal assent (excluding 33 at close)	87	18	105
	152	28	180
	GEORGE III 1760–1811		
Opening	46	8	54
Approval of Speaker	8	12	20
Close	43	11	54
Royal assent (excluding 51 at close)	94	409	503
	191	440	631

★excluding 15 March 1695 when Speaker approved on same day on which royal assent given.

Chapter 7. The Edmunds Case and the House of Lords

If one is fortunate enough to occupy an office of some antiquity it is perhaps natural to enquire into the lives and circumstances of one's predecessors. The first certainly identifiable Reading Clerk was John Relfe (died 1711), an industrious individual who compiled impressive collections of 'Relfe's Book of Orders' now deposited in the Parliamentary Archives.[1] By far the most distinguished person ever considered for the post was the poet William Cowper. He was offered it in 1763 but declined it on the ground of his 'incapacity to execute a business of so public a nature'.[2] No such scruples were entertained by William Stewart Rose, another individual with literary aspirations, who accepted the appointment in 1800. Rose seems never to have allowed his duties at the Table of the House seriously to interfere with his activities as a poet and translator of mediaeval French literature. In 1816 a permanent deputy was appointed to relieve him of such duties as he still performed. In 1824 he was permitted to retire on pension on the plea of ill-health. He lived on until 1843.[3] The only other Reading Clerk who is worthy of particular notice is Leonard Edmunds whose rather unusual career is the subject of this essay.

Edmunds was born about 1802, the son of John Edmunds of Ambleside, Westmorland. John Edmunds was the election agent of the Whig politician, Henry Brougham, and lost his life while canvassing on his behalf during the general election campaign of 1826. In the circumstances Brougham felt an obligation to make provision for the Edmunds children and Leonard was accordingly articled to Brougham's solicitor, William Vizard (1774–1859), a partner in the firm of James and Henry Leman of Lincoln's Inn Fields.[4]

Four years later, in November 1830, the Whigs were returned to power and Brougham became Lord Chancellor. In this capacity he had at his disposal a number of places in his official entourage. He was thus able to nominate Edmunds to the office of Pursebearer and also to that of Secretary of Commissions with responsibility for the administrative arrangements for appointing justices of the peace. The combined income from these two posts was about £1,000 a year – a very respectable sum in the values of the time for a man still under thirty.[5] However, both offices were held on a precarious tenure and Edmunds was therefore at risk should there be a change of administration. Consequently it was important for him to take steps to obtain more employment while

---

[1] M.F. Bond, *The Records of Parliament* (1971), 191, 280.

[2] Memoir of William Cowper, ed. M.J. Quinlan, *Proceedings of the American Philosophical Society*, xcii (1953), 369–70.

[3] *Dictionary of National Biography*, xlix, 244–5.

[4] *Report of select committee of house of lords on the resignation of Mr Edmunds* (hereafter cited as *Edmunds Report*), HL 1865, xxii, 387; *Gentleman's Magazine* (1826), new ser., xcvi, 94; F. Boase, *Modern English Biography* (1892–1921), i, 963; vi, 747.

[5] *Edmunds Report*, QQ. 1768, 1769, 1857, p. 387.

Brougham remained Lord Chancellor. In this he was successful. In August 1833 he was appointed Clerk of the Patents with a salary of £400 while in November of the following year, a few days before the fall of the Whig Government, he obtained the additional office of clerk of the Crown in Chancery with a salary of £500. Both these offices were concerned with the preparation and authorisation of chancery documents, the Patent Office primarily with patents of invention and the Crown Office primarily with patents of creation and appointment and parliamentary writs. While the work involved was mainly of a routine kind which could be largely delegated to subordinate clerks, a considerable amount of financial responsibility fell upon Edmunds because most of the documents attracted fees payable by the public which had to be passed on to the Exchequer.[6]

Edmunds never married and from the time that Brougham ceased to be Lord Chancellor he boarded at his London house and acted as his confidential secretary.[7] Although Brougham never again held office he remained a very active member of the House of Lords and it is likely that Edmunds assisted him with his many schemes for the reform of the law.

In 1844 Edmunds presented a petition to the House of Lords representing that the financial arrangements made for the Crown Office were inadequate. The petition was referred to a select committee which recommended that steps should be taken to improve the situation. Later in the same year an Act was passed doubling the salary of the Clerk of the Crown.[8] In 1848 Edmunds negotiated through the agency of William Brougham, a Master in Chancery and brother of the former Lord Chancellor, an arrangement whereby he gave up the office of Clerk of the Crown in favour of the son of the then Lord Chancellor, Lord Cottenham, on condition that Cottenham appointed him Reading Clerk in the House of Lords, an office to which a salary of £1,500 was attached.[9]

In 1852 an Act of Parliament reformed the Patent Office and placed it under a body of Commissioners headed by the Lord Chancellor. Edmunds was appointed Clerk to the Commissioners at a salary of £600 in addition to the £400 he already enjoyed as Clerk of the Patents.[10]

Thus at mid century Edmunds's affairs appeared to be prospering. He had a total income from public funds of £2,500 a year. Since he lodged at Brougham's house his living expenses were small. Although he was responsible for the welfare of two sisters he had apparently no other commitments and his future seemed secure. However, in 1863 a cloud appeared on the horizon in the shape of a charge of embezzlement in the Patent Office. An investigation revealed that the charge was well founded and that Edmunds had to some degree condoned the conduct of the individual concerned. Edmunds at first offered to resign but, finding that he was unable to obtain the pension he desired, decided to remain in office. But this was not the end of the matter. There were quarrels amongst the staff of the Patent Office and accusations of maladministration were made

---

[6] *Edmunds Report*, QQ. 1645, 1778; *London Gazette* No. 19211; *Report of select committee of house of lords on the petition of the clerk of the crown in chancery*, HL, 1844, xix, 1–18.

[7] *Edmunds Report*, Q. 1550.

[8] *LJ*, lxxvi, 10; *Clerk of the Crown in Chancery Act 1844*. See also *Report of select committee of house of commons on the clerk of the crown in chancery*, HC 1844, xiv, 111–70.

[9] *Edmunds Report*, QQ. 1507–8, 1778.

[10] Patent Law Amendment Act 1852; *Edmunds Report*, Q. 1857.

against Edmunds who demanded an independent enquiry into his conduct. Two Queen's Counsel, Messrs. Greenwood and Hindmarch, were appointed to undertake the enquiry in May 1864.[11]

On 24 June, Edmunds went to the Lord Chancellor, Lord Westbury, 'to state his great anxiety to resign immediately'. After some hesitation the Lord Chancellor agreed and signed the necessary memorial to the Treasury seeking a retiring allowance. Before the memorial could be acceded to Greenwood called upon the Lord Chancellor and told him that there were circumstances 'of a very fearful character' which made it essential that all further proceedings on the memorial should be stayed.[12]

On 12 July the preliminary report of the enquiry was made and made clear the reasons for concern. It found the charges of maladministration against Edmunds established and, what was much more serious, uncovered evidence that he had used public money for his own private purposes. Edmunds was thereupon summoned to appear before the Commissioners of Patents to show cause why he should not be removed from office upon four charges founded on the report. However, acting on the advice of his solicitor, Edmunds asked to be able to resign and the Commissioners permitted him to do so on condition that he undertook to account for and pay over to the Treasury all sums of money due from him as Clerk of the Patents. In September Edmunds paid to the Bank of England £7,872 5s. 6d. as representing the full amount of his indebtedness to the Treasury. However, in a supplementary report made on 31 January 1865 Greenwood and Hindmarch identified a further £9,617 15s. 4d. as owing from him.[13]

In the meantime the Lord Chancellor had been giving consideration to Edmunds's position as Reading Clerk. He was initially under the false impression that he possessed the power to dismiss Edmunds himself. On this assumption he consulted two Law Lords, Lords Cranworth and Kingsdown, as to the course which he should take. Both considered that Edmunds should be invited to show cause why he should not be dismissed. Edmunds was told that he would be given the opportunity of making his defence and in due course delivered his reply to the charges contained in the preliminary report. This reply was never sent to the two Law Lords as the Lord Chancellor had discovered that the power of dismissal in fact rested with the House and not with him.[14]

At about this time William Brougham intervened on Edmunds's behalf. Brougham, like his brother, had for many years been on intimate terms with Edmunds. However, in October 1864, on learning of Edmunds's misconduct in the Patent Office, Lord Brougham had ordered him to leave his London house. This caused Edmunds to harbour a most violent dislike for both the Brougham brothers.[15] Despite this, William Brougham wrote a letter to the Lord Chancellor in which he said 'if you think, looking at all the circumstances of the case, that Mr Edmunds's wisest course is to resign and

---

[11] *Edmunds Report*, iii.

[12] *Edmunds Report*, iv.

[13] *Edmunds Report*, iv, ix.

[14] *Edmunds Report*, x–xi.

[15] *Edmunds Report*, QQ. 1781–8.

petition the Parliament Office Committee to be allowed to retire on a pension, and if you will do what you can to help him to a pension, I will advise him to resign'. In reply the Lord Chancellor said that, if Edmunds decided to resign, he would do all that he could 'with propriety' to obtain a pension for him.[16]

Once the Lord Chancellor became aware that Edmunds's fate was in the hands of the House which also had the power to award a retiring allowance, he consulted the cabinet as to the course which he should follow. The cabinet were of the opinion that he should bring the matter before the House and accordingly he wrote to Edmunds's solicitor to inform him that at the beginning of the next session he would lay on the Table the charges which had been made together with Edmunds's answers and move for a select committee to be appointed to take the matter into consideration.[17]

By the time the new session opened on 7 February Edmunds's solicitor had persuaded him to resign. The Lord Chancellor was of the opinion that this absolved him from the obligation to raise the matter in the House on the ground that he was required to take this course only if Edmunds remained an officer of the House. He further decided to 'throw no obstacle in the way of the pension'. On this basis he presented to the House without comment Edmunds's petition expressing his wish to retire and praying the House to grant him such retiring allowance as it should think fit. This petition was referred to the Parliament Office Committee which without enquiry recommended a pension of £800. This was agreed to by the House on 24 February.[18]

However, in the course of the next few weeks the Edmunds case became so publicly notorious that the Lord Chancellor felt constrained to raise the whole question in the House. On 7th March he made a statement outlining on his own conduct and moved for the appointment of a select committee to enquire into all the circumstances of Edmunds's resignation of his various offices and also the circumstances surrounding the grant of his pension. The motion was agreed to and a strong committee was nominated which included the Leader of the House, Lord Granville, who was chosen Chairman, and the Leader of the Opposition, Lord Derby. The Committee held fourteen meetings during the course of the next two months and took a large amount of revealing evidence from, amongst others, the Lord Chancellor, the Chancellor of the Exchequer, the Master of the Rolls and the Attorney General.[19]

The Committee made its report to the House on 4 May 1865. Their principal conclusions related to the charges against Edmunds which, in the main, they found fully substantiated. The Committee went on to criticise the conduct of the Lord Chancellor in failing to make the Parliament Office Committee aware of the circumstances which had prompted Edmunds to resign and leaving the Committee to decide the question of a pension 'with no clearer light than that which could be derived from vague and uncertain rumours'. It must be rare for a select committee with a Cabinet Minister as its Chairman to express such criticism of one of his colleagues. Nor did the report spare the Parliament Office Committee stating that 'It is to be regretted that the Committee did not consider it to be their duty under the circumstances to act upon their general

---

[16] *Edmunds Report*, xi.

[17] *Edmunds Report*, xii.

[18] *Edmunds Report*, xii, xiii; QQ. 1790–1826; *LJ*, xcvii, 22, 27, 38.

[19] Hansard, *Parl. Debs*, 3rd ser. clxxvii, cols 1203–21; *Edmunds Report*, xix–xxvi.

knowledge or impression so far as to interpose some delay before the question was finally disposed of in favour of a pension'.[20]

The Committee also investigated an arrangement made at the time of Edmunds's appointment as Clerk of the Patents in 1833 whereby it had been agreed between him and James Brougham, one of the former Lord Chancellor's brothers, that £300 a year out of his salary should be applied either for the benefit of the family of John Brougham, another brother, or be available towards the liquidation of the debts of James Brougham. This arrangement was linked to a proposal made in 1863 that Edmunds should resign his post in the Patent Office in favour of William Brougham's son who should hold it on the same terms. On this question the Committee expressed itself in the following terms: 'Any private arrangement that a portion of the salary of a public officer which is the remuneration for his services shall be applied to the benefit of any other person is a grave offence against public morality, and deserves the severest condemnation'.[21]

The Committee had, however, a word to say in extenuation of Edmunds's conduct. They found from Treasury witnesses that there was no proper legal framework for ensuring the accountability of the Clerk of the Patents. Gladstone, the Chancellor of the Exchequer, stated that the Clerk 'may hold in his hands just as much money as he thinks fit, and pay it if he thinks fit, and if he pay nothing at all there are no means of calling him to account for such non-payment'. Gladstone agreed that the law in this field was in certain respects extremely unsatisfactory. The Committee commented that this state of affairs should not be allowed to continue 'as it not only imperils the custody of public money, but offers to various persons employed in the public service temptation to misconduct'.[22]

The report was debated in the House on 9 May.[23] In spite of a petition from Edmunds seeking to be allowed to be heard in his own defence the House agreed to a motion moved by Lord Granville rescinding his pension.[24]

The report had repercussions that went beyond the fate of Edmunds. It was one of the factors which led to Lord Westbury's resignation as Lord Chancellor and it occasioned in the following year the passage of the Exchequer and Audit Departments Act which tightened up the procedures for accounting for public money.

The proceedings ruined Edmunds. Apart from the damage to his moral character he was deprived of any kind of retiring allowance. However, his tribulations did not end there. The Treasury pursued its claims against him. In the event the matter was sent to arbitration which was concluded in November 1869.

The arbitrators found that he was still indebted to the Crown for more than £7,000. In January 1870 a Treasury minute was published in the press which recorded this fact and also commented adversely on Edmunds's conduct, particularly his attempts to blacken the character of Greenwood, the Treasury Solicitor, who had been jointly responsible for the investigation into the Patent Office in 1864–5. Edmunds thereupon initiated proceedings for libel against the Prime Minister, Gladstone, and the other

[20] *Edmunds Report*, xiii, xiv.

[21] *Edmunds Report*, xiv–xviii.

[22] *Edmunds Report*, ix.

[23] Hansard, *Parl. Debs*, clxxix, cols 6–45.

[24] T.A. Nash, *Life of Lord Westbury* (1888), ii, 112–13, 129; Hansard, *Parl. Debs*, clxxxi, col. 276.

Treasury Commissioners who had signed the Minute. In May Edmunds was arrested for debt and imprisoned for a period of eight months, a development which led to a lengthy debate in the House of Commons where there was a widespread impression that imprisonment for debt had been abolished. Edmunds's action against Gladstone and his colleagues was eventually brought to trial in July 1872 but he was non-suited.[25]

Edmunds still had friends in the House of Lords. His most persistent supporter was the Chairman of Committees, Lord Redesdale, who in August 1872 moved an address with the object of having Edmunds's accounts audited by the Comptroller and Auditor General whose office had been created by the Act of 1866. This course was resisted by the Lord Chancellor, Lord Selborne, on the ground that there was no case for reopening the matter after the arbitration of 1869 and, in view of the fact that the session was nearing its close, Redesdale did not press the matter. However, he returned to the charge in June of the following year after Edmunds had petitioned the House to the same effect. Once again he met with the opposition of Selborne and his motion was negatived.[26]

In June 1874 the youthful Lord Rosebery, who was later to become Prime Minister, presented a further petition from Edmunds seeking an enquiry into his case by the Parliament Office Committee and moved that it be referred to that Committee. On this occasion the government's view was expressed by the new Lord Chancellor, Lord Cairns. It was as unfavourable to Edmunds as that of his predecessor. Rosebery's motion was negatived.[27]

Five years were to elapse before one final effort was made on Edmunds's behalf. Redesdale secured the printing by the House of his own correspondence with the Chancellor of the Exchequer about the case and also a document prepared by Edmunds setting out his view of the past history of the matter. This curious document, which runs to eighty-seven pages, is full of virulent and intemperate accusations against a whole range of public officials from cabinet ministers downwards. Having thus prepared the ground Redesdale moved for a select committee to re-examine the case. He was firmly opposed by Lord Chancellor Cairns and his motion was rejected by the House.[28]

Edmunds at last gave up the struggle. In 1885 the House of Lords Offices Committee, the successor to the Parliament Office Committee, awarded him a compassionate allowance of £2 10s. a week which he enjoyed until his death on 19 June 1887.[29]

Edmunds's case was a sad one. He was a man of uneven temper and poor judgment at least where his own affairs were concerned. His violence of language and extreme partisanship obviously lost him the sympathy of the officials who had to deal with his problems. On the other hand, while it is impossible to defend his conduct over the affairs of the Patent Office, it is only fair to say that Edmunds was to some extent a victim of the changing morality of the Victorian era. He was perhaps unfortunate to have owed his introduction to the public service to the Brougham family whose standards of probity, as revealed by the investigation of 1865, were not of the highest.

---

[25] HC 1870, lvii, 97–8; 1872, i, 195–8; HL 1878–9, xii, 241–9; Hansard, *Parl. Debs*, cciii, cols 509–35.

[26] Hansard, *Parl. Debs*, ccxiii, cols 831–4; ccxvi, cols 963–79.

[27] Hansard, *Parl. Debs*, cclxx, cols 1500–16.

[28] HL 1878–9, xii, 213–308; Hansard, *Parl. Debs*, cclxvii, cols 1407–14.

[29] *LJ*, cxvii, 68; *Modern English Biography*, i, 963.

When he was first appointed in 1830 the earlier concept of office as a species of property still had some currency. The practice of using balances of public money for private purposes, however heinous it may have appeared subsequently, was commonplace in the eighteenth and not unknown in the early nineteenth century. As already noted the absence of any proper provision for the auditing of the Patent Office accounts offered serious temptations to financial laxity. However his culpability is assessed there is no doubt that Edmunds suffered severely. Perhaps his only consolation in his old age was the fact that nobody impugned his conduct as an officer of the House of Lords.[30]

[30] Both the Chairman of Committees, the Clerk of the Parliaments and the Lord Chancellor testified to his good conduct as Reading Clerk at the time of the enquiry of 1865: *Edmunds Report*, QQ. 1813, 1856, 1955.

Chapter 8. The Parliamentary Office in the Early Nineteenth and Twentieth Centuries: Biographical Notes on Clerks in the House of Lords 1800 to 1939

Preface

In 1971 the House of Lords Record Office published memorandum no. 45 entitled *Officers of the House Lords 1485–1971* which provided handlists of those who served the House during that period. In the course of compiling these lists a considerable amount of biographical material was assembled from a variety of sources. In 1977 that which related to clerks who served in the Parliament Office between 1600 and 1800 was published by the Record Office under the title *The Parliament Office in the Seventeenth and Eighteenth Centuries*. The present memorandum continues this work from 1800 to 1939. It is preceded by an Introduction which gives a brief account of the history of the office during that period. An Appendix contains information supplementing and correcting that published for the earlier period which has come to light since 1977.

References

In Manuscript

Parliamentary Archives
  Braye MSS
  Certificates of Fee Fun
  Chief Usher of Exchequer Papers
  Committee Books
  Parliament Office Papers
    PO 51/10
    PO 56/35A
    PO 56/45
    PO 83/28
    PO 106
    PO 549/1, 2

The National Archives, Kew

C 66	Patent Rolls
E 351/1670	Declared Accounts: Hanaper
Prob. 6	Prerogative Court of Canterbury: administrations
Prob. 11	Prerogative Court of Canterbury: registered copies of wills

Westminster Abbey Library
  Registers of St Margaret's, Westminster

Westminster City Library
  Registers of St John's, Westminster

Works in Print

Al. Cant.	*Alumni Cantabrigienses*, pt ii, 1752–1900, ed. J.A. Venn (6 vols, Cambridge, 1940–54).
Al. Ox.	*Alumni Oxonienses 1715–1886*, ed. J. Foster (4 vols, 1888).
Burke's Landed Gentry	4th, 7th, 15th, 17th and 18th edns.
Burke's Peerage	41st, 49th, 97th, 103rd and 105th edns.
Commons Clerks	W.R. McKay, *Clerks in the House of Commons 1363–1989: A Biographical List* (1989).
Complete Peerage	2nd edn, ed. G.E.C. (13 vols, 1910–59).
DNB	*Dictionary of National Biography*, ed. L. Stephen and S. Lee (66 vols, 1885–1901).
Eton Register	Pts i–viii, 1841–1919 (1903–32).
Lincoln's Inn Register	*Admissions to Lincoln's Inn 1420–1799* (1846).
LJ	*Lords Journal.*
MEB	*Modern English Biography*, ed. F. Boase (6 vols, 1892–1921).
Men at the Bar	*Men at the Bar: A Biographical Handlist of Members of the Various Inns of Court*, 2nd edn, ed. J. Foster (1885).
Middle Temple Register	*Register of Admissions to the Middle Temple*, ed. H.A.C. Sturgess (3 vols, 1949).
RK	*Royal Kalendar.*
Westminster Register	*Record of Old Westminsters*, ed. G.F.R. Barker and others (3 vols, 1928–63) and supplementary vol., ed. J.B. Whitmore and G.R.Y. Radcliffe.
Who Was Who	7 vols, 1920–81.

Introduction

In 1800 the clerks attached to the service of the House of Lords, known collectively as the Parliament Office, were nine in number. They consisted of three Clerks at the Table, the Clerk of the Parliaments, the Clerk Assistant and the Reading Clerk, and six other clerks, the Clerk of the Journals, the Copying Clerk and four Writing Clerks. In addition there were an indeterminate number of Extra Clerks who did not form part of the establishment. By the terms of his patent the Clerk of the Parliaments enjoyed the right of appointing all the other clerks. However, his freedom of action in this field had to some extent been circumscribed by 1800 since, as a result of pressure exerted during the course of the previous century, he was obliged to submit his nominations to the offices of Clerk Assistant and Reading Clerk to the House for its approbation before they could enter upon their duties. While most of the clerks received small salaries the bulk of their remuneration was derived from fees which arose from business transacted in the House.[1]

By the early years of the nineteenth century it was accepted that appointments to the Table would be made from outside the office. This long remained the general rule. Only after 1930 did it become usual for these places to be filled by promotion from within the Parliament Office. The other clerks seem usually to have begun their careers as Extra Clerks often at what would now be regarded as a very youthful age. After some years' service they could expect to be placed on the establishment with the prospect of rising eventually to become Clerk of the Journals or Copying Clerk.

In 1800 the Clerk of the Parliaments was George Rose, a long serving politician of the middle rank who had secured the reversion of the office in 1783 from the vantage point of his position as one of the Joint Secretaries of the Treasury. He had succeeded to the office in 1788 but his membership of the House of Commons and the demands of his ministerial posts prevented him from officiating at the Table. Relying on the right conferred by his patent to exercise his duties by deputy he entrusted the day to day direction of the office to the Clerk Assistant, Henry Cowper, who had served in that capacity since 1785. The Reading Clerk, appointed in 1800, was William Stewart Rose, younger son of George Rose, a minor poet and friend of Sir Walter Scott. The younger Rose enjoyed poor health. As early as 1804 it was necessary to make temporary provision for carrying out the duties of his post during his absence while from 1816 his place was taken by a permanent deputy, John William Birch.

In 1818 George Rose died and was succeeded as Clerk of the Parliaments by his eldest son, George Henry, by virtue of a reversionary grant made in 1795. George Henry Rose never made any pretence of carrying out his duties in person, being preoccupied with his career as a diplomat and member of the House of Commons. On Rose's succession the opportunity was taken to regulate the arrangements at the Table. The complement was fixed at three. The first place was filled by Cowper as Clerk Assistant and Deputy Clerk of the Parliaments; the second by Benjamin Currey occupying the newly-created post of Additional Clerk Assistant; the third by Birch, the Deputy Reading Clerk.[2] Shortly afterwards the emergence of two new posts in the lower part of the office was publicly acknowledged, those of the Clerk of the Ingrossments and Clerk of the Inrolments.[3] The origin of these posts is obscure.

---

[1] For the history of the Parliament Office before 1800, see M.F. Bond, 'Clerks of the Parliaments, 1509–1953', *EHR*, lxxiii (1958), 78–85; *Manuscripts of the House of Lords*, xii (1977), xvii–xxiii. See also Chapter 5.

[2] *LJ*, li, 488–9.

[3] *RK* (1820), 44.

In 1824 the general dissatisfaction of the House at the state of affairs in the Parliament Office resulted in the appointment of a select committee. This committee was the precursor of the sessional committee, known at first as the Parliament Office Committee and after 1890 as the House of Lords Offices Committee, which has continued to exercise supervision of the office until the present day. The select committee of 1824 entered into negotiations with Sir George Rose, as he had now become, as a result of which a compromise was worked out. Rose was to remain Clerk of the Parliaments and to enjoy the remuneration attached to the office but was to surrender the patronage with the exception of the right to make one further appointment to the Table. For the remainder of his life the functions of the office were to be carried out by the Clerk Assistant who was to be appointed by the Crown and to be removable on an address by the House of Lords for that purpose. Otherwise the right of appointment to the Table was to be vested in the Lord Chancellor subject to the approbation of the House with provision for removal by order of the House while the remaining patronage was to be exercised by the Clerk Assistant during Rose's lifetime and by the Clerk of the Parliaments thereafter. Rose's successor as Clerk of the Parliaments was to exercise his duties in person and to be removable on an address by the House.[4] These provisions were embodied in the Clerk of the Parliaments Act passed in the same year.[5]

The Select Committee of 1824 also made new arrangements for financing the office. The fees enjoyed by officers other than the Clerk of the Parliaments were to be carried to a common fund to be used for the payment of fixed salaries. Any deficiency in the fund was to be made good by the Treasury following an application to the Crown by way of address. This arrangement continued until 1831 when provision was made for an estimate of the amount of the deficiency to be submitted annually to the House of Commons.[6]

Following the recommendations of the Select Committee of 1824 the number of Clerks at the Table was fixed at four, the Clerk Assistant (Cowper), the Additional Clerk Assistant (Currey), the Reading Clerk (Charles Philip Rose, on the retirement of his uncle, William Stewart Rose) and – a new office – the Assistant Reading Clerk (Birch, the former deputy Reading Clerk). Each was granted a fixed salary (£4,000 plus residence, £2,500 plus residence, £1,800 and £1,200 respectively) together with provision for a retirement pension. The remaining clerks on the establishment, the Clerk of the Journals, the Copying Clerk, the Clerk of Ingrossments, the Clerk of Inrolments and the Writing Clerks were to be appointed and be removable by the Clerk of the Parliaments and were to be promoted on merit with no claim of right to advancement by seniority. Their remuneration was to consist in part of fixed salaries and in part of fees, the total to be equal to their average receipts over the previous five years. Provision was made for superannuation in suitable circumstances.[7]

Early in 1826 the Clerk Assistant, Cowper, retired after a career of over forty years in the service of the House. His successor as effective head of the office was William

---

[4] *LJ*, lvi, 322–4.

[5] Clerk of the Parliaments Act 1824 (5 Geo. IV, c. 82).

[6] *LJ*, lvi, 441–2; lxiii, 223; D. Dewar, *The Financial Administration and Records of the Parliament Office, 1824–1868* (House of Lords Record Office Memorandum no. 37, 1967).

[7] *LJ*, lvi, 323.

Courtenay, a former Master in Chancery and Member of the Commons.[8] Later in the same year Courtenay was authorised to add six clerks to the establishment. These were selected from amongst the Extra Clerks employed on the business of the House. At the same time the first steps were taken in the creation of a Library and the Clerk Assistant was authorised to appoint one of the clerks on the establishment as Librarian.[9]

Courtenay was obliged to relinquish his office in June 1835 on his succession to the earldom of Devon. Shortly before his departure he made a number of alterations in the internal administration of the office, the most important of which was the creation of the post of Cashier and Accountant which was conferred upon one of the clerks on the establishment, William Atkinson Green.[10] The office of Clerk Assistant remained vacant while the Parliament Office Committee considered the number and salaries of the Clerks at the Table. In July the Committee reported their opinion that for the future three Clerks at the Table would be sufficient and that, in view of the recent reductions in the salaries of other public officials, their salaries should be reduced, that of the Clerk Assistant from £4,000 to £3,000, that of the Additional Clerk Assistant from £2,500 to £1,800 and that of the Reading Clerk from £1,800 to £1,200. They recommended that, since Charles Philip Rose wished to retire from the position of Reading Clerk, his father should be invited to exercise his remaining right of appointment to the Table by nominating his successor. Finally it was proposed that one of the Clerks at the Table should take responsibility for committee work with the additional title of Principal Committee Clerk and that the Clerk Assistant should be authorised to spend an additional £500 on clerks for servicing select committees.[11]

New appointments to the Table were not made until August 1835. It had apparently been the original intention to appoint Currey, the Additional Clerk Assistant, as Courtenay's successor. But it was, it seems, a condition of Currey's appointment that he should give up his position as solicitor and agent to the Duke of Devonshire and this he was unwilling to do. The choice, therefore, fell upon Birch, the Assistant Reading Clerk. Currey remained Additional Clerk Assistant while Sir George Rose replaced his second son, Charles Philip, by his youngest son, William, as Reading Clerk.[12]

Birch presided over the office for the next thirteen years. Various changes took place during this time. In October 1835 the post of Copying Clerk was abolished and replaced by that of Chief Clerk ranking immediately after the Clerk of the Journals.[13] In the following year increasing business led to the addition of two clerks to the establishment while at the same time the Clerk Assistant was authorised to obtain temporary assistance from Extra Clerks for committee work.[14] In 1837 a special salary was made available to the Principal Assistant Committee Clerk whose office appears to have originated in 1826 and who seems increasingly to have taken charge of this work and to have become in

---

[8] *LJ*, lviii, 18, 31.

[9] *LJ*, lviii, 512.

[10] Dewar, *Financial Administration*, 6–7; PO 549/1, p. 9.

[11] *LJ*, lxvii, 314.

[12] PO 106, p. 4; *LJ*, lxvii, 620–2.

[13] PO 549/1, p. 11.

[14] *LJ*, lxviii, 542.

effect Clerk of Committees.[15] In 1840 the salary of the Reading Clerk was raised from £1,200 to £1,500.[16] In April 1845 the continuing expansion of committee work, particularly that arising from Opposed Private Bills, occasioned the appointment of two more clerks.[17]

In August 1845 a comprehensive revision of the establishment took place. The department of the Librarian which had hitherto formed part of the Parliament Office was now separated from it. The officials responsible for collecting fees and copying documents were placed on a special footing. The Clerk of the Journals and the Chief Clerk retained their positions at the head of the office. The remaining clerks were classified according to length of service and divided into three grades with improved salaries. Provision was made for a first class consisting of seven clerks selected from amongst those who had served for at least fourteen years with salaries of £280 rising by annual increments of £30 to £500; a second class consisting of seven clerks selected from amongst those who had served for at least seven years with salaries of £140 rising by annual increments of £10 to £280; and a third class consisting of the remaining clerks with salaries of £70 rising by annual increments of £10 to £140. In addition the clerks were to continue to be entitled to further remuneration for work performed according to the established rates. Finally, the distinction between Extra Clerks and Clerks on the establishment was abolished. As a result four further clerks were added to the establishment.[18]

In 1846 a further expansion of the business of the House led to increases in the salaries of the Chief Clerk and the Principal Assistant Committee Clerk and the addition of four clerks to the establishment.[19]

In March 1848 Birch retired from the office of Clerk Assistant. The choice of his successor fell upon Currey, the Additional Clerk Assistant, who presumably now felt able to shed his outside commitments. However, within three days of his appointment, he died. The office was left vacant for a month while a replacement was sought. In the meantime Lord Chancellor Cottenham exercised for the first time the right of appointment vested in the holder of his office by the Clerk of the Parliaments Act 1824. He promoted William Rose from the post of Reading Clerk to that of Additional Clerk Assistant, appointing to the former office Leonard Edmunds, the Clerk of the Crown in Chancery.[20]

In April 1848 a new Clerk Assistant was appointed in the person of John George Shaw Lefevre, brother of the Speaker of the House of Commons, who voluntarily accepted a reduction in his salary from £3,000 to £2,500.[21] After periods as a member of the Commons, Under Secretary to the Colonial Office and Poor Law Commissioner, he had since 1841 served as one of the Joint Secretaries at the Board of Trade. He had also been Vice Chancellor of the University of London since 1841 and an Ecclesiastical Commissioner since 1847. Shaw Lefevre immediately turned his attention to the

---

[15] *RK* (1827), 46; PO 106, p. 46; Certificates of Fee Fund 1836–7, 1837–8.

[16] *LJ*, lxxii, 550.

[17] *LJ*, lxxvii, 97–8.

[18] *LJ*, lxxvii, 1130.

[19] *LJ*, lxxviii, 1338.

[20] *LJ*, lxxx, 80, 122.

[21] *LJ*, lxxx, 177, 814.

organisation of the Parliament Office. His views formed the basis of a report made by the Parliament Office Committee to the House in the following year. The main feature of the existing arrangements to which exception was taken was the system whereby clerks were remunerated in part by insufficient fixed salaries and in part by specific payments for each function or item of work performed. This made it difficult to conduct business methodically and economically because any contraction of work reduced the income of some clerks while any increase added to expenditure. The solution put forward was to discontinue payments for work performed and to allot to each clerk a salary sufficient to compensate him for all the work he might be called upon to perform.

With this end in view the establishment was remodelled. In its new form it was to be headed by a Chief Clerk with a salary of £1,500; five First Class Clerks with salaries of £700, £750, £800, £850 and £900; seven Second Class Clerks, two with salaries of £450, three with salaries of £500 and the remaining two with salaries of £550 and £600; six Third Class (First Division) Clerks, two with salaries of £250, two with salaries of £300 and two with salaries of £400; and six Third Class (Second Division) Clerks with salaries of £100 rising after eight years to £200. Within each class clerks were to rise by seniority but promotion from one class to another was to take place only following a favourable report from the Clerk Assistant, acting as Clerk of the Parliaments. No clerk was to be promoted to the first division of the third class until he had reached the age of twenty-one. The office of Clerk of the Journals was to be abolished on the next vacancy. These changes were agreed to by the House subject to certain transitional arrangements for those already on the establishment.[22]

From the mid nineteenth century the emergence of a number of departmental heads within the Parliament Office may be discerned. Some such positions had, of course, originated long before. The offices of Clerk of the Journals and Copying Clerk (the predecessor of the Chief Clerk) are traceable to the early eighteenth century.[23] As already noted the office of Clerk Committees or Principal Assistant Comittee Clerk apparently originated in 1826.[24] Additional posts of this nature developed after about 1849 although, in view of the inadequate documentation, it is not always possible to be precise about their origin. The designation Clerk of Bills or Clerk of Public Bills appears to have originated in 1849 at the time of the discontinuation of the ingrossment of bills. Thereafter the former Clerk of Ingrossments, William Elyard Walmisley, was so described.[25] The special position of the Clerk of Printed Papers appears to have been due to the activities of a particularly gifted clerk, William John Thoms, who joined the office relatively late in life and was rewarded with a special salary in view of his poor prospects of advancement within the ordinary establishment.[26] The office of Clerk of Private Bills may be said to have originated in 1850 when the position of Bartholomew Samuel Rowley Adam, who had long acted as Private Secretary to Lord Shaftesbury, the

---

[22] *LJ*, lxxxi, 595–7.

[23] Sainty, *Parliament Office*, 5; PO 106, pp. 39, 40.

[24] See p. 170.

[25] *RK* (1850), 61; *LJ*, lxxxii, 113; PO 106, p. 49.

[26] PO 106, p. 56.

Chairman of Committees, was accorded special recognition.[27] The first acknowledged Clerk of the Judicial Office, Edward Meredith Parratt, had become the senior clerk in that department by 1854.[28]

In June 1855 Sir George Rose finally died and was succeeded by Shaw Lefevre as Clerk of the Parliaments. Thus the acting head of the office became also its titular head as contemplated by the Clerk of the Parliaments Act over thirty years before. Apart from the fact that William Rose now became Clerk Assistant with a salary increased from £1,800 to £2,000 instead of Additional Clerk Assistant there was no other change in the position of the Clerks at the Table.[29]

Shortly afterwards, Shaw Lefevre was appointed one of the original Civil Service Commissioners serving as such until 1862. He had for some time been interested in the reform of the public service, having served on the enquiry into the Indian Civil Service which resulted in the adoption of open competition for entrants. It was natural, therefore, that Shaw Lefevre should insist that future candidates for clerkships in the Parliament Office should submit themselves to the selection processes administered by the Commission. This development had considerable effects on recruitment to the office. Previously clerks had come from relatively obscure social backgrounds and, so far as can be established, had seldom been educated at public schools. Since they were usually appointed well before reaching the age of twenty they had rarely had a university education. So far as is known they underwent no form of qualifying examination. After 1855 candidates were required to reach a certain minimum standard in examinations administered by the Civil Service Commission.[30] Under the new system most recruits were of noticeably higher social standing and had been educated at public schools. Because they had also usually attended either Oxford or Cambridge, even if they had not always graduated, they usually joined the office at a more advanced age than their predecessors.

No further changes of significance took place in the Parliament Office until 1865. In that year, Edmunds, the Reading Clerk, retired and was succeeded by the Hon. Slingsby Bethell, son of the Lord Chancellor, Lord Westbury, with a salary reduced from £1,500 to £1,200. As was customary, Edmunds was granted a pension by the House. Shortly afterwards, however, allegations of misconduct on his part began to circulate. As a result a select committee was appointed by the House to look into his case. The committee found that Edmunds had been guilty of financial malpractices in connection with the employment in the Patent Office which he had held since 1833 and which he had been allowed to retain after his appointment as Reading Clerk in 1848. In consequence he was deprived of his pension. Edmunds made unavailing attempts to re-establish his reputation, even going so far as to sue Mr Gladstone for libel. Eventually the House made him a small compassionate allowance which he enjoyed until his death in 1888.[31]

The year 1866 was notable for the consideration by the Parliament Office Committee of a memorial from the clerks in the office. In this they complained of the adverse effects

---

[27] *LJ*, lxxxii, 107–8; PO 106, p. 45.

[28] *LJ*, lxxxvi, 516; PO 106, p. 48.

[29] *LJ*, lxxxvii, 243.

[30] *LJ*, lxxxviii, 82.

[31] *LJ*, xcvii, 27, 179–89, 232; cxvii, 68.

of the revised establishment of 1849. They alleged that promotion had been retarded and financial hardship inflicted by the reduction of the First Class Clerks from seven to five, the abolition of the office of Clerk of the Journals and the absence of automatic annual increments in salary. In order to meet these criticisms a further revision was authorised. The office of Chief Clerk was retained but with the proviso that its salary should be reduced, on a vacancy, to £1,200. The three classes were amalgamated. The five Senior Clerks were to continue to receive the salaries provided for the first class in 1849. The remainder were to receive salaries of £100 rising to £600 over a period of twenty-five years. Additional allowances of £150 were to be paid to heads of departments and clerks with special responsibilities who were to be chosen on grounds of fitness.[32]

In 1868 a substantial change took place in the manner in which the administrative services of the House of Lords were financed. Since 1831 it had been the practice for an annual estimate to be submitted by the Treasury to the House of Commons in this connection. This consisted of a number of items: £5,500 for the salaries of the Chairman of Committees, the Chairman's Counsel and the Serjeant at Arms; a sum, fixed at £2,300 from 1861, for Black Rod's expenses; and a further sum designed to make good any deficiency in the fee fund out of which the remaining salaries of the staff and certain other expenses were paid. The amount required for this purpose varied. Until 1860 it averaged about £15,000 a year. Thereafter, the increase in private business and the consequential increase in the total fees was such that from 1863 it was unnecessary for the House to ask for any sum in aid of the fee fund.

In view of these developments the Treasury stated in 1868 that it was no longer prepared to pay the fixed charges borne on the vote, thus throwing these charges on the fee fund. After considering the situation the Parliament Office Committee reported to the House that, although the fund would be able to meet this additional burden in the current year, there was little expectation of its being able to do so in subsequent years because there was no certainty that the income from fees on private bills would continue at its existing level. The Committee therefore recommended that the House sould acquiesce in the Treasury's wish that the finances of the House of Lords should be placed on the same basis as those of the House of Commons. The House agreed with this recommendation and the new arrangements came into effect in the following year. These provided that the Clerk of the Parliaments should submit annually to the Treasury a detailed estimate of all the salaries and expenses of the office together with a statement of the balance of the fee fund. After reserving a sufficient amount for the fund to cover pensions to former members of the staff all fees payable to the House of Lords were to be handed over to the Treasury. The previously accumulated balance of the fee fund was to be invested and to remain under the control of the House to provide an additional source of finance to pay retiring allowances.[33]

One of the effects of these changes was to provide the Commons by means of the detailed estimate with full details of the Lords' establishment. For the next thirty years a Commons debate on the estimate was almost an annual event, sometimes directed to

---

[32] *LJ*, xcviii, 513.

[33] *LJ*, c, 465; ci, 569; Dewar, *Financial Administration*, 10.

real or supposed differences in salaries of those holding comparable offices in the two Houses and sometimes used as a vehicle for a general attack on the House of Lords.

The year 1871 witnessed a change in the manner of recruiting clerks. Since 1856 no candidate proceeded to the civil service examination unless he had been first nominated by the Clerk of the Parliaments. In 1870 an order in council was passed introducing the system of open competition for clerkships in most government departments. In the following year Shaw Lefevre applied this system to candidates for clerkships in the House of Lords.[34]

In 1875 Shaw Lefevre retired after having presided over the office for twenty years. He was succeeded by the Clerk Assistant, Sir William Rose, who was in turn replaced by Ralph Disraeli, a brother of the Prime Minister and a former official of the Court of Chancery. The Clerk Assistant's salary was reduced from £2,000 to £1,800 with £300 in lieu of a residence.[35] Rose's tenure of the office was comparatively uneventful. In the field of recruitment he reversed Shaw Lefevre's decision of 1871 and reinstated the system of nominated candidatures.[36]

In 1885 Rose died. He had served for only ten years as Clerk of the Parliaments but had completed a total of fifty years' continuous service at the Table – a record that has never been equalled. His place was taken by Henry John Lowndes Graham, a barrister who had served as Principal Secretary to Lord Chancellor Cairns from 1874 to 1880 and had since been a Master in Lunacy.[37]

In July 1887, on the occasion of the consideration by the Commons of the annual estimate for the House of Lords Offices, objections were made that the officers of the House of Lords enjoyed higher salaries than their counterparts in the Commons. The government undertook to have the matter examined and in February 1888 it was remitted to a sub-comittee of the Parliament Office Committee. The sub-committee made a careful comparison between the two establishments and found that considerable economies had been made in the Lords since the last major revision of the clerical structure in 1866. The number of clerks, other than those at the Table, had been reduced from 28 to 19. As four of them were assigned to judicial work for which there was no equivalent in the Commons, there were 15 clerks employed on ordinary parliamentary work compared with 32 in the Commons. The sub-committee acknowledged that the salaries of the clerks in the two houses were not identical but expressed the view that the emoluments of Lords' clerks, especially in the case of heads of departments, were certainly not higher than those of Commons' clerks.

The sub-committee, nevertheless, recommended a number of further economies. The remuneration of the Clerk of the Parliaments and the Clerk Assistant should be reduced. The right of appointment to one of the two junior posts at the Table should revert to the Clerk of the Parliaments who should promote one of the clerks in the Parliament Office to fill it, such a clerk continuing to carry out his other duties in the office. The number of Junior Clerks should be reduced from 13 to 11 over a period of time. All

---

[34] PO 106, p. 59.
[35] *LJ*, cvii, 126–7, 299.
[36] PO 106, p. 60.
[37] *LJ*, cxviii, 5.

these recommendations were approved first by the main committee and ultimately by the House during the course of 1889.[38]

In 1890 Disraeli, the Clerk Assistant, retired and was replaced by Edward Peirson Thesiger, a junior clerk in the Parliament Office with a salary reduced from £1,800 to £1,500 without a residential allowance. The circumstances surrounding this somewhat surprising appointment are obscure. It may have been intended to represent compliance with the recommendations of the previous year on the subject of the Clerks at the Table. However, it did so only to the extent that it involved a promotion from within the office. The actual appointment was made by the Lord Chancellor and not by the Clerk of the Parliaments and Thesiger was not given any of the departmental responsibilities envisaged. Thesiger had long held a position in the Lord Chancellor's Office concurrently with his clerkship. Since 1866 he had held the post of Secretary of Presentations with responsibility for administering the Lord Chancellor's ecclesiastical patronage. This post was, however, abolished in 1890 and Thesiger's appointment as Clerk Assistant is probably to be seen at least in part as compensation for loss of this office.[39]

In 1891 an economy was made in the establishment when it was provided that the holder of the office of Chief Clerk should, in addition to the duties of that post, retain responsibility for one of the departments of the office.[40]

In 1893 there was sustained criticism in the Commons of the size of the salaries of the officers of the House of Lords compared with those of the House of Commons and the amount of the House of Lords vote was reduced by £500. As a consequence the Treasury declined to submit the proposed estimate for 1894–5 to the Commons on the ground that it was in excess of the amount granted for the current year. It was pointed out that the sole reason for the increase was that it was required to pay the salaries of the staff together with the automatic increments to which they were entitled and that any reduction would involve a breach of faith with them. The contention that the Lords' clerks were more favourably treated than the Commons' clerks was not accepted. However, the Treasury expressed the view that it would be useless to submit an estimate which, on the basis of recent experience, the Commons would refuse to sanction. As a way out of the impasse the Chairman of Committees, Lord Morley, suggested that a joint committee should be appointed to examine the position of the officers of the two Houses but this proposal did not bear fruit. In the event the House of Lords Offices Committee were obliged to acquiesce in a scheme whereby the classification and pay of the Lords' clerks were assimilated to those of the Commons. Under this scheme the establishment was fixed at five principals with salaries of £850 rising by annual increments of £50 to £1,000, six assistants with salaries of £300 rising by annual increments of £20 to £600 and six juniors with salaries of £100 rising by annual increments of £15 to £250.[41]

At the same time the House of Lords agreed to adopt the rules for the compulsory retirement of staff which had been introduced into the civil service in 1890. These

---

[38] Hansard, *Parl. Debs*, 3rd ser., cccxvii, cc. 681–99; *LJ*, cxxi, 351.

[39] *LJ*, cxxii, 31.

[40] PO 106, p. 40; PO 549/2, p. 46.

[41] *LJ*, cxxvi, 116–21.

provided that all clerks appointed by the Clerk of the Parliaments should retire at sixty-five but that the House of Lords Offices Committee should have the discretion, at the instance of the Clerk of the Parliaments, to extend an officer's employment for a further period of not more than five years on being satisfied that his retirement would be detrimental to the service of the House or that there were special circumstances which would render a relaxation of the rule expedient.[42]

In 1896 the Clerk of the Parliaments was given the use of the residence in the Palace of Westminster formerly occupied by Black Rod and had his salary reduced from £2,500 to £2,000 in consequence.[43] In the same year Bethell, the Reading Clerk, died and the opportunity was taken fully to implement the recommendation of 1889 on the subject of the Clerks at the Table. The Lord Chancellor refrained from making an appointment and the Clerk of the Parliaments nominated Owen Edward Grant, the Chief Clerk, to execute the duties of the post with a salary of £1,200. Following Grant's retirement later in the same year the Clerk of the Parliaments nominated Merton Anthony Thoms, one of the Examiners of Standing Orders, as his successor.[44] In 1899 a joint committee on the permanent staff of the two Houses, which had originally been proposed in 1894, was finally appointed. Their report proved to be largely a factual survey of the current position with which the committee professed themselves generally satisfied. In particular they rejected the idea of open competition for clerkships and approved the existing arrangements whereby only those candidates who had been nominated by the Clerks of the two Houses were permitted to compete in the civil service examination. The committee found that there was no longer any justification for the view that the remuneration of officers of the House of Lords was higher than that of their counterparts in the House of Commons.[45] This assurance had the effect of bringing to an end the recurrent questioning of the House of Lords vote in the Commons.

Thoms, the acting Reading Clerk, retired at the end of 1899 and no immediate steps were taken to replace him. It was evident that there was opposition to the arrangements adopted in 1896. In July 1900 the House of Lords Offices Committee reported that 'after considering a letter addressed to the Clerk of the Parliaments by the Clerk Assistant, and certain proposals made by the Lord Chancellor, it was resolved that the Committee having heard the proposals of the Lord Chancellor has no recommendation to make to the House'. The recommendation of 1889 became a dead letter and at the beginning of the next session in January 1901 the Lord Chancellor exercised his statutory right and appointed Edward Hall Alderson, his former private secretary, to the post of Reading Clerk with a reduced salary of £900.[46]

In 1916 Thesiger, the Clerk Assistant, retired. Alderson was promoted to fill his post. The new Reading Clerk was Montague Ronald Alfred Muir Mackenzie, nephew of a

---

[42] *LJ*, cxxvi, 121–2.

[43] *LJ*, cxxi, 352; cxxviii, 75.

[44] *LJ*, cxxviii, 176; cxxix, 66.

[45] *LJ*, cxxxi, 317–19.

[46] *LJ*, cxxxi, 379; cxxxii, 324. In 1905 the salary was increased to £1,000 rising to £1,200 after ten years' service (*LJ*, cxxxvii, 288).

former Permanent Secretary to the Lord Chancellor, who had been an official of the Lord Chancellor's department.[47]

In 1917 Graham relinquished his position as Clerk of the Parliaments. He was succeeded by Sir Arthur Theodore Thring who had been First Parliamentary Counsel since 1903. The terms of Thring's patent required him to retire at seventy-five, the first occasion on which such a limitation was applied to the office. He was deprived of the use of the residence in the Palace and granted an allowance of £500 in lieu.[48] Soon after the end of the First World War the establishment of the Parliament Office was revised. In March 1919 Thring submitted to the House of Lords Offices Committee a memorandum setting out his views on the subject. In it he drew attention to the shortcomings of the establishment as regulated in 1894. In his opinion the system was open to objection on the grounds that it did not ensure any even or continuous increase in pay and that there was a danger of a block being created owing to the simultaneous promotion of clerks from one class to another. The existing structure of the office provided graphic evidence of the problem. Between March 1918 and June 1919 six Senior Clerks would have retired with the result that, once their places had been filled, there would be little prospect of a vacancy in the highest class for many years. As a consequence the chances of a newly appointed clerk receiving a salary of more than £250 within a reasonable period of time were very remote. Thring felt that the difference in pay between clerks in the highest and lowest classes was too large and that the starting salary of £100 was far too low. He also felt that the existing organisation of the office was too rigid and offered insufficient variety of work to the junior clerks.

As a remedy Thring proposed that the number of separate departments should be reduced to three, namely the Public Bill Office which should absorb the Journal Office and the Printed Paper Office, the Private Bill Office which should be combined with the Committee Office and the Judicial Office. He further proposed to amalgamate the existing classes of Assistant and Junior Clerks, to reduce the number of clerkships and to give the clerks, in consideration of higher pay, more continuous and more varied employment. To this end he recommended that the establishment should be remodelled to consist of three Senior Clerks with salaries of £1,000 and ten other clerks with salaries of £200 rising by £15 a year for the first ten years, by £25 a year for the next ten years and by £30 a year thereafter to a maximum of £800 a year. Special provision should be made to safeguard the position of existing clerks. These proposals were approved by the House of Lords Offices Committee and provided the basic framework of the office until the end of the Second World War.[49]

The implementation of this reorganisation was assisted by the retirements to which Thring had drawn attention. It was thus possible immediately to abolish the offices of Chief Clerk, Clerk of the Journals and Clerk of Printed Papers.[50] The departmental heads were thus reduced to the Clerks of Public Bills, Private Bills, Committees and the Judicial Office.

[47] *LJ*, cxlviii, 294.

[48] *LJ*, cxlix, 94, 73.

[49] *LJ*, cli, 67. Thring's memorandum is included amongst the proceedings of the House of Lords Offices Committee.

[50] The title of Clerk of the Journals was revived in 1935 but without the rank which was previously attached to the office.

In November 1917 the House of Lords Offices Committee had directed Thring to fill one of the vacancies on the establishment with 'some suitable candidate who had been serving in His Majesty's Forces, but who was no longer able to serve'.[51] This course was followed in the case of all the appointments made during the next two years. Several of these new clerks had not attended universities and none appears to have been examined by the Civil Service Commission. Indeed the system of examination seems to have been discontinued from this period until 1973 except in the case of the clerks appointed in 1935 and 1938.[52]

In 1922 two clerks, John Beaumont Hotham and Arthur O'Neill Cubitt Chichester, were transferred to the service of the newly established parliament of Northern Ireland.[53] In 1925 a further vacancy was created when Cuthbert Morley Headlam, the Clerk of Public Bills, was elected a member of the House of Commons.[54]

In 1930 Thring retired and was replaced as Clerk of the Parliaments by the Clerk Assistant, Alderson, with a salary increased from £2,000 to £2,500 and a residential allowance of £500 and a requirement to retire at seventy. The new Clerk Assistant was Henry John Fanshawe Badeley, the Clerk of the Judicial Office, with a salary increased from £1,500 to £1,800.[55] This was the first occasion since the eighteenth century (if the special cases of Thesiger (1890) and Grant and Thoms (1896) are left out of account) on which an office at the Table was filled by a clerk who had made his career in the Parliament Office. Badeley remained at the head of the Judicial Office thus initiating the modern practice whereby in most cases the Clerks at the Table combine their duties at the Table with departmental responsibilities within the Parliament Office. Badeley's appointment also resulted in an economy since it occasioned no vacancy in the office.

In 1932 the retirement of Edward Alexander Stonor, the Clerk of Private Bills, provided the occasion for the amalgamation of the Committee and Private Bill Offices recommended in principle in 1919.[56]

In 1934 Alderson retired and was replaced as Clerk of the Parliaments by Badeley whose place at the Table was taken by Muir Mackenzie who had been Reading Clerk since 1916. At the same time the salary of the Clerk Assistant was reduced from £1,800 to £1,500. The new Reading Clerk was Robert Leslie Overbury who had previously been Chief Clerk in the Lord Chancellor's Office.[57] On Muir Mackenzie's death in 1937 Overbury was promoted to succeed him, being replaced as Reading Clerk by Francis William Lascelles, the Clerk of Public Bills. Like Badeley, Lascelles, whose salary was increased to £1,650, combined his duties at the Table with his departmental responsibilities.[58] This appointment occasioned a further reduction of one in the size of the establishment which was then composed of three clerks at the Table and nine other

---

[51] *LJ*, cxlix, 270; cl, 54.

[52] PO 549/2, pp. 121, 126.

[53] *LJ*, cliv, 38.

[54] *LJ*, clvii, 95.

[55] *LJ*, clxii, 252, 258, 387.

[56] *LJ*, clxiv, 262.

[57] *LJ*, clxvi, 215–16.

[58] *LJ*, clxix, 234, 251.

clerks. No further changes of any significance occurred in the office before the outbreak of war in 1939 which marks the end of the period covered by this account.

Lists of Appointments 1800–1939

Clerk of the Parliaments

1788	Rose, G.
1818	Rose, G.H.
1855	Shaw Lefevre, J.G.
1875	Rose, Sir W.
1885	Graham, H.J.L.
1917	Thring, Sir A.T.
1930	Alderson, Sir E.H.
1934	Badeley, H.J.F.

Clerk Assistant

1785	Cowper, H.
1826	Courtenay, W.
1835	Birch, J.W.
1848	Currey, B.
1848	Shaw Lefevre, J.G.
1855	Rose, W.
1875	Disraeli, R.
1890	Thesiger, Hon. E.P.
1916	Alderson, E.H.
1930	Badeley, H.J.F.
1934	Muir Mackenzie, M.R.A.
1937	Overbury, R.L.

Additional Clerk Assistant 1818–55

1818	Currey, B.
1848	Rose, W.

Reading Clerk

1800	Rose, W.S.
1824	Rose, C.P.
1835	Rose, W.
1848	Edmunds, L.
1865	Bethell, Hon. S.
1896	Grant, O.E. (acting)
1896	Thoms, M.A. (acting)
1901	Alderson, E.H.
1916	Muir Mackenzie, M.R.A.
1934	Overbury, R.L.
1937	Lascelles, F.W.

Clerk of the Journals

1797	Parratt, E.
1819	Walmisley, E.G.
1835	Parratt, E.
	–
1866	Walmisley, W.E.
1873	Birch, L.
1884	Webb, G.J.
1897	Austen Leigh, W.
1908	Hamilton Gordon, W.
	–
1935	St George, C.F.L.

Copying Clerk 1800–35

1799	Walmisley, W.
1819	Payne, W.C.
1822	Parratt, E.

Chief Clerk 1835–1918

1835	Walmisley, R.
1840	Smith, H.S.
1874	Parratt, E.M.
1886	Haines, W.H.
1891	Grant, O.E.
1896	Malkin, H.C.
1901	Monro, R.W.
1903	Harrison, A.B.
1910	Lloyd Anstruther, C.

Clerk of Committees 1826–1932

1826	Smith, H.S.
1840	Courtenay, E.
1848	Birch, P.
1862	Haines, W.H.
1886	Thoms, M.A.
1896	Symons Jeune, J.F.
1914	McDonnell, Hon. A.
1918	Stonor, Hon. E.A.
1921	Vigors, E.C.

Clerk of Public Bills 1849–1939

1849	Walmisley, W.E.
1866	Walmisley, H.
1871	Malkin, H.C.
1901	Skene, H.J.F.

1902	Harrison, A.B.
1910	Headlam, C.M.
1925	Lascelles, F.W.

Clerk of Printed Papers 1849–1918

1849	Thoms, W.J.
1862	Grant, O.E.
1896	Harrison, A.B.
1902	Lloyd Anstruther, C.

Clerk of Private Bills 1850–1932;
Clerk of Private Bills and Committees 1932–9

1850	Adam, B.S.R.
1886	Monro, R.W.
1901	Robinson, A.H.
1919	Hotham, J.B.
1921	Stonor, Hon. E.A.
1932	Vigors, E.C.
1939	Davidson, C.K.

Clerk of Judicial Office c. 1854–1939

By 1854	Parratt, E.M.
1874	Dubourg, A.W.
1895	Taylor, E.F.
1902	Skene, F.J.H.
1908	St John, H.P.
1919	Badeley, H.J.F.

Alphabetical List of Clerks 1800–1939

ADAM, Bartholomew Samuel Rowley *Extra Clerk* 1833–29 Aug. 1843 (PO 106, p. 50). *Clerk* 29 Aug. 1843–1850 (PO 549/1, p. 16). *Clerk of Private Bills* 1850–25 Nov. 1886 (*LJ*, lxxxii, 107–8). Died 25 Nov. 1886.

Private Secretary to Chairman of Committees 27 Aug. 1839–25 Nov. 1886 (PO 549/1, p. 14).

Son of Arthur Adam, bootmaker. Born about 1811 being aged 75 at death. Married 23 May 1839 Harriet Larke (died 1 Dec. 1886), daughter of Robert Howe, Clerk of the Works and Professor of Practical Architecture at the Royal Engineer Establishment, Chatham.

ALDERSON, Edward Hall (ktd 1925) *Reading Clerk* 15 Mar. 1901–7 Dec. 1916 (*LJ*, cxxxiii, 72). *Clerk Assistant* 7 Dec. 1916–3 Mar. 1930 (*LJ*, cxlviii, 294). *Clerk of the Parliaments* 3 Mar. 1930–2 June 1934 (*LJ*, clxii, 252). Retired 2 June 1934 (*LJ*, clxvi, 214).

Son of Francis John Alderson. Grandson of Sir Edward Hall Alderson, Baron of Exchequer. Nephew of Georgina Charlotte, wife of 3rd Marquess of Salisbury. Born 2

June 1864. Married 9 Oct. 1900 Mary Emily (died 24 Oct. 1935), 2nd daughter of Sir Cosmo Bonsor, 1st Bart. Died 7 Mar. 1951.

Educated: Brasenose College, Oxford. BA. Inner Temple. Bar 1890.

Private Secretary to Lord Chancellor and Secretary of Commissions 1895–1900.

CB 1919. KBE 1925. KCB 1931.

Al. Ox., i, 13; *Who Was Who*, v, 13; *The Times*, 9 Mar. 1951, p. 8.

ANSTRUTHER *see* LLOYD ANSTRUTHER

ANTRIM, Randal John Somerled (McDonnell) 8th Earl of *Clerk* 8 May 1933–1 Jan. 1935 (PO 549/2, p. 119). Resigned 1 Jan. 1935 (*LJ*, clxvii, 66).

1st son of 7th Earl of Antrim and Margaret Isobel, 6th daughter of John Gilbert Talbot. Nephew of Alexander McDonnell (q.v.). Born 22 May 1911. Married 11 May 1934 Angela Christina, 3rd daughter of Sir Mark Sykes, 6th Bart. Died 26 Sept. 1977.

Educated: Eton. Christ Church, Oxford.

Who Was Who, vii, 23; *The Times*, 27 Sept. 1977, p. 17.

AUSTEN LEIGH, William *Clerk* 1 Dec. 1869–2 Nov. 1897 (PO 549/2, p. 13). *Clerk of Journals* 2 Nov. 1897–11 May 1908 (PO 549/2, p. 56). Retired 11 May 1908 (*LJ*, cxl, 104).

Son of Rev. James Edward Austen Leigh, Vicar of Bray, Berks and Emma, daughter of Charles Smith of Suttons. Brother of Charles Edward Austen Leigh and uncle of Richard Arthur Austen Leigh, Clerks in the House of Commons. Great nephew of Jane Austen, the novelist. Born 11 May 1843. Died 27 Nov. 1921.

Educated: Eton. King's College, Cambridge. BA 1865. MA 1868.

Fellow 1864–1921 and Bursar 1875–87, King's College, Cambridge. Clerk, Legacy Duty Office 1868–9.

Eton Register 1853–9, p. 53; *Register of Admissions to King's College, Cambridge 1797–1925*, 2nd edn, ed. J.J. Withers, 61; *Commons Clerks*, 20.

BADELEY, Henry John Fanshawe (ktd 1934) *Clerk* 3 Feb. 1897–1 Apr. 1919 (PO 549/2, p. 53). *Clerk of Judicial Office* 1 Apr. 1919–24 June 1941 (PO 549/2, 89).

Clerk Assistant 6 Mar. 1930–2 June 1934 (*LJ*, clxii, 258). *Clerk of the Parliaments* 2 June 1934–30 May 1949 (*LJ*, clxvi, 215). Retired 30 May 1949 (*LJ*, clxxxi, 242).

Only son of Captain Henry Badeley of Guy Harlings, Chelmsford, Essex and Blanche, daughter of Christian Augustus Allhusen of Stoke Court, Stoke Poges, Bucks. Born 27 June 1874. Died 27 Sept. 1951.

Educated: Radley. Trinity College, Oxford.

Private Secretary to Permanent Secretary to Lord Chancellor 1903–7.

Lieutenant Colonel, RAMC 1917–20. Fellow, Royal Society of Painters, Etchers and Engravers.

CBE 1920. KCB 1934. Created Lord Badeley 1949.

Burke's Landed Gentry (15th edn), 73; *Radley Register 1847–1962*, ed. R.W. Robertson-Glasgow (1965), 130; *Who Was Who*, v, 50; *The Times*, 28 Sept. 1951, p. 6.

BETHELL, Hon. Slingsby *Reading Clerk* 17 Feb. 1865–3 Apr. 1896 (*LJ*, cxvii, 27). Died 3 Apr. 1896.

2nd son of 1st Lord Westbury, Lord Chancellor 1861–5 and Elinor Mary, 1st daughter of Robert Abraham. Born 4 Oct. 1831. Married (1) 9 May 1855 Caroline (died 28 July 1886), 5th daughter of William James Chaplin of Ewhurst Park, Hants; (2) 6 Sept. 1888 Laura Beatrice (died 16 July 1925), 1st daughter of Rev. Frederick Webster Maunsell, Rector of Symondsbury, Dorset.

Educated: University College, Oxford. BA 1853. Middle Temple. Bar 1857.

Registrar of Bankruptcy Court 1861–5.

CB 1887.

Burke's Peerage (105th edn), 2792–3; *Al. Ox.*, i, 104; *Middle Temple Register*, ii, 518; *Men at the Bar*, 36.

BIDDULPH *see* MYDDLETON BIDDULPH

BIRCH, James Nicholas Francis *Extra Clerk* Aug. 1836–5 Apr. 1839 (PO 549/1, p. 13). *Clerk* 5 Apr. 1839–5 Aug. 1861 (PO 549/1, p. 13). Retired 5 Aug. 1861 (*LJ*, lxxxii, 355; lxxxvii, 439; xciii, 633).

1st son of Captain James Birch of Colchester, Essex. Born about 1820 being aged 41 at death 30 Oct. 1861.

Educated: Tonbridge. Middle Temple. Bar 1844.

Tonbridge Register 1820–93, ed. W.O. Hughes-Hughes (1893), 38; *Middle Temple Register*, ii, 483.

BIRCH (from 31 May 1847 NEWELL BIRCH), John William *Deputy Reading Clerk* 26 Mar. 1816–16 Feb. 1824 (*LJ*, i, 524; lvi, 31). *Assistant Reading Clerk* 9 June 1824–26 Aug. 1835 (*LJ*, lvi, 368). *Clerk Assistant* 26 Aug. 1835–28 Feb. 1848 (*LJ*, lxvii, 620). Retired 28 Feb. 1848 (*LJ*, lxxx, 80).

3rd son of George Birch of St Leonard's Hill, Berks and Mary, daughter of Thomas Newell of Henley Park, Oxon. 2nd cousin once removed of Lawrence Birch, Peregrine Birch and Charles Henry Congreve. Probably related to James Nicholas Francis Birch (qq.v.). Born 30 Apr. 1775. Married 13 Dec. 1821 Diana Eliza, daughter of James Bourchier of Little Berkhamsted, Herts. Died 24 Jan. 1864.

Educated: Eton. Middle Temple. Inner Temple.

Burke's Landed Gentry (7th edn), i, 141–2; *Eton Register 1753–90*, ed. R.A. Austen-Leigh (Eton, 1921), 47; *Middle Temple Register*, ii, 413.

BIRCH, Lawrence *Clerk* 26 Aug. 1846–25 Feb. 1873 (PO 549/1, p. 27). *Clerk of Journals* 25 Feb. 1873–31 Mar. 1884 (PO 549/2, p. 19). Retired 31 Mar. 1884 (*LJ*, cxvi, 322).

6th son of Wyrley Birch of West Wretham Hall, Norfolk and Katherine Sarah, daughter of Jacob Reynardson of Hollywell Hall, Lincs. Brother of Peregrine Birch. 1st cousin of Charles Henry Congreve. 2nd cousin once removed of John William Birch. Probably related to James Nicholas Francis Birch (qq.v). Born 19 Feb. 1824. Married 1856 Gertrude, daughter of David Powell. Died 28 Mar. 1895.

Educated: Rugby. St John's College, Cambridge.

Burke's Landed Gentry (7th edn), i, 141–2; *Rugby Register 1675–1857*, ed. G.A. Solly (Rugby, 1933), 344; *Al. Cant.*, i, 267.

BIRCH, Peregrine *Clerk* 17 June 1836–1848 (PO 549/1, p. 12). *Clerk of Committees* 1848–1862 (PO 106, p. 46). *Index Clerk* 1862–12 Apr. 1878 (PO 106, p. 44). Retired 12 Apr. 1878 (*LJ*, cx, 139, 149).

5th son of Wyrley Birch of West Wretham Hall, Norfolk and Katherine Sarah, daughter of Jacob Reynardson of Hollywell Hall, Lincs. Brother of Lawrence Birch. 1st cousin of Charles Henry Congreve. 2nd cousin once removed of John William Birch. Probably related to James Nicholas Francis Birch (qq.v.). Born 1817. Married Anna Charlotte, daughter of Major General James Grant CB and sister of Owen Edward Grant (q.v.). Died 26 June 1898.

Educated: Rugby. Middle Temple. Bar 1842.

Burke's Landed Gentry (7th edn), i, 141–2; *Rugby Register 1675–1857*, ed. G.A. Solly (Rugby, 1933), 300; *Middle Temple Register*, ii, 478; *Men at the Bar*, 38.

BROUGHAM, Henry Charles (*styled Hon.* from 7 May 1868) *Clerk* 2 June 1857–31 Dec. 1876 (PO 549/2, p. 5). Resigned 31 Dec. 1876 (PO 106, p. 51).

1st son of 2nd Lord Brougham and Vaux and Emily Frances, only daughter of Sir Charles William Taylor, 1st Bart. Born 2 Sept. 1836. Married 18 Apr. 1882 Adora Frances Olga (died 17 Dec. 1925), daughter of Peter Wells of Forest Farm, Windsor, Berks and widow of Sir Richard Courtenay Musgrave, 11th Bart. Succeeded as 3rd Lord Brougham and Vaux 3 Jan. 1886. Died 24 May 1927.

Educated: Eton. Trinity College, Cambridge.

KCVO 1905.

Burke's Peerage (105th edn), 374; *Eton Register 1841–50*, p. 95; *Al. Cant.*, i, 399; *Who Was Who*, ii, 131.

BURROWS, Henry Montagu *Clerk* 16 Nov. 1925–1 Oct. 1945 (PO 549/2, p. 111). *Clerk, Chairman of Committees Office* 1 Oct. 1945–1 Jan. 1950 (PO 549/2, p. 133). *Clerk of Public Bills* 1 Jan. 1950–20 Jan. 1959 (*LJ*, clxxxii, 59). *Reading Clerk* 20 Jan. 1959–18 Oct. 1961 (*LJ*, cxci, 82). *Clerk Assistant* 18 Oct. 1961–1 Jan. 1964 (*LJ*, cxciii, 429). Retired 1 Jan. 1964 (*LJ*, cxcvi, 44).

1st son of Rev. Montagu John Burrows, Diocesan Society, Ceylon and Lydia Anthonitz, daughter of Frederick William de Vos. Born 24 Mar. 1899. Married 4 Jan. 1939 Harriet Elizabeth (died May 1984), daughter of Ker George Russell Vaizey of Star Stile, Halstead, Essex. Died 16 Aug. 1979.

Educated: Osborne. Dartmouth.

Served World War I. Navy. Transferred to RAF 1923. Served World War II. Lieutenant Commander 1939. Commander 1945.

CBE 1956. CB 1964.

Burke's Landed Gentry (18th edn), i, 108: *Who Was Who*, vii, 114.

BUTLER, Arthur Hugh Montagu *Clerk* 30 Apr. 1895–1 Nov. 1897 (PO 549/2, p. 49). Resigned 1 Nov. 1897 on appointment as Assistant Librarian, House of Lords (PO 549/2, p. 56).

2nd son of Rev. Henry Montagu Butler and Georgina Isabella, 1st daughter of Edward Francis Elliot. Born 23 Nov. 1873. Married 6 Dec. 1900 Margaret Edith, daughter of Francis Latham of Gad's Hill Place, Rochester, Kent. Died 28 May 1943.

Educated: Harrow.

Assistant Librarian 1897–1914 and Librarian 1914–22, House of Lords. Private Secretary to Permanent Secretary to Lord Chancellor 1901–2. Secretary of Statute Law Committee 1902–22. Secretary of Commissions 1909–14.

Burke's Landed Gentry (18th edn), ii, 74; *Harrow Register 1800–1911*, 3rd edn, ed. M.G. Dauglish and P.K. Stephenson (1911), 658; *Who Was Who*, iv, 171.

CHICHESTER, Arthur O'Neill Cubitt *Clerk* 1 May 1919–16 Sept. 1921 (PO 549/2, p. 94). Resigned 16 Sept. 1921 on appointment as Clerk, Northern Ireland Parliament (*LJ*, cliv, 39).

1st son of Rev. Edward Arthur Chichester, Rural Dean and Hon. Canon of Winchester and Mary Agnes, 2nd daughter of 1st Lord Ashcombe. Great nephew of 1st Lord O'Neill. Born 14 July 1889. Married 31 July 1924 Hilda Grace, only daughter of William Robert Young of Golgona Castle, Ballymena, Antrim. Died 9 Mar. 1972.

Educated: Wellington. Trinity College, Cambridge.

Served World War I. Clerk 1921–8 and Clerk of the Parliaments 1928–45. Northern Ireland Parliament.

MC 1918. OBE 1941.

Burke's Peerage (105th edn), 2033; *Burke's Irish Family Records* (1976), 230; *Wellington Register 1859–1962*, 8th edn, ed. M. Allen (1965), 88; *Who Was Who*, vii, 145.

CONGREVE, Charles Henry *Clerk* 8 Apr. 1845–6 Apr. 1875 (PO 549/1, pp. 18–19). Died 6 Apr. 1875.

5th son of Richard Congreve of Congreve, Staffs and Mary Anne, daughter of George Birch of Hampstead Hall, Staffs. 1st cousin of Lawrence Birch and Peregrine Birch. 2nd cousin once removed of John William Birch (qq.v.). Born about 1821 being aged 64 at death. Married 6 July 1864 Ethelred Victoria (died 20 Jan. 1893), 3rd daughter of Hon. Sir Edward Cust, 1st Bart.

Burke's Landed Gentry (7th edn), i, 141; (18th edn), ii, 114.

COURTENAY, Edward *Extra Clerk* 1831–May 1833 (PO 106, p. 50). *Clerk* May 1833–24 July 1840 (PO 549/1, p. 1). *Clerk of Committees* 24 July 1840–7 Dec. 1848 (PO 549/1, p. 1). Died 7 Dec. 1848.

5th son of Thomas Peregrine Courtenay and Ann, daughter of Mayow Wynell Mayo of Sydenham, Kent. Nephew of William Courtenay (q.v.). Born 26 July 1818.

Burke's Peerage (105th edn), 793.

COURTENAY, William *Clerk Assistant* 8 Feb. 1826–26 May 1835 (*LJ*, lviii, 31). Resigned 26 May 1835 on succeeding as 10th Earl of Devon (*LJ*, lxvi, 232).

1st son of Henry Reginald Courtenay, Bishop of Exeter and Elizabeth, 1st daughter of 2nd Earl of Effingham. Uncle of Edward Courtenay (q.v.). Born 19 June 1777.

Married (1) 29 Nov. 1804 Harriet Leslie (died 16 Dec. 1839), daughter of Sir Lucas Pepys, 1st Bart; (2) 30 Jan. 1849 Elizabeth Ruth (died 17 Mar. 1914), daughter of Rev. John Middleton Scott. Died 26 Mar. 1859.

Educated: Westminster. Christ Church Oxford. BA 1798. MA 1801. Lincoln's Inn. Bar 1799.

Master of Subpoena Office in Chancery 1778–1852. Commissioner of Bankrupts 1802–17. MP Exeter 1812–26. Master in Chancery 1817–26. Ecclesiastical Commissioner 1842–50.

Complete Peerage, iv, 336–7; *Westminster Register*, i, 221; *Al. Ox.*, i, 305; *Lincoln's Inn Register*, i, 548.

COWPER, Henry *Clerk Assistant* 25 Jan. 1785–6 Feb. 1826 (*LJ*, xxxvii, 177). Retired 6 Feb. 1826 (*LJ*, lviii, 18).

3rd son of General Spencer Cowper and Charlotte, daughter of John Baber. Born about 1753 being aged 87 at death. Married Maria Judith (died 22 Mar. 1815), daughter of William Cowper of Hertingfordbury Park, Herts. Died 28 Nov. 1840.

Educated: Exeter College, Oxford. Middle Temple. Bar 1775.

Commissioner of Bankrupts 1777–85. Bencher, Middle Temple 1811.

Victoria County History, *Hertfordshire*, genealogical volume, 148; *Al. Ox.*, i, 307; *Middle Temple Register*, i, 167.

CURREY, Benjamin *Additional Clerk Assistant* 3 Mar. 1818–10 Mar. 1848 (*LJ*, li, 488–9). *Clerk Assistant* 10–13 Mar. 1848 (*LJ*, lxxx, 122). Died 13 Mar. 1848.

8th son of Rev. John Currey, Vicar of Dartford, Kent and Mary Eliott. Born 2 May 1786. Married 20 July 1813 Anna (died 16 Jan. 1865), daughter of Robert Pott of Bridge Street, Southwark.

Educated: Rugby. Lincoln's Inn.

Temporary Deputy Reading Clerk, House of Lords 1810. Solicitor. Partner in firm of Dubary, Scudamore and Currey 1814. Solicitor to Duke of Gloucester. Solicitor and Agent to Duke of Devonshire 1816–48.

Rugby Register 1675–1857, ed. G.A. Solly (Rugby, 1933), 130; *Lincoln's Inn Register*, ii, 61; *Al. Cant.*, ii, 202; *LJ*, xlviii, 4; PO 106, p. 4; D. Cannadine, *Lords and Landlords: The Aristocracy and the Towns 1774–1967* (Leicester, 1980), 305; Monumental Inscription, Eltham, Kent; information supplied by Mr T.J. Burrows of Currey and Co., 21 Buckingham Gate, London, SW1 and Mrs G.G. More, Flat B, 78 Warwick Gardens, London, W14 8PR.

DAVIDSON, Colin Keppel *Clerk* 1 Mar. 1919–1 June 1939 (PO 549/2, p. 90). *Clerk of Private Bills and Committees* 1 June 1939–2 Mar. 1943 (PO 549/2, p. 127). Died 2 Mar. 1943.

2nd son of Lieutenant Colonel William Leslie Davidson and Theodora, 2nd daughter of 7th Earl of Albemarle. Born 1 Sept. 1895. Married 31 July 1939 Mary Rachel, 1st daughter of 15th Duke of Norfolk.

Educated: Dover College.

Served World War I. Captain RA. World War II. Lieutenant Colonel RA. OBE 1919. CIE 1935.

Burke's Landed Gentry (18th edn), i, 191; *Dover Register 1871–1924*, ed. C.L. Evans (1924), 74: *Who Was Who*, iv, 290–1.

DAVIS, Thomas William *Clerk* 31 Dec. 1846–31 Oct. 1859 (PO 549/1, p. 29). Died 31 Oct. 1859.

Youngest son of Thomas Davis of Boxmoor House, Hemel Hempstead, Herts. Under 21 on 1 Aug. 1849.

LJ, lxxxi, 597; *The Times*, 12 Nov. 1859, p. 1.

DIKE, George John *Extra Clerk* 1819–1826 (PO 106, p. 50). *Clerk* 1826–31 Jan 1850 (*RK* (1827), 46). Died 31 Jan. 1850.

Clerk of Inrolments 14 Aug. 1840–1849 (PO 549/1, p. 15; *RK* (1849), 61).

Probably son of George Dike of Millbank Street, Westminster, Deputy Doorkeeper, House of Lords and brother of William Henry Dike (q.v.). Born about 1806 being aged 44 at death.

DIKE, William Henry *Extra Clerk* 1813–13 Aug. 1844 (PO 106, p. 50). *Clerk* 13 Aug. 1844–5 Oct. 1854 (PO 549/1, pp. 16, 17). Retired 5 Oct. 1854 (*LJ*, lxxxvi, 516).

Son of George Dike of Millbank Street, Westminster, Deputy Doorkeeper, House of Lords. Probably brother of George John Dike (q.v.). Died 6 Feb. 1856.

DISRAELI, Ralph *Clerk Assistant* 27 Apr. 1875–18 Feb. 1890 (*LJ*, cvii, 127). Retired 18 Feb. 1890 (*LJ*, cxxii, 31).

3rd son of Isaac Disraeli of Hughendon Manor, Bucks and Maria, daughter of Nathan Basevi of Billiter Square, London. Brother of Benjamin Disraeli, later Earl of Beaconsfield. Born 9 May 1809. Married 15 Aug. 1861 Katharine (died 20 July 1930), daughter of Charles Trevor of Somerset House. Died 18 Oct. 1898.

Educated: Winchester.

Clerk in Registrar's Office in Chancery 1841–56. Registrar in Chancery 1856–75.

Burke's Landed Gentry (17th edn), 666; *Winchester Commoners 1800–35*. ed. C.W. Holgate (1893), 10; *MEB*, v, 111; *The Times*, 19 Oct. 1898, p. 6.

DUBOURG, Augustus William *Clerk* 23 June 1845–1 July 1874 (PO 549/1, p. 19). *Clerk of Judicial Office* 1 July 1874–31 Mar. 1895 (PO 549/2, 21, 22). Retired 31 Mar. 1895 (*LJ*, cxxvii, 81).

Only son of Charles Seymour Dubourg of Pimlico, London. Born 10 Mar. 1830. Married 6 Sept. 1854 Ellen (died 3 Feb. 1917), youngest daughter of James Nightingale of Wilton, Wilts. Died 8 July 1910.

Gentleman's Magazine (1854), new ser., xlii, 618; *The Times*, 12 July 1910, p. 1.

EASTWOOD, Geoffrey Hugh *Clerk* 1 Jan. 1925–21 June 1946 (PO 549/2, p. 109). *Clerk, Special Procedure Orders Office* 21 June 1946–28 Oct. 1953 (PO 549/2, p. 137). *Clerk of Judicial Office* 28 Oct. 1953–1 Jan. 1959 (*LJ*, clxxxvi, 38). Retired 1 Jan. 1959 (*LJ*, cxci, 49).

5th son of John Edmund Eastwood of Gosden House, Surrey and Ethel Mary Emily, daughter of Thomas Lowes of Eastbank, Eltham, Kent. Born 17 May 1895. Died 1 Aug. 1983.

Served World War I. 3rd King's Own Hussars. Hon. Attaché, British Embassy, Paris 1919–21. Comptroller, Governor General of Canada 1941–6. Comptroller, Princess Royal 1959–65. Extra Equerry to Queen 1959.

CBE 1945. CVO 1956. KCVO 1965.

Burke's Landed Gentry (18th edn), i, 222; *Who's Who*; *The Times*, 9 Aug. 1983, p. 10.

EDMUNDS, Leonard *Reading Clerk* 19 Mar. 1848–14 Feb. 1865 (*LJ*, lxxx, 122). Resigned 14 Feb. 1865 (*LJ*, xcvii, 23).

1st son of John Edmunds of Ambleside, Westmorland. Born about 1802 being aged 85 at death 19 June 1887.

Articled to William Vizard, Solicitor of Lincoln's Inn Fields. Purse Bearer to Lord Chancellor and Secretary of Commissions 1830–4. Clerk of Patents 1833–64. Clerk of Crown in Chancery 1834–48. Clerk to Commissioners of Patents 1852–64.

MEB, i, 963. See also Chapter 5.

FEARY, Fenwick William *Clerk* c. 1781–c. 7 Aug. 1802 (*RK* (1781), 67; (1802), 38). Died by 7 Aug. 1802.

Parentage unknown. Probably brother of John Feary (died 1762), Vestry Clerk of St Margaret's, Westminster. Buried 7 Aug. 1802.

Prob 11/874, f. 104, will of John Feary 1762; Prob 11/1379, f. 615, will of Fenwick William Feary 1802; *Gentleman's Magazine* (1762), xxxii, 94; Burial register of St Margaret's, Westminster.

FLINT, Andrew Guisti *Extra Clerk* 1824–1 June 1835 (PO 106, p. 500). *Clerk* 1 June 1835–13 Dec. 1854 (PO 549/1, p. 10). Died 13 Dec. 1854.

Parentage unknown. Born about 1792 being aged 62 at death.

Gentleman's Magazine (1855), new ser., xliii, 219; Prob. 6/231, f. 146, administration granted to brother, Alexander Flint.

FRERE, Constantine *Clerk* 30 June 1836–c. 5 Apr. 1839 (PO 549/1, p. 12). Resigned by 5 Apr. 1839 (PO 549/1, p. 13).

5th son of James Hatley Frere of Cambridge Terrace, London, Chief Clerk in Army Pay Office and Marian, daughter of Matthew Martin of Poet's Corner, Westminster, Commissioner for S. Domingo Affairs. Brother of Charles Frere and uncle of Charles Edward Vansittart Frere, Clerks in the House of Commons. Born 12 Oct. 1817. Married 13 May 1847 Antonina Mary (died 7 Mar. 1885), daughter of Don Antonino Gadiano of Palermo, Sicily. Died 27 Oct. 1905.

Educated: Westminster. Blackheath Old Proprietary School. King's College, London. Corpus Christi College, Cambridge. BA 1843. MA 1846.

Fellow, Corpus Christi College, Cambridge 1845. Curate, Hailsham, Sussex 1846–7. Rector, Finningham, Suffolk 1847. Hon. Canon, Norwich 1881. Proctor, Archdeaconry of Suffolk 1886.

Burke's Landed Gentry (18th edn), ii, 229; *Westminster Register*, i, 354; *Al. Cant.*, ii, 578; *Commons Clerks*, 47.

GOODMAN, Victor Martin Reeves (ktd 1959) *Clerk* 1 Apr. 1920–1 Jan. 1946 (PO 549/2, p. 97). *Clerk of Judicial Office* 1 Jan. 1946–27 Oct. 1953 (PO 549/2, 134).

Reading Clerk 31 May 1949–27 Oct. 1953 (*LJ*, clxxxi, 249). *Clerk Assistant* 27 Oct. 1953–1 Jan. 1959 (*LJ*, clxxxv, 289). *Clerk of the Parliaments* 1 Jan. 1959–17 June 1963 (*LJ*, cxci, 81). Retired 17 June 1963 (*LJ*, cxcv, 345).

Son of George Henry Goodman and Mary Alice Reeves. Born 14 Feb. 1899. Married (1) 1928 Julian (divorced 1946), daughter of Philip Edward Morrell; (2) Anstice, daughter of Canon Arthur Stafford Crawley. Died 29 Sept. 1967.

Educated: Eton.

Served World War I. Coldstream Guards. Intelligence Officer. Trustee British Museum 1949–63.

MC 1919. OBE 1946. CB 1951. KCB 1959.

Eton Register 1909–19, p. 100; *Who Was Who*, vi, 437; *The Times*, 30 Sept. 1967, p. 12.

GORDON *see* HAMILTON GORDON

GOWER *see* LEVESON GOWER

GRAHAM, Henry John Lowndes (ktd 1902) *Clerk of the Parliaments* 22 Dec. 1885–8 Feb. 1917 (*LJ*, cxviii, 5). Retired 8 Feb. 1917 (*LJ*, cxlix, 20).

6th son of William Graham MP of Burntshields and Ann Matilda, 1st daughter of John Lowndes of Arthurlie. Born 15 Jan. 1842. Married (1) 15 June 1869 Elizabeth Edith (died 8 Jan. 1875), 2nd daughter of 1st Earl of Cranbrook; (2) 30 Dec. 1884 Margaret Georgiana (died 15 Nov. 1931), 2nd daughter of 4th Marquess of Northampton. Died 5 Dec. 1930.

Educated: Harrow. Balliol College, Oxford. BA 1864. MA 1867. Inner Temple. Bar 1868.

Principal Secretary to Lord Chancellor 1874–80. Master in Lunacy 1880–5.

CB 1895. KCB 1902.

Burke's Landed Gentry (18th edn), i, 329; *Harrow Register 1800–1911*, 3rd edn, ed. M.G. Dauglish and P.K. Stephenson (1911), 282; *Al. Ox.*, ii, 548; *Men at the Bar*, 184; *Who Was Who*, iii, 540; *The Times*, 8 Dec. 1930, p. 14.

GRANT, Owen Edward *Clerk* 23 June 1845–1862 (PO 549/1, p. 19). *Clerk of Printed Papers* 1862–19 May 1896 (*LJ*, xciv, 276). *Acting Reading Clerk* 19 May–7 Oct. 1896 (PO 549/2, p. 50). Retired 7 Oct. 1896 (*LJ*, cxxviii, 410).

Chief Clerk 1 May 1891–7 Oct. 1896 (PO 549/2, pp. 46, 51).

Son of Major General James Grant CB and Mary Penelope, daughter of Robert Willis Blencowe of Hayes Park, Middlesex. Brother in law of Peregrine Birch (q.v.). Born 7 Oct. 1831. Married Adelaide Georgiana, daughter of General George Powell Higginson. Died 14 Nov. 1921.

Educated: Marlborough.

Marlborough Register 1843–1952, 9th edn, ed. L.W. James, 4; *Kelly's Handbook to the Titled, Landed and Official Classes* (1921), 734; *The Times*, 16 Nov. 1921, p. 1.

GREEN, Charles William *Extra Clerk* 1839–19 July 1845 (PO 106, p. 50). *Clerk* 19 July 1845–17 Feb. 1865 (PO 549/1, pp. 19–21). Retired 17 Feb. 1865 (*LJ*, xcvii, 28).
  1st son of William Atkinson Green and brother of Frederick George Green (qq.v.). Born about 1825 being aged 41 at death 5 May 1866.
  The Times, 14 May 1866, p. 1.

GREEN, Frederick George *Clerk* 29 July 1846–31 Mar. 1869 (PO 549/1, pp. 27–9). Retired 31 Mar. 1869 (*LJ*, ci, 570).
  Younger son of William Atkinson Green and brother of Charles William Green (qq.v.). Born 2 July 1829. Died 1 Dec. 1869.
  Educated: Westminster.
  Westminster Register, i, 395.

GREEN, William Atkinson *Extra Clerk* 1819–1826 (PO 106, p. 50). *Clerk* 1826–9 Oct. 1869 (*RK* (1827), 46). Died 9 Oct. 1869.
  Cashier and Accountant 1 June 1835–9 Oct. 1869 (PO 549/1, p. 9).
  Son of Hatton Green and Mary ---. Father of Charles William Green and Frederick George Green (qq.v.). Born 23 Mar. 1798. Married Marian Elizabeth ---.
  Registers of St John's, Westminster, iii, 38.

HAINES, William Henry *Clerk* 8 Apr. 1845–1862 (PO 549/1, p. 18). *Clerk of Committees* 1862–18 Nov. 1886 (*LJ*, xciv, 276). *Chief Clerk* 18 Nov. 1886–18 Apr. 1891 (PO 549/2, pp. 37, 46). Died 18 Apr. 1891.
  Son of Henry Haines of 44 Sussex Gardens, London W. Born 1825. Married 1845 Mary Ann (living 18 Apr. 1891), only daughter of P. Mullins of Orger House, Acton, London W.
  Kelly's Handbook to the Titled, Landed and Official Classes (1891), 523.

HALLIDAY, Michael Frederick *Extra Clerk* 1839–17 Aug. 1843 (PO 106, p. 50). *Clerk* 17 Aug. 1843–1 June 1869 (PO 549/1, pp. 15, 16; *RK* (1844), 61). Died 1 June 1869.
  Son of Captain Michael Halliday RN of Epsom, Surrey and Jane Hester ---. Born 1822. Artist.
  Prob. 11/1758, f. 425, will of Michael Halliday; *MEB*, i, 1295; *DNB*, ix, 112.

HAMILTON GORDON, William *Clerk* 27 Jan. 1876–11 May 1908 (PO 549/2, p. 24). *Clerk of Journals* 11 May 1908–30 Apr. 1919 (PO 549/2, p. 73). Retired 30 Apr. 1919 (*LJ*, cli, 67).
  3rd son of Hon. and Rev. Douglas Hamilton Gordon, Canon of Salisbury and Ellen Susan, 2nd daughter of 19th Earl of Morton. Grandson of 4th Earl of Aberdeen. Born 1 Oct. 1855. Married 6 Aug. 1890 Florence Evelyn (died 15 May 1947), daughter of T.E. Vickers of Bolsover Hill, Sheffield. Died 25 June 1936.
  Educated: Eton.
  Burke's Peerage (105th edn), 9: *Eton Register 1871–80*, p. 47.

HARRISON, Alfred Bayford *Temporary Clerk* 24 Feb. 1864–24 Feb. 1865 (PO 106, p. 51; *LJ*, xcvii, 28). *Clerk* 24 Feb. 1865–19 May 1896 (PO 549/2, p. 12). *Clerk of Printed Papers* 19 May 1896–28 Jan. 1902 (PO 549/2, p. 50). *Clerk of Public Bills* 28 Jan. 1902–30 Apr. 1910 (PO 549/2, p. 63). Retired 30 Apr. 1910 (*LJ*, cxlii, 66).

   Chief Clerk 1 Apr. 1903–30 Apr. 1910 (PO 549/2, pp. 66, 79).

   3rd son of George Harrison FRCS, surgeon, of Walton on Thames, Surrey. Born 24 Apr. 1845. Married 6 Sept. 1871 Frances Annie, daughter of Inspector General Robert Taylor CB. Died 6 May 1928.

   Educated: Cheltenham. Inner Temple. Bar 1869.

   Cheltenham Register 1841–1910, ed. A.A. Hunter (1911), 204; *Men at the Bar*, 205; *Who Was Who*, ii, 468; *The Times*, 8 May 1928, p. 1.

HEADLAM, Cuthbert Morley *Clerk* 1 Nov. 1897–1 May 1910 (PO 549/2, p. 56). *Clerk of Public Bills* 1 May 1910–14 Nov. 1924 (PO 549/2, 80). Resigned 14 Nov. 1924 on election as MP.

   3rd son of Francis John Headlam of Manchester and Matilda Ann, daughter of S. Pincoffs of Ardwick, Manchester. Born 27 Apr. 1876. Married 22 Mar. 1904 Georgiana Beatrice, daughter of George Baden Crawley. Died 27 Feb. 1964.

   Educated: King's School, Canterbury. Magdalen College, Oxford. BA 1899. Inner Temple. Bar 1906.

   Served World War I. MP (Conservative) Barnard Castle 1924–9, 1931–5; North Newcastle 1940–52. Parliamentary and Financial Secretary, Admiralty 1926–9. Parliamentary Secretary, Ministry of Pensions 1931–2. Parliamentary Secretary, Ministry of Transport 1932–4.

   DSO 1918. OBE 1919. TD 1926. PC 1945. Created Bart 1935.

   Burke's Peerage (103rd edn), 1189; *King's School Canterbury Register 1859–1931* (1932), 108; *Who Was Who*, vi, 510; *The Times*, 28 Feb. 1964, p. 15.

HEALEY, Charles Hugh Courtney *Clerk* 1 Feb. 1922–7 Oct. 1925 (PO 549/2, p. 105). Resigned 7 Oct. 1925 (*LJ*, clvii, 429).

   Son of Colonel Charles Healey CMG of Bishop's Stortford, Essex and Ella, daughter of Baron Ernst Poellnitz. Great grandson of 17th Lord Forbes. Born 4 July 1890. Died 2 Jan. 1973.

   Educated: Malvern.

   With Parry and Co., Madras 1911–13. Served World War I. 2nd Lieutenant, 4th Battalion, Bedfordshire Regiment. Captain, Grenadier Guards; Military Attaché's Office, British Embassy, Paris. With Messrs Knoedler & Co. Inc. in 1934. Temporary Deputy Serjeant at Arms, House of Commons 1940.

   Malvern Register First Supplement (1934), 211; *Who Was Who*, vii, 616.

HINCHLIFFE, Alfred Walter Gunner *Clerk* 1 Oct. 1914–26 Feb. 1919 (PO 549/2, p. 86). Died 26 Feb. 1919.

   Only son of Walter Hinchliffe of Upper Tooting, Surrey and Emma ---. Born 30 Dec. 1889.

   Educated: Westminster. Christ Church, Oxford. BA 1912. MA 1918.

   Westminster Register, i, 461.

HODGSON, Patrick Kirkman *Clerk* 1 July 1908–1914 (PO 549/2, p. 73). Last occurs 1914 (*Imperial Kalendar* (1914), 52).

4th son of Robert Kirkman Hodgson of Gavelacre, Hants and Honora Janet, 3rd daughter of 9th Earl of Cork and Orrery. Born 4 July 1884. Died 13 Apr. 1963.

Educated: Radley. Trinity College, Oxford. BA 1907. MA 1908. Inner Temple. Bar 1911.

Served World War I. Major, Suffolk Yeomanry. Assistant Secretary to GOC, 3rd Army, BEF. Private Secretary and Comptroller to Governor General of Canada 1922–5. Private Secretary to Duke of York 1926–33.

OBE 1918. CMG 1926. CVO 1927.

Burke's Landed Gentry (17th edn), 1247; *Radley Register 1847–1962*, ed. R.W. Robertson-Glasgow, 179; *Who was Who*, vi, 536.

HOTHAM, John Beaumont *Clerk* 1 Nov. 1898–1 June 1919 (PO 549/2, p. 57). *Clerk of Private Bills* 1 June 1919–16 Sept. 1921 (PO 549/2, p. 95). Resigned 16 Sept. 1921 on appointment as Clerk, Northern Ireland Parliament (*LJ*, clvii, 95).

1st son of Admiral Sir Charles Frederick Hotham KCB and Margaret, daughter of D. Milne Home of Wedderburn. Great great great nephew of 1st Lord Hotham. Born 15 Sept. 1874. Married 5 Aug. 1905 Gladys Mary, 2nd daughter of Colonel John Gerald Wilson CB of Cliffe Hall, Yorks. Died 30 Dec. 1924.

Educated: Eton. Trinity College, Cambridge. BA 1896.

Clerk Assistant and Clerk of the Senate, Northern Ireland Parliament 1921–4.

Burke's Peerage (105th edn), 1379; *Eton Register 1883–9*, p. 114.

JEFFREYS, Anthony Henry *Clerk* 11 Mar. 1919–1 Oct. 1945 (PO 549/2, p. 91). *Clerk of Private Bills and Committees* 1 Oct. 1945–1 Apr. 1960 (PO 549/2, 133; *LJ*, cxcii, 258).

Reading Clerk 27 Oct. 1953–20 Jan. 1959 (*LJ*, clxxxv, 289). *Clerk Assistant* 20 Jan. 1959–18 Oct. 1961 (*LJ*, cxci, 82). Retired 18 Oct. 1961 (*LJ*, cxciii, 429).

2nd son of Major General Henry Byron Jeffreys CB, CMG and Marian, only daughter of Captain William Charles Burlton Bennet. Born 13 Aug. 1896. Married 5 Oct. 1922 Dorothy Bertha (died 1983), youngest daughter of Lieutenant Colonel Edward Tufnell. Died 7 Feb. 1984.

Educated: Eton. Inner Temple. Bar 1924.

Served World War I. 2nd Lieutenant RFA 1915. Lieutenant 'D' Battery RHA 1917–19. World War II. Staff Captain GHQ, France and War Office 1939–41.

CB 1961.

Burke's Landed Gentry (17th edn), 1376; *Eton Register 1909–19*, p. 56; *Who's Who*.

JEUNE (from 28 Oct. 1878 SYMONS JEUNE), John Frederick *Clerk* 1 Dec. 1869–7 Oct. 1896 (PO 549/2, p. 13). *Clerk of Committees* 7 Oct. 1896–10 Dec. 1914 (PO 549/2, p. 52). Retired 10 Dec 1914 (*LJ*, cxlvi, 347).

3rd son of Francis Jeune, Bishop of Peterborough and Margaret, only daughter of Henry Symons of Axbridge, Somerset. Brother of Lord St Helier. Born 10 Dec. 1849. Married 27 Mar. 1873 Frances Susannah (died 2 May 1915), daughter of Captain Richard Hanmer Bunbury RN. Died 8 Feb. 1925.

Educated: Rugby. Inner Temple. Bar 1884.

Examiner of Standing Orders 1900–25.

Burke's Landed Gentry (17th edn), 1385: *Rugby Register 1842–74*, ed. A.T. Mitchell (Rugby, 1902), 220; *Men at the Bar*, 244.

KITSON, George *Clerk* 1815–c. 9 Jan. 1819 (*RK* (1816), 48; (1819), 44). Died by 9 Jan. 1819.

Parentage unknown. Born about 1787 being aged 32 at death. Married 29 July 1810 Jane (living 1 July 1822), daughter of William Charles Payne (q.v.). Buried 9 Jan. 1819.

Registers of St John's, Westminster, xxvi, 241; lvi, 78; Prob 11/1659, f. 394, will of William Charles Payne 1822.

LASCELLES, Francis William (ktd 1954) *Clerk* 1 Jan. 1919–1 Jan. 1925 (PO 549/2, p. 90). *Clerk of Public Bills* 1 Jan. 1925–1 Jan. 1950 (PO 549/2, p. 109; *LJ*, clxxxii, 59).

Reading Clerk 1 June 1937–31 May 1949 (*LJ*, clxix, 234). *Clerk Assistant* 31 May 1949–27 Oct. 1953 (*LJ*, clxxxi, 249). *Clerk of the Parliaments* 27 Oct. 1953–31 Dec. 1958 (*LJ*, clxxxv, 288). Retired 31 Dec. 1958 (*LJ*, cxci, 42).

3rd son of Lieutenant Colonel Henry Arthur Lascelles CVO of Woolbeding, Sussex and Cordelia Matilda, 2nd daughter of Hon. Charles Alexander Gore. Great grandson of 2nd Earl of Harewood. Born 23 Mar. 1890. Married 30 Sept. 1924 Esmee Marion, daughter of C.A. Bury of Downings, Kildare. Died 16 May 1979.

Educated: Winchester. Christ Church, Oxford. MA.

Served World War I. Sussex Yeomanry.

Secretary of Statute Law Committee 1922–40.

MC. CB 1937. KCB 1954.

Burke's Peerage (105th edn), 1251; *Winchester Register 1884–1934*, ed. M.S. Leigh (Winchester, 1940), 269; *Who Was Who*, vii, 453.

LEFEVRE *see* SHAW LEFEVRE

LEIGH *see* AUSTEN LEIGH

LEVESON GOWER, William George Gresham *Clerk* 1 May 1908–9 Oct. 1918 (PO 549/2, p. 72). Died 9 Oct. 1918.

1st son of Arthur Francis Leveson Gower and Caroline Frederica, 2nd daughter of George Savile Foljambe of Osberton, Notts. Great great great grandson of 1st Earl Gower. Born 12 Mar. 1883.

Educated: Eton. Christ Church, Oxford. MA 1905. Inner Temple. Bar.

Served World War I. Lieutenant, Grenadier Guards.

Burke's Peerage (105th edn), 2586; *Eton Register 1893–9*, p. 77.

LLOYD ANSTRUTHER, Cecil *Clerk* 1 Apr. 1876–28 Jan. 1902 (PO 549/2, p. 25). *Clerk of Printed Papers* 28 Jan. 1902–1 June 1918 (PO 549/2, p. 63). Retired 1 June 1918 (*LJ*, cl, 54).

Chief Clerk 1 May 1910–1 June 1918 (PO 549/2, p. 79).

5th son of Lieutenant Colonel James Hamilton Lloyd Anstruther of Hintlesham Hall, Suffolk and Georgiana Christina, 4th daughter of 5th Viscount Barrington. Grandson of

Sir Robert Anstruther, 3rd Bart. Born 1 Dec. 1852. Married 4 Aug. 1904 Bertha Mary (died 26 July 1958), youngest daughter of John Capel Philips of Stoke on Trent. Died 24 Feb. 1939.

Educated: Haileybury. Lincoln College, Oxford. BA 1876.

Burke's Peerage (105th edn), 87; *Haileybury Register 1862–1910*, 4th edn, ed. L.S. Milford (1910), 26; *Al. Ox.*, i, 27.

LUARD, Geoffrey Dundas *Clerk* 17 Apr. 1902–1944 (PO 549/2, p. 64). *Acting Clerk of Private Bills and Committees* 1944–5 (*House of Lords Official Report*, cxxxiii, iv). Retired 1945 (*House of Lords Official Report*, cxxxvi, vi; *LJ*, clxxvii, 17).

3rd son of Colonel Charles Henry Luard and Amelia Juliana, daughter of W.H. Martin. Born 28 Dec. 1879. Married (1) 11 Sept. 1920 Dorothea Cecil Radclyffe (died Nov. 1930), youngest daughter of Caledon Josias Radclyffe Dolling of Edenmore, Magherlin, Down; (2) 4 Feb. 1937 Dulce Annette, only daughter of Hubert Charles Jones of Red House, Apsley Guise, Beds. Died 22 Feb. 1956.

Educated: Harrow. Christ Church, Oxford. BA 1901.

Served World War I. Lieutenant RASC.

Burke's Landed Gentry (18th edn), i, 467; *Harrow Register 1800–1911*, 3rd edn, ed. M.G. Dauglish and P.K. Stephenson (1911), 746.

MCDONNELL, Hon. Alexander *Clerk* 1 June 1877–10 Dec. 1914 (PO 549/2, p. 26). *Clerk of Committees* 10 Dec. 1914–31 Aug. 1918 (PO 549/2, p. 87). Retired 31 Aug. 1918 (*LJ*, cl, 212).

4th son of 5th Earl of Antrim and Emma Hannah, 2nd daughter of Major Turner Macan of Carrif, Armagh. Uncle of 8th Earl of Antrim (q.v.). Born 23 June 1857. Died 9 Dec. 1945.

Educated: Eton.

Burke's Peerage (105th edn), 91; *Eton Register 1871–80*, p. 28.

MACKENZIE *see* MUIR MACKENZIE

MALKIN, Herbert Charles *Clerk* 16 Apr. 1861–9 Feb. 1871 (PO 549/2, p. 9). *Clerk of Public Bills* 9 Feb. 1871–1 Oct. 1901 (PO 549/2, p. 16). Retired 1 Oct. 1901 (*LJ*, cxxxiii, 305).

Chief Clerk 7 Oct. 1896–1 Oct. 1901 (PO 549/2, pp. 51, 60).

1st son of Sir Benjamin Heath Malkin, Judge of Supreme Court, Calcutta and Elizabeth Whitehorne. Born 21 Sept. 1836. Married 7 Oct. 1879 Elizabeth (died 3 Apr. 1925), 3rd daughter of George Percy Elliott of Egland, Awliscombe, Devon. Died 18 Aug. 1913.

Educated: Charterhouse. Trinity College, Cambridge. BA 1859. MA 1862. Lincoln's Inn. Bar 1876.

Secretary of Statute Law Committee 1872–96. Editor, Annual Statutes 1887–96.

Burke's Landed Gentry (17th edn), 2689; *Charterhouse Register 1769–1872*, ed. R.L. Arrowsmith (1974), 248; *Al. Cant.*, iv, 301; *Lincoln's Inn Register*, ii, 362; *Men at the Bar*, 302.

MALONY, William *Extra Clerk* 1835–19 July 1845 (PO 106, p. 50). *Clerk* 19 July 1845–12 Apr. 1878 (PO 549/1, pp. 19–21). Retired 12 Apr. 1878 (*LJ*, cx, 139, 149).

Parentage unknown. Father of William Alfred Malony (died 1915), Receiver of Fees and Accountant. House of Lords 1859–80. Born about 1800 being aged 79 at death 12 Jan. 1879. Wife dead by 15 Feb. 1870 when will made.

MARSHALL, Francis Ord *Clerk* 5 Apr. 1831–c. 6 Mar. 1835 (PO 549/1, p. 1). Absconded by 6 Mar. (PO 549/1, p. 3; PO 56/35A).

No further information available.

MITCHELL, George *Clerk* 29 July 1836–5 Jan. 1846 (PO 549/1, p. 13). Dismissed 5 Jan. 1846 (PO 549/1, p. 27).

Probably related to Richard Mitchell (q.v.).

MITCHELL, Richard *Extra Clerk* 1815–29 Aug. 1835 (PO 106, p. 37). *Clerk* 29 Aug. 1835–5 Apr. 1845 (PO 549/1, p. 10). Retired 5 Apr. 1845 (*LJ*, lxxvii, 39).

Parentage unknown. Probably related to George Mitchell (q.v.) and identical with Richard Mitchell who died 15 Mar. 1852 at Ipswich aged 79.

LJ, lxxxiv, 91; Committee Book 168, p. 18.

MONRO, Robert Webber *Clerk* 22 July 1862–6 Dec. 1886 (PO 549/2, p. 12). *Clerk of Private Bills* 6 Dec. 1886–1 Oct. 1901 (PO 549/2, p. 38). *Chief Clerk* 1 Oct. 1901–1 Apr. 1903 (PO 549/2, pp. 60, 66). Retired 1 Apr. 1903 (*LJ*, cxxxv, 73).

Only son of John Boscawen Monro of London, barrister. Born 28 Mar. 1838. Married 2 June 1870 Frances Mary, daughter of Duncan Davidson of Tilliechetly, Aberdeen. Died 10 June 1908.

Educated: Harrow. Balliol College, Oxford. BA 1861. MA 1865. Lincoln's Inn. Bar 1864.

Harrow Register 1800–1911, 3rd edn, ed. M.G. Dauglish and P.K. Stephenson (1911), 248; *Balliol College Register 1833–1933*, 2nd edn, ed. I. Elliot (1934), 20; *Lincoln's Inn Register*, ii, 294; *Men at the Bar*, 322.

MUIR MACKENZIE, Montague Ronald Alfred *Reading Clerk* 21 Dec. 1916–5 June 1934 (*LJ*, cxlviii, 318). *Clerk Assistant* 5 June 1934–4 May 1937 (*LJ*, clxvi, 215). Died 4 May 1937.

1st son of Sir John William Pitt Muir Mackenzie KCSI and Fanny Louisa, 2nd daughter of Lieutenant General Montague Cholmeley Johnstone. Grandson of Sir John William Pitt Muir Mackenzie, 2nd Bart. Nephew of Lord Muir Mackenzie. Born 22 Apr. 1881. Married 17 Nov. 1910 Felicity, 3rd daughter of Samuel Henry Romilly of Huntingdon Park, Hereford.

Educated: St Paul's. Jesus College, Cambridge. BA 1903.

Private Secretary to Permanent Secretary to Lord Chancellor 1907–16. Deputy Serjeant at Arms, House of Lords 1909–16. Secretary of Commissions 1914–15. Secretary for Ecclesiastical Patronage to Lord Chancellor 1915–16.

Burke's Peerage (105th edn), 1708; *St Paul's Register 1876–1905*, ed. R.B. Gardiner (1906), 312; *Al. Cant.*, iv, 493; *The Times*, 6 May 1937, p. 18.

MYDDLETON BIDDULPH, Victor Alexander Frederick *Clerk* 5 June 1884–31 Mar. 1918 (PO 549/2, p. 36). Retired 31 Mar. 1918 (*LJ*, cl, 54).

Only son of Sir Thomas Myddleton Biddulph and Mary Frederica, only daughter of Frederick Charles William Seymour. Born 8 June 1860. Died 13 Feb. 1919.

Educated: Eton. New College, Oxford. BA 1882.

Burke's Landed Gentry (18th edn), iii, 673; *Eton Register 1871–80*, p. 92; *Al. Ox.*, i, 107.

NEWELL BIRCH *see* BIRCH

OVERBURY, Robert Leslie (ktd 1950) *Reading Clerk* 5 June 1934–1 June 1937 (*LJ*, clxvi, 216). *Clerk Assistant* 1 June 1937–31 May 1949 (*LJ*, clxix, 234). *Clerk of the Parliaments* 31 May 1949–1 Oct. 1953 (*LJ*, clxxx, 248). Retired 1 Oct. 1953 (*LJ*, clxxxv, 287).

Son of Robert Overbury. Born 26 July 1887. Married 1913 Ethel (died 9 Sept. 1960), daughter of J.E. Stapleton. Died 11 Jan. 1955.

Clerk, Central Office Supreme Court of Judicature 1910–19. Clerk, Crown Office in Chancery 1919–23. Secretary of Commissions 1923–30. Chief Clerk, Lord Chancellor's Office 1930–4.

CB 1941. KCB 1950.

Who Was Who, v, 840; *The Times*, 13 Jan. 1955, p. 11.

PALK, Wilmot Henry *Temporary Clerk* 13 Aug. 1857–Nov. 1859 (PO 549/2, p. 6). *Clerk* Nov. 1859–13 June 1876 (PO 549/2, p. 9). Died 13 June 1876.

2nd son of Robert Malet Palk, Counsel to Chairman of Committees, House of Lords 1832–66 and Harriet, youngest daughter of George Hibbert of Portland Place, London. Grandson of Sir Lawrence Palk, 2nd Bart. First cousin of Augustus Palk, Clerk in the House of Commons. Born 1836. Married Elizabeth Alexandrina Grieg, youngest daughter of William Mackenzie of Aberdeen.

Educated: Eton.

Burke's Peerage (97th edn), 1179; *Eton Register 1841–50*, p. 87; *Commons Clerks*, 78.

PARRATT, Edward *Clerk* c. 1781–1797 (*RK* (1781), 67; (1797), 68). *Clerk of Journals* 1797–18 Mar. 1819 (*RK* (1798), 68; (1819), 44). Died 18 Mar. 1819.

4th son of Thomas Parratt of Barton Street, Westminster and Elizabeth, only daughter of James Meredith of St Margaret's, Westminster, peruke maker. Uncle of Edward Parratt (died 1853) and great uncle of Edward Meredith Parratt (qq.v.). Born 27 Nov. 1748. Married by 22 Oct. 1796 Elizabeth – (died 1 Apr. 1816).

Baptismal Register of St Margaret's, Westminster; *Registers of St John's, Westminster*, iii, 29; Monumental Inscription St Margaret's, Westminster; *Westminster Register Supplement*, 110.

PARRATT, Edward *Clerk* 1802–c. 1820 (*RK* (1803), 36; (1819), 44). *Clerk of Ingrossments* c. 1820–1822 (*RK* (1820), 44: (1822), 46). *Copying Clerk* 1822–5 Oct. 1835 (*RK* (1823), 46). *Clerk of Journals* 5 Oct. 1835–23 Feb. 1853 (PO 549/1, p. 11). Died 23 Feb. 1853.

3rd son of James Meredith Parratt of Bridge Street, Westminster, apothecary and Sophia Maria, daughter of Henry Cowper. Nephew of Edward Parratt (died 1819) and uncle of Edward Meredith Parratt (qq.v.). Born 28 Oct. 1787. Married Henrietta Christina – (died 20 Feb. 1892).

Baptismal Register of St Margaret's, Westminster; *Westminster Register Supplement*, 110; *Huntingdon Library Quarterly*, xix (1955), 189–90.

PARRATT, Edward Meredith *Extra Clerk* 1830–16 Aug. 1839 (PO 106, p. 50). *Clerk* 16 Aug. 1839–c. 1854 (PO 549/1, pp. 14, 17). *Clerk of Judicial Office* c. 1854–1 July 1874 (*LJ*, lxxxvi, 516). *Chief Clerk* 1 July 1874–10 Nov. 1886 (PO 549/2, p. 21). Retired 10 Nov. 1886 (*LJ*, cxix, 53).

Son of Thomas Parratt of the Customs House by 1st wife, Eliza. Nephew of Edward Parratt (died 1853). Great nephew of Edward Parratt (died 1819) (qq.v.). Baptised 1 Jan. 1815. Died 12 Mar. 1896.

Registers of St John's, Westminster, iv, 20; Prob. 11/2258, f. 702, will of Maria Sophia Parratt 1857.

PAYNE, William Charles *Clerk* 1793–1819 (*RK* (1794), 68; (1819), 44). *Copying Clerk* 1819–22 May 1822 (*RK* (1820), 44; (1822), 46).

Parentage unknown. Father in law of George Kitson (q.v.). Born about 1757 being aged 65 at death. Married by 5 Oct. 1788 Jane (living 1 July 1822). Died 22 May 1822.

Registers of St John's, Westminster, ii, 260; *Gentleman's Magazine* (1822), xcii, 572; Prob. 11/1659, f. 394, will of William Charles Payne 1822.

PECHELL, Augustus *Clerk* 20 Jan. 1847–31 Mar. 1876 (PO 549/1, p. 30). Retired 31 Mar. 1876 (*LJ*, cviii, 131).

1st son of Rev. Horace Robert Pechell, Chancellor of Brecon, and Caroline Mary, 3rd daughter of Rear Admiral Lord Mark Kerr. Great grandson of Sir Paul Pechell, 1st Bart. Born 21 Jan. 1828. Married 7 Apr. 1863 Lucy (died Dec. 1872), daughter of Rev. Charles Douglas Beckford. Died 4 Apr. 1894.

Burke's Peerage (105th edn), 2078.

PEMBERTON, Richard Oliver Walpole *Clerk* 1 May 1910–24 Mar. 1920 (PO 549/2, p. 80). Resigned 24 Mar. 1920 on appointment as Principal, Treasury (*LJ*, clii, 92).

2nd son of Colonel Arthur Ralph Pemberton of 15A Basil Street, London, SW and Mary Frances, daughter of Andrew Cockerell. Born 18 Aug. 1885. Married 1922 Daphne Joan, daughter of William Trevor of Lathbury Park, Newport Pagnell. Died 15 Mar. 1960.

Educated: Eton. Balliol College, Oxford. BA 1910.

Assistant Master, Eton 1910. Principal, Treasury 1920–6. Inspector of Schools 1926–47.

R.C.B. Pemberton, *Pemberton Pedigrees* (Bedford, 1923), Table 14; *Eton Register 1899–1909*, p. 55; *Balliol College Register 1833–1933*, 2nd edn, ed. I. Elliot (1934), 282; *Balliol College Register 1916–67*, 4th edn, ed. E. Lemon (1969), 19.

PEPYS, Hon. William John *Clerk* 1 Dec. 1854–1861 (PO 549/2, p. 5). Last occurs 1861 (*RK* (1861), 60).

2nd son of 1st Earl of Cottenham and Caroline Elizabeth, daughter of William Wingfield Baker. Born 15 Aug. 1825. Married 11 Oct. 1870 Theodosia Selina (died 27 Feb. 1919), only daughter of Sir Robert Charles Dallas, 2nd Bart. Succeeded as 3rd Earl of Cottenham 18 Feb. 1863. Died 20 June 1881.

Educated: Eton. Magdalene College, Cambridge. MA 1848.

Complete Peerage, iii, 460; *Eton School Lists 1791–1850*, 2nd edn, ed. H.E.C. Stapylton (1864), 194; *Al. Cant.*, v, 90.

PERCEVAL, Robert Westby *Clerk* 21 Nov. 1938–28 Oct. 1953 (PO 549/2, p. 126). *Clerk, Special Procedure Orders Office* 28 Oct. 1953–31 July 1956 (*LJ*, clxxxvi, 38). *Clerk, Chairman of Committees Office* 3 July 1956–20 Jan. 1959 (*House of Lords Official Report*, cxix, lv). *Clerk of Public Bills* 20 Jan. 1959–10 Aug. 1963 (*LJ*, cxci, 144: cxcvi, 44).

Reading Clerk 17 June 1963–14 Jan. 1964 (*LJ*, cxcv, 346). *Clerk Assistant* 14 Jan. 1964–12 June 1974 (*LJ*, cxcvi, 70).

Retired 12 June 1974 (*LJ*, ccvii, 193).

1st son of Major Francis Westby Perceval OBE of Bishop's Lydeard, Somerset and Dorothy Anne Cecilia, daughter of George Thornton of Fairlawn, Eltham, Kent. Born 28 Aug. 1914. Married (1) 1 May 1940 Rosemary (divorced 1946), daughter of Allen Clerk of Treparett House, Cornwall; (2) 1 Sept. 1948 Joanna Ida Louisa, 1st daughter of 5th Lord Hatherton.

Educated: Ampleforth. Balliol College, Oxford. BA 1937. Middle Temple.

Served World War II. Royal Artillery 1939–44. General Staff, War Office 1944–5. Secretary of Statute Law Committee 1950–74.

Burke's Landed Gentry (17th edn), 2012; *Middle Temple Register*, iii, 986; *Who's Who*.

PROBY, Granville *Clerk* 1 Feb. 1907–24 June 1941 (PO 549/2, p. 71). *Clerk of Judicial Office* 24 June 1941–31 Dec. 1945 (*LJ*, clxxiii, 137). Retired 31 Dec. 1945 (*LJ*, clxxviii, 118).

1st son of Major Douglas James Hamilton (from 1904 Proby) of Elton Hall, Hunts and Margaret Frances, 2nd daughter of 4th Earl of Donoughmore. Great nephew of 1st Duke of Abercorn. Born 13 Sept. 1883. Died 9 Mar. 1947.

Educated: Eton. Trinity College, Cambridge. MA 1912. Inner Temple. Bar 1920.

Served World War I. Captain, Bedfordshire Yeomanry. Lord Lieutenant of Huntingdon 1945–7.

Burke's Peerage (105th edn), 4; *Eton Register 1899–1909*, p. 6; *Who Was Who*, iv, 941.

ROBINSON, Arthur Hildyard *Clerk* 1 Dec. 1877–1 Oct. 1901 (PO 549/2, p. 29). *Clerk of Private Bills* 1 Oct. 1901–31 May 1919 (PO 549/2, p. 61). Retired 31 May 1919 (*LJ*, cli, 67).

1st son of John Harding Robinson (q.v.) and Lucy Harriette, 2nd daughter of Henry Hildyard of Rio de Janeiro. Born 28 May 1859. Married 19 July 1892 Ethel Fanny, daughter of Walter Long of The Holt, Bishop's Waltham, Hants and Muchelney, Somerset. Died 7 Dec. 1939.

Educated: Charterhouse.

Burke's Landed Gentry (15th edn), 1930; *Charterhouse Register 1872–1931*, 3rd edn (Guildford, 1932), Long Quarter, 1875; *Who Was Who*, iii, 1156.

ROBINSON, John Harding *Clerk* 23 June 1845–9 Aug. 1869 (PO 549/1, p. 19). Left office 9 Aug. 1869 on appointment as Examiner of Standing Orders (*LJ*, ci, 582).

Son of Colonel Daniel William Robinson and Mary Ann Greathead. Father of Arthur Hildyard Robinson (q.v.). Born 17 May 1834. Married 8 Oct. 1856 Lucy Harriette, 2nd daughter of Henry Hildyard of Rio de Janeiro. Died 8 Apr. 1890.

Examiner of Standing Orders 1869–90.

Burke's Landed Gentry (15th edn), 1930.

ROSE, Charles Philip *Deputy Reading Clerk* 16 Feb.–9 June 1824 (*LJ*, lvi, 31). *Reading Clerk* 9 June 1824–27 Aug. 1835 (*LJ*, 368). Retired 27 Aug. 1835 (*LJ*, lxvii, 622).

2nd son of George Henry Rose (q.v.) and Frances, daughter of Thomas Duncombe of Duncombe Park, Yorks. Grandson of George Rose. Nephew of William Stewart Rose. Brother of William Rose (qq.v.). Born 27 Nov. 1799. Died 12 Sept. 1835.

Educated: St John's College, Cambridge. BA 1821. Lincoln's Inn.

Burke's Landed Gentry (18th edn), ii, 537; *Burke's Peerage* (41st edn), 1161; *Al. Cant.*, v. 536; *Lincoln's Inn Register*, ii, 94.

ROSE, George *Clerk of the Parliaments* 6 June 1788–13 Jan. 1818 (M.F. Bond, 'Clerks of the Parliaments, 1509–1953'; *EHR*, lxxiii (1958), 85; *LJ*, xxxviii, 215–16).

2nd son of Rev. David Rose of Lethnot, Forfar and Margaret, daughter of Donald Rose of Westerclunie. Father of George Henry Rose and William Stewart Rose. Grandfather of Charles Philip Rose and William Rose (qq.v.). Born 17 June 1744. Married 7 July 1769 Theodora (died 6 Nov. 1834), daughter of John Dues of Antigua. Died 13 Jan. 1818.

Educated: Westminster.

Secretary, Board of Taxes 1777–82. Secretary, Treasury 1782–3, 1783–1801. Clerk of Pleas, Exchequer 1784–97. MP Launceston 1784–8, Lymington 1788–90, Christchurch 1790–1818. PC 1802. Joint Paymaster of Forces and Vice President of Board of Trade 1804–6. Treasurer of Navy and Vice President of Board of Trade 1807–18.

Burke's Landed Gentry (18th edn), ii, 537; *Burke's Peerage* (41st edn), 1161; *Westminster Register*, ii, 800–1; *DNB*, xlix, 226–30; *The History of Parliament: The House of Commons 1754–90*, ed. L.B. Namier and J. Brooke (1964), iii, 375–6.

ROSE, George Henry (ktd 1819) *Clerk of the Parliaments* 13 Jan. 1818–17 June 1855 (M.F. Bond, 'Clerks of the Parliaments, 1509–1953'; *EHR*, lxxiii (1958), 85: *LJ*, li, 481–2). Died 17 June 1855.

1st son of George Rose (q.v.) and Theodora, daughter of John Dues of Antigua. Brother of William Stewart Rose. Father of Charles Philip Rose and William Rose (qq.v.). Born 3 May 1770. Married Frances (died 12 Oct. 1861), daughter of Thomas Duncombe of Duncombe Park, Yorks.

Educated: Winchester. St John's College, Cambridge. BA 1792. MA 1795. Lincoln's Inn.

MP Southampton 1794–1813, Christchurch 1818–32, 1837–44. Deputy Paymaster of Forces 1804–6. British Minister, Munich 1813, Berlin 1815. PC 1818.

GCH 1819.

Burke's Landed Gentry (18th edn), ii, 537; *Burke's Peerage* (41st edn), 1161; *Al. Cant.*, v, 537; *MEB*, iii, 284–5; *DNB*, xlix, 231–2.

ROSE, William (ktd 1867) *Reading Clerk* 27 Aug. 1835–13 Mar. 1848 (*LJ*, lxvii, 622). *Additional Clerk Assistant* 13 Mar. 1848–17 June 1855 (*LJ*, lxxx, 122). *Clerk Assistant* 17 June 1855–27 Apr. 1875 (*LJ*, lxxxviii, 82). *Clerk of the Parliaments* 27 Apr. 1875–19 Nov. 1885 (*LJ*, cvii, 126). Died 19 Nov. 1885.

4th son of George Henry Rose (q.v.) and Frances, daughter of Thomas Duncombe of Duncombe Park, Yorks. Grandson of George Rose. Nephew of William Stewart Rose. Brother of Charles Philip Rose (qq.v.). Born 19 July 1808. Married 15 Mar. 1856 Sophia Andalusia Mary (died 13 Nov. 1900), 2nd daughter of 2nd Lord Rendlesham.

Educated: St John's College, Cambridge. BA 1830. Lincoln's Inn. Bar 1839.

KCB 1867.

Burke's Landed Gentry (18th edn), ii, 537; *Burke's Peerage* (41st edn), 1161; *Al. Cant.* v, 356; *Lincoln's Inn Register*, ii, 152; *Men at the Bar*, 51; *MEB*, iii, 288.

ROSE, William Stewart *Reading Clerk* 25 Apr. 1800–9 June 1824 (PO 51/10; *LJ*, xlii, 519). Retired 9 June 1824 (*LJ*, lvi, 368).

2nd son of George Rose (q.v.) and Theodora, daughter of John Dues of Antigua. Brother of George Henry Rose. Uncle of Charles Philip Rose and William Rose (qq.v.). Born 1775. Died 30 Mar. 1843.

Educated: Eton. St John's College, Cambridge. Lincoln's Inn. Clerk of Pleas, Exchequer 1797–1837. MP Christchurch 1796–1800.

Poet. Friend of Sir Walter Scott.

Burke's Landed Gentry (18th edn), ii, 537; *Burke's Peerage* (41st edn), 1161; *Eton School Lists 1791–1850*, 2nd edn, ed. H.E.C. Stapylton (1864), 3; *Al. Cant.*, v. 359; *Lincoln's Inn Register*, i; 556; *DNB*, xlix, 244–5.

RYDER, Algernon Frederick Roland Dudley *Clerk* 1 Dec. 1921–1 Jan. 1950 (PO 549/2, p. 104). *Clerk, Chairman of Committees Office* 1 Jan. 1950–31 July 1956 (*LJ*, clxxxii, 59). Retired 31 July 1956 (*LJ*, clxxxviii, 335).

1st son of Rev. Algernon Charles Dudley Ryder and Constance Eugenia, daughter of Rowland Smith of Duffield Hall, Derby. Great grandson of 1st Earl of Harrowby. Born 25 May 1891. Married 19 Mar. 1921 Olive, daughter of John Baillie of Montreal, Canada. Died 16 Apr. 1957.

Educated: Eton. Trinity College, Cambridge. BA 1913.

Served World Wars I and II.

MC (Bar).

Burke's Peerage (105th edn), 1267; *Eton Register 1899–1909*, p. 184.

ST GEORGE, Clifford Fortescue Loftus *Clerk* 1 Apr. 1918–1935 (PO 549/2, p. 87). *Clerk of Journals* 1935–1 Apr. 1960 (*House of Lords Official Report*, cxcix, p. ix). Retired 1 Apr. 1960 (*LJ*, cxcii, 258).

1st son of Loftus St George and Marguerite Isabel Clifford, daughter of Clifford Fortescue Borrer of Pickwell, Cuckfield, Sussex. Great grandson of Sir Richard Bligh St George, 2nd Bart. Born 22 July 1894. Married 29 July 1931 Gwen Marjorie Chisholm (died June 1982), youngest daughter of Rev. William Edward Dalton, Vicar of Glynde, Sussex. Died 1 June 1966.

Educated: Eastbourne. Merton College, Oxford. MA 1920.

Served World War I. 4th Battalion, Royal Sussex Regiment, TF.
CBE 1948.
Burke's Peerage (105th edn), 2350.

ST JOHN, Henry Percy *Clerk* 23 Apr. 1878–1 Aug. 1908 (PO 549/2, p. 30). *Clerk of Judicial Office* 1 Aug. 1908–1 Apr. 1919 (PO 549/2, p. 74). Retired 1 Apr. 1919 (*LJ*, cli, 67).

1st son of Rev. Maurice William Ferdinand St John, Canon of Gloucester and Charlotte Lucy, daughter of John Dalyell. Great grandson of 3rd Viscount Bolingbroke. Born 23 Mar. 1854. Married 12 Oct. 1887 Maud Louisa (died 28 Oct. 1938), 1st daughter of Hon. Charles Pascoe Glyn. Died 9 Sept. 1921.

Educated: Marlborough.

Burke's Peerage (105th edn), 298; *Marlborough Register 1843–1952*, 3rd edn, ed. L.W. James, 160; *Who Was Who*, ii, 925.

SHAW LEFEVRE, John George (ktd 1857) *Clerk Assistant* 6 Apr. 1848–17 June 1855 (*LJ*, lxxx, 177). *Clerk of the Parliaments* 17 June 1855–11 Mar. 1875 (*LJ*, lxxxvii, 243). Retired 11 Mar. 1875 (*LJ*, cvii, 63).

2nd son of Charles Shaw MP and Helena, daughter of John Lefevre of Heckfield Hall, Hants. Brother of Viscount Eversley. Born 24 July 1797. Married 1824 Rachel Emily, daughter of Ichabod Wright of Mapperley, Notts. Died 20 Aug. 1879.

Educated: Eton. Trinity College, Cambridge. BA 1818. MA 1821. Inner Temple. Bar 1825.

MP Petersfield 1832–3. Under Secretary, Colonial Office 1833–4. Poor Law Commissioner 1833–41. Joint Secretary, Board of Trade 1841–8. Vice Chancellor, London University 1842–62.

Emigration Commissioner 1843. Ecclesiastical Commissioner 1847. Church Commissioner 1850. Civil Service Commissioner 1855–62.

KCB 1857.

Burke's Peerage (49th edn), 511–12; *Eton School Lists 1791–1850*, 2nd edn, ed. H.E.C. Stapylton (1864), 60; *Al. Cant.*, v, 483; *MEB*, ii, 367; *DNB*, li, 451–2.

SKENE, Felix James Henry *Clerk* 1 Oct. 1871–1 Oct. 1901 (PO 549/2, p. 18). *Clerk of Public Bills* 1 Oct. 1901–28 Jan. 1902 (PO 549/2, p. 61). *Clerk of Judicial Office* 28 Jan. 1902–31 July 1908 (PO 549/2, p. 62). Retired 31 July 1908 (*LJ*, cxl, 286).

1st son of James Henry Skene, Vice Consul at Constantinople and Consul General at Aleppo and Rhalou, daughter of Jakovaki Rizo Rangabe of Athens. Born 5 July 1843. Married 15 Dec. 1871 Jane Elizabeth Huddleston, 2nd daughter of Angus Hossack. Died 26 Mar. 1927.

Educated: Harrow.

Private Secretary to Governor of New Brunswick. Clerk in office of Queen's Remembrancer for Scotland 1868–71. Secretary of Statute Law Committee and Editor of Annual Statutes 1897–1902.

Memorials of the Family of Skene, ed. W.F. Skene (Aberdeen, 1887), 141; *Burke's Landed Gentry* (4th edn), 1381; (7th edn), ii, 1676; *Harrow Register 1800–1911*, 3rd edn, ed. M.G. Dauglish and P.K. Stephenson (1911), 295.

SMITH, Henry Stone *Clerk* 1819–1826 (PO 106, p. 50; *RK* (1820), 44). *Clerk of Committees* 1826–24 July 1840 (*RK* (1827), 46). *Chief Clerk* 24 July 1840–22 May 1874 (PO 549/1, p. 14). Retired 22 May 1874 (*LJ*, cvi, 255).

Clerk of Inrolments probably appointed 1831 on retirement of Robert Harvey Strachan; first occurs 1833 (*RK* (1833), 48); left office 24 July 1840 (PO 549/2, pp. 14, 15).

Only son of Captain John Langdale Smith RN and Sarah Stone. Born 4 Feb. 1795. Married 21 Feb. 1816 Sophia Sheppard (living 12 Aug. 1837). Died 4 Sept. 1881.

Educated: Westminster.

Clerk, Prisoners of War Department, Transport Office 15 Feb. 1810–24 June 1818. Deputy Chief Usher of Court of Exchequer 1836–42.

Registers of St John's, Westminster, iii, 19; xxviii, 84; *Westminster Register*, ii, 859; PO 56/45; PO 83/28; Chief Usher of Exchequer Papers; *The Times*, 6 Sept. 1881, p. 4.

STEPHENS, David (ktd 1964) *Clerk* 1 Jan. 1935–21 Nov. 1938 (PO 549/2, p. 121). Resigned 21 Nov. 1938 on appointment as Member of Runciman Mission (*LJ*, clxxi, 47).

Reading Clerk 18 Oct. 1961–17 June 1963 (*LJ*, cxciii, 430). *Clerk of the Parliaments* 17 June 1963–31 July 1974 (*LJ*, cxcv, 345). Retired 31 July 1974 (*LJ*, ccvii, 328).

Only son of Berkeley John Byng Stephens CIE and Gwendolen Elizabeth, daughter of Edmund William Cripps of Ampney Park, Oxon. Born 25 Apr. 1910. Married (1) 25 Mar. 1941 Mary Clemency (died 1966), 1st daughter of Sir Eric Gore Browne DSO, OBE of Glaxton House, Uppingham, Rutland; (2) 28 Oct. 1967 Charlotte Evelyn, daughter of Rev. A.M. Baird-Smith of Wheathampstead and widow of Henry Manisty.

Educated: Winchester. Christ Church, Oxford. BA 1933.

Travelling Fellow, Queen's College, Oxford 1932–4. Member of Runciman Mission to Czechoslovakia 1938. Transferred to Treasury 1938. Political Warfare Executive 1941–3. Principal Private Secretary to Lord President of Council 1947–9. Assistant Secretary, Treasury 1949. Secretary for Appointments to Prime Minister 1955–61. Chairman, Redundant Churches Fund 1976–81.

CVO 1960. KCB 1964.

Burke's Landed Gentry (17th edn), 2402; *Winchester Register 1915–60*, ed. L.H. Lamb (1974), 149; *Who's Who*.

STONOR, Hon. Edward Alexander *Clerk* 1 Jan. 1891–1918 (PO 549/2, p. 44). *Clerk of Committees* 1918–1 Nov. 1921 (*House of Lords Official Report*, xxxiii, p. ix; xliv, p. viii). *Clerk of Private Bills* 1 Nov. 1921–16 Oct. 1932 (PO 549/2, p. 104). Retired 16 Oct. 1932 (*LJ*, clxiv, 262).

3rd son of Hon. Francis Stonor (q.v.) and Eliza, 2nd daughter of Sir Robert Peel, 2nd Bart. Born 16 Oct. 1867. Granted precedence as younger son of Baron May 1881. Married 16 Jan. 1899 Christine Alexandra (died 9 Dec. 1958), daughter of Richard Ralli and widow of Ambrose Ralli. Died 12 May 1940.

Educated: Woburn Park, Weybridge.

Served World War I. Major, RAF 1914–19. Secretary, Anti-Socialist and Anti-Communist Union. Had Orders of Legion of Honour of France, Leopold of Belgium, St Maurice and St Lazarus of Italy, Crown of Roumania, St Anne of Russia and St Sava of Yugoslavia.

Burke's Peerage (105th edn), 457; Who Was Who, iii, 1299.

STONOR, Hon. Francis Clerk 23 Mar. 1846–10 Jan. 1881 (PO 549/1, p. 27). Died 10 Jan. 1881.

2nd son of 5th Lord Camoys and Frances, daughter of Peregrine Edward Towneley of Towneley, Lancs. Father of Edward Alexander Stonor (q.v.). Born 5 Jan. 1829. Married 25 Sept. 1855 Eliza, 2nd daughter of Sir Robert Peel, 2nd Bart.

Burke's Peerage (105th edn), 457.

STRACHAN, Robert Harvey Extra Clerk 1806–13 (LJ, lxiii, 1090). Clerk 1813–22 (RK (1814), 48; (1822), 46). Clerk of Inrolments 1822–25 Apr. 1831 (RK (1823), 46; (1832), 48). Retired 25 Apr. 1831 (LJ, lxiii, 1090).

Parentage unknown. Born about 1789 being aged 46 at death. Married c. 22 May 1822 Elizabeth Nettlefold of St Marylebone (living 23 Oct. 1835). Buried 30 Aug. 1835.

Lambeth Palace Library: Faculty Office Marriage Allegations Jan.–June 1822, f. 336; Burial Register of Ripley, Surrey; Prob. 11/1853, f. 624, will of Robert Harvey Strachan.

SYMONS JEUNE see JEUNE

TAYLOR, Edward Fairfax Clerk 7 Mar. 1865–1 Apr. 1895 (PO 549/2, p. 12). Clerk of Judicial Office 1 Apr. 1895–27 Jan. 1902 (PO 549/2, p. 48). Died 27 Jan. 1902.

Only son of John Edward Taylor of Weybridge, Surrey, printer and translator. Born 10 July 1845. Married Olivia Harriet (living 27 Mar. 1902).

Educated: Marlborough.

Translator from German and Latin.

Marlborough College Register 1843–1952, 9th edn, ed. L.W. James, 107; British Museum Catalogue of Printed Books, liii; Vergil's Aeneid, translated by E.F. Taylor (Everyman's Library), xvi–xvii.

THESIGER, Hon. Edward Peirson (ktd 1911) Clerk 21 Feb. 1862–18 Feb. 1890 (PO 549/2, p. 10). Clerk Assistant 18 Feb. 1890–7 Dec. 1916 (LJ, cxx, 31). Retired 7 Dec. 1916 (LJ, cxlviii, 294).

5th son of 1st Lord Chelmsford and Anna Maria, youngest daughter of William Tinling of Southampton. Born 19 Dec. 1842. Married 13 May 1869 Georgiana Mary (died 22 Dec. 1916), 3rd daughter of William Bruce Stopford Sackville. Died 11 Nov. 1928.

Educated: Eton.

Clerk, Lord Chancellor's Office 1862–6. Secretary of Presentations to Lord Chancellor 1866–90.

CB 1886. KCB 1911.

Burke's Peerage (105th edn), 529; Eton Register 1853–9, p. 36; Who Was Who, ii, 1032; The Times, 12 Nov. 1928, p. 18.

THOMPSON, Lionel Hill Extra Clerk 1825–6 (PO 196, p. 50). Clerk 1826–5 Jan. 1856 (RK (1827), 46). Retired 5 Jan. 1856 (LJ, lxxxvii, 441; lxxxviii, 81).

Parentage unknown. Born about 1801 being aged 64 at death. A widower at death. Died 17 Dec. 1865.

THOMS, Merton Antony *Extra Clerk* 11 Aug. 1854–3 May 1858 (PO 106, p. 51). *Clerk* 3 May 1858–6 Dec. 1886 (PO 549/2, p. 5). *Clerk of Committees* 6 Dec. 1886–7 Oct. 1896 (PO 549/2, p. 38). *Acting Reading Clerk* 7 Oct. 1896–31 Dec. 1899 (PO 549/2, p. 51). Retired 31 Dec. 1899 (*LJ*, cxxxi, 165, 380).

Son of William John Thoms (q.v.) and Laura, youngest daughter of John Bernard Sale. Born 12 May 1834. Died 30 Nov. 1909.

Examiner of Standing Orders 1890–9.

The Times, 2 Dec. 1909, p. 1.

THOMS, William John *Extra Clerk* 1844–19 July 1845 (PO 106, p. 50). *Clerk* 19 July 1845–1849 (PO 549/1, pp. 19–21). *Clerk of Printed Papers* 1849–10 Mar. 1862 (PO 106, p. 56). Left office 10 Mar. 1862 on appointment as Assistant Librarian, House of Lords (PO 549/2, p. 10).

Son of Nathaniel Thoms, Treasury Clerk. Father of Merton Anthony Thoms (q.v.). Born 16 Nov. 1803. Married 1828 Laura, youngest daughter of John Bernard Sale. Died 15 Aug. 1885.

Clerk, Secretary's Office, Chelsea Hospital 1819–44. Secretary, Camden Society 1838–72. Editor, *Notes and Queries* 1849–72. Assistant Librarian, House of Lords 1862–80.

FSA 1838.

LJ, cxii, 354; *MEB*, iii, 943; *DNB*, lvi, 230–2.

THRING, Sir Arthur Theodore, Kt. *Clerk of the Parliaments* 25 Apr. 1917–26 Feb. 1930 (*LJ*, cxlix, 94). Retired 26 Feb. 1930 (*LJ*, clxii, 245).

3rd son of Theodore Thring of Alford House, Somerset and Julia Jane, 4th daughter of William Mills of Saxham House, Suffolk.

Nephew of Lord Thring. Born 7 Feb. 1860. Married 25 Sept. 1902 Georgiana Baxendale (died 4 Jan. 1942), 4th daughter of Edward Bovill of Sondes Place, Dorking, Surrey. Died 17 Apr. 1932.

Educated: Winchester. New College, Oxford. BA. Lincoln's Inn. Bar 1887.

Assistant Parliamentary Counsel 1902–3. First Parliamentary Counsel 1903–17.

CB 1902. KCB 1908.

Burke's Landed Gentry (18th edn), iii, 899; *Winchester College Register 1867–1920*, ed. J.H. Hardy (Winchester, 1923), 96; *Al. Ox.*, iv, 1417; *Lincoln's Inn Register*, ii, 408; *Who Was Who*, iii, 1351; *The Times*, 18 Apr. 1932, p. 17.

TUBB, William *Clerk* 1824–29 July 1836 (*RK* (1825), 46). Died 29 July 1836.

Son of John Tubb of Barton Street, Westminster, Deputy Chief Usher of Court of Exchequer and Margaret —. Born 9 Dec. 1802.

Educated: Westminster.

Deputy Chief Usher of Court of Exchequer c. 1831–6.

Registers of St John's, Westminster, iii, 61; lxi, 83; *Westminster Register*, ii, 933; PO 549/1, p. 13; Chief Usher of Exchequer Papers; Prob. 11/1867, will of William Tubb 1836.

VANE, Frederick Nicholson *Clerk* 8 Apr. 1845–10 Feb. 1878 (PO 549/1, p. 18). Died 10 Feb. 1878.

2nd son of John Henry Vane and Elizabeth, 3rd daughter of Richard Nicholson. Great great grandson of 2nd Lord Barnard. Born 19 Dec. 1809.

Educated: Richmond School, Yorks. Trinity College, Cambridge. BA 1832.

Burke's Peerage (105th edn), 183; *Al. Cant.*, vi, 276.

VIGORS, Edward Cliffe *Clerk* 1 Oct. 1901–1921 (PO 549/2, p. 61). *Clerk of Committees* 1921–1932 (*House of Lords Official Report*, xlviii, p. ix). *Clerk of Private Bills and Committees* 1932–31 May 1939 (*House of Lords Official Report*, lxxxv, p. iii). Retired 31 May 1939 (*LJ*, clxiv, 262).

1st son of Thomas Mercer Cliffe Vigors of Burgrave, Carlow and Mary Louisa Helen, 1st daughter of Hon. Robert French Handcock. Born 9 Oct. 1878. Married 6 June 1914 Mary Selina, daughter of Lieutenant General Henry Ellenborough Dyneley. Died 6 Mar. 1945.

Educated: Charterhouse. Christ Church, Oxford.

Examiner of Standing Orders 1925–40.

CB 1936.

Burke's Irish Family Records (1976), 1169; *Charterhouse Register 1872–1931*, 3rd edn (Guildford, 1932), i; Oration Quarter 1892; *Who Was Who*, iv, 1183.

WALKER, Charles Michael *Clerk* 5 June 1939–1 Mar. 1947 (PO 549/2, p. 127). Resigned 1 Mar. 1947 on appointment to Dominions Office (*LJ*, clxxix, 179).

1st son of Colonel Charles William G. Walker CMG, DSO. Born 22 Nov. 1916. Married 1945 Enid Dorothy, daughter of W.A. McAdam CMG.

Educated: Charterhouse. New College, Oxford.

Served World War II. RA 1939–46. Dominions Office 1947. First Secretary, British Embassy, Washington 1949–51. Office of United Kingdom High Commissioner, Calcutta and New Delhi 1952–5. Establishment Officer, Commonwealth Relations Office 1955–8. Imperial Defence College 1958. Assistant Under Secretary of State, Commonwealth Relations Office 1959–62. British High Commissioner, Ceylon 1962–5, Malaysia 1965–71. Secretary, Overseas Development Administration 1971–3. High Commissioner, India 1974–6. Chairman, Commonwealth Scholarship Commission 1976–87.

CMG 1960. KCMG 1963. GCMG 1976.

Charterhouse Register 1872–1931, 3rd edn (Guildford, 1932), ii; Oration Quarter 1930; *Who's Who*.

WALMISLEY, Edward George *Clerk* 1799–1819 (*RK* (1800), 32; (1819), 44). *Clerk of Journals* 1819–19 Sept. 1835 (*RK* (1820), p. 44). Died 19 Sept. 1835.

1st son of William Walmisley (died 1819) (q.v.) and Mary, daughter of Thomas Jackson of Bewdley, Worcs. Brother of William Walmisley (died 1822) and Robert Walmisley. Uncle of William Elyard Walmisley and Henry Walmisley (qq.v.). Born 26 Dec. 1778. Married (1) 9 Nov. 1810 Amelia Matilda, widow of Frederick Fox of Westminster; (2) 29 Aug. 1825 Mary Selina Sybella (died 5 Mar. 1834), daughter of Thomas Harris Bradshaw, Senior Clerk in Post Office.

Educated: Westminster.
Westminster Register, ii, 960.

WALMISLEY, Francis *Clerk* 1826–1833 (*RK* (1827), 46; (1833), 48).
Relationship to other Walmisleys, if any, unknown.

WALMISLEY, Henry *Extra Clerk* 1826–19 July 1845 (PO 106, p. 50). *Clerk* 19 July 1845–1866 (PO 549/1, pp. 19–21). *Clerk of Public Bills* 1866–26 Nov. 1870 (PO 106, p. 49). Died 26 Nov. 1870.

Son of William Walmisley (died 1822) (q.v.) and Eleanor, daughter of – Elyard of the London Stock Exchange. Grandson of William Walmisley (died 1819). Nephew of Edward George Walmisley and Robert Walmisley. Brother of William Elyard Walmisley (qq.v.). Born 9 Oct. 1810. Married 23 Mar. 1842 Ann (died 17 Aug. 1882), daughter of T.W. Hodgson and widow of C. Wilkinson.

Registers of St John's, Westminster, iii, 94; *Westminster Register*, ii, 960; Prob. 11/1857, f. 56, will of Edward George Walmisley 1836.

WALMISLEY, John Hayden *Clerk* 1815–19 (*RK* (1816), 48; (1819), 44).

Possibly identical with John Angus (*sic*) Walmisley, 5th son of William Walmisley (died 1819) (q.v.) and Mary, daughter of Thomas Jackson of Bewdley, Worcs. who was born 23 Nov. 1791, married 6 Sept. 1816 Anna Maria, daughter of Colonel William Lambert E.I.C.S and died 6 Feb. 1862.

John Angus Walmisley was educated at Westminster and was a parliamentary agent, Extra Clerk to Clerk of Privileges and Elections, House of Commons c. 1823–36 and Deputy Chief Usher of Court of Exchequer 1842–52.

Westminster Register, ii, 960; *House of Commons Papers* (1833), xii, 230–1, 255; (1834), xi, 405; *RK* (1824), 89; (1836), 90; Chief Usher of Exchequer Papers; *Commons Clerks*, 96.

WALMISLEY, Robert *Extra Clerk* 1800–13 (PO 106, p. 37). *Clerk* 1813–22 (*RK* (1814), 48; (1822), 46). *Clerk of Ingrossments* 1822–5 Oct. 1835 (*RK* (1823), 46). *Chief Clerk* 5 Oct. 1835–5 July 1840 (PO 549/1, p. 11). Retired 5 July 1840 (*LJ*, lxxii, 551).

4th son of William Walmisley (died 1819) (q.v.) and Mary, daughter of Thomas Jackson of Bewdley, Worcs. Brother of Edward George Walmisley and William Walmisley (died 1822). Uncle of William Elyard Walmisley and Henry Walmisley (qq.v.). Born 28 Jan. 1786. Married 16 Nov. 1811 Elizabeth, 1st daughter of Robert Selby of Kingsbury, Middlesex. Died 1 Dec. 1843.

Educated: Westminster.

Messenger, Court of Exchequer 1823–43.

Westminster Register, ii, 960; Chief Usher of Exchequer Papers.

WALMISLEY, William *Clerk* 1777–99 (MI Bromley, Kent; *RK* (1781), 67; (1799), 68). *Copying Clerk* 1799–17 Jan. 1819 (*RK* (1800), 32; (1819), 44). Died 17 Jan. 1819.

Parentage unknown. First cousin of Edward Blackstock, Copying Clerk 1765–99. Father of Edward George Walmisley, William Walmisley (died 1822) and Robert Walmisley. Grandfather of William Elyard Walmisley and Henry Walmisley (qq.v.).

Born about 1745 being in 74th year at death. Married (2) 15 Mar. 1778 Mary (died 4 Apr. 1822), daughter of Thomas Jackson of Bewdley, Worcs.

Westminster Abbey Registers, ed. J.L. Chester (Harleian Society, x, 1876), 462 n. 5; *Westminster Register*, ii, 960; Marriage Register of St Margaret's, Westminster; Monumental Inscription, Bromley, Kent.

WALMISLEY, William *Clerk* 1797–c. 1820 (*RK* (1798), 68; (1819), 44). *Clerk of Inrolments* c. 1820–16 Apr. 1822 (*RK* (1820), 44; (1822), 46). Died 16 Apr. 1822.

2nd son of William Walmisley (died 1819) (q.v.) and Mary, daughter of Thomas Jackson of Bewdley, Worcs. Brother of Edward George Walmisley and Robert Walmisley. Father of William Elyard Walmisley and Henry Walmisley (qq.v.). Born 9 May 1780. Married 26 Apr. 1808 Eleanor, daughter of – Elyard of the London Stock Exchange.

Educated: Westminster

Westminster Register, ii, 960; *Registers of St John's, Westminster*, xxvi, 188.

WALMISLEY, William Elyard *Clerk* 1 Jan. 1823–5 Oct. 1835 (PO 106, p. 50; *RK* (1823), 46). *Clerk of Ingrossments* 5 Oct. 1835–1849 (PO 549/1, p. 12; *RK* (1849), 46). *Clerk of Public Bills* 1849–1866 (*RK* (1850), 61; *LJ*, lxxxii, 113). *Clerk of Journals* 1866–24 Feb. 1873 (PO 106, p. 39). Retired 24 Feb. 1873 (*LJ*, cv, 206).

Son of William Walmisley (died 1822) (q.v.) and Eleanor, daughter of – Elyard of the London Stock Exchange. Grandson of William Walmisley (died 1819). Nephew of Edward George Walmisley and Robert Walmisley. Brother of Henry Walmisley (qq.v.). Born 29 Jan. 1809. Died 16 Jan. 1875.

Registers of St John's, Westminster, iii, 87; *Westminster Register*, ii, 960; Prob. 11/1857, f. 56, will of Edward George Walmisley 1836.

WEBB, Godfrey John *Clerk* 17 Oct. 1856–31 Mar. 1884 (PO 549/2, p. 5). *Clerk of Journals* 31 Mar. 1884–1 Nov. 1897 (PO 549/2, p. 35). Retired 1 Nov. 1897 (*LJ*, cxxix, 379).

2nd son of Lieutenant Colonel Robert Smith Webb of Milford House, Surrey. Born 1 Nov. 1832. Died 25 Oct. 1901.

Educated: Marlborough. Brasenose College, Oxford. BA 1854.

Marlborough College Register 1843–1952, 9th edn, ed. L.W. James, 27; *Al. Ox.*, iv, 1516.

WHITE, William Frederick *Extra Clerk* 1824–6 Mar. 1835 (PO 106, p. 50). *Clerk* 6 Mar. 1835–26 Mar. 1862 (PO 549/1, p. 3). Retired 26 Mar. 1862 (*LJ*, xciv, 276).

Parentage unknown. Born about 1809 being aged 73 at death. Married Jane Lawn – (living 29 July 1882). Died 29 July 1882.

Appendix

Additions and corrections to *The Parliament Office in the Seventeenth and Eighteenth Centuries: Biographical Notes on Clerks in the House of Lords 1600–1800*

ARNOTT, Matthew Robert. Died 24 Apr. 1800 (N.H. Nicolas, *History of the Orders of Knighthood* (1842), iii (Thistle), xxxvi).

BLACKSTOCK, Edward. Married (1) 1 Sept. 1757 at St Martin's in the Fields, Mary Bridgewater; (2) 21 Jan. 1781 at St Marylebone, Sarah Hinks, widow; (3) 18 Sept. 1795 at Sunbury, Middlesex, Harriet Willis Strangeways.

BOWYER, Robert. Died in office 14 Mar. 1621 (W. Camden, *Annalium Apparatus*, 69) or 15 Mar. 1621 (Braye MS 99).

CANE, Henry. Eldest son of Henry Cane of Great Marlow, Bucks and Elizabeth Brauhinge. Born 24 Apr. 1655. Married Mary, daughter of Rev. Robert Jones, Rector of Rotherfield Greys, Oxon. Died 16 Apr. 1724. 'He was for many years Clerk of the House of Lords which place he kept so long as his health would suffer him, but being much subject to an asthma he retired into the country to Little Hillingdon (Middlesex)'. (Information communicated by Mr Michael Davies from a manuscript source).

CROFT, John. Married 5 Apr. 1756 at St George's, Hanover Square, Sarah Jones, aged 30.

ELSYNG, Henry. Died in office between 29 Sept. 1635, the last quarter day for which he received his salary (E 351/1670) and 1 Dec. 1635, the day on which the reversion of the office was granted to Daniel Bedingfield (C 66/2693).

KEN, Thomas. Son of Matthew Ken of London and Elizabeth, daughter of Richard Barret of London. An Attorney in the Court of Common Pleas (*Visitation of London 1633–5* (Harleian Society, xxvii, 1883), 27). Protonotary and Clerk of the Crown, Glamorgan, Brecon and Radnor: grant of reversion 21 Dec. 1616 (C 66/2092); entered office 1624 (C 66/2338, grant to Simon Thelwall 30 Dec. 1624); still in office 29 Jan. 1645 (C 66/2905, grant to Charles Hughes).

MACKLAY, Francis. Born about 1715 being aged 48 at death (Monumental Inscription, St Margaret's, Lee, Kent).

MACKLAY, William. Baptised 3 Dec. 1737 (*sic*) at St Margaret's, Westminster.

RELFE, John. Brother of Joseph Relfe, steward to Duke of Somerset at Cockermouth, Cumberland (*The London Diaries of William Nicolson*, ed. C. Jones and G. Holmes (Oxford, 1985), 10, 240 n. 182).

Chapter 9. New Light on the Office of Chairman of Committees in the House of Lords

In 1974 the House of Lords Record Office published memorandum No. 52 entitled 'The Origin of the Office of Chairman of Committees in the House of Lords'. This was primarily directed to the identification of holders of the office before 1800 and was based on a statistical analysis of Lords chairing Committees, supplemented by such other evidence as was then available. The purpose of this note is to make known material which has subsequently come to light serving to corroborate some of the conjectures put forward in that Memorandum. Most of this new information relates to Viscount Wentworth, whose role as Chairman between 1770 and 1774 had only been deduced from the statistical analysis. This was drawn to my attention by the kindness of Mr Michael McCahill and is to be found in the papers of Lord Denbigh deposited in the Warwickshire Record Office (Denbigh Letter Book, CR2017 C243).

Lord Delamer, who had been Chairman since 1765, died in office on 9th January 1770. On 30th January following, Lord Denbigh wrote to Lord Weymouth, Government 'Leader of the House', recommending Wentworth 'for the chair' stating that he (Weymouth) 'will find him a Man of Solid understanding, and it will also please the Country Lords much'. That the recommendation was acted upon is clear from a notice that appeared in the *Gazeteer and New Daily Register* for 21 May 1770 in these terms: 'Lord Wentworth is appointed Chairman of the Committee of the House of Lords, with a salary of £800 per annum, in the room of the late Baron Delamere'. Subsequent correspondence explains Wentworth's lack of assiduity in the chair, to which attention was drawn in the Memorandum. On 4th December, 1771, Lord Rochford, Weymouth's successor as 'Leader of the House', wrote to Denbigh to say that he had been informed that Wentworth would not be returning to England that winter and to ask what alternative arrangements had been made. Replying on 7th December, Denbigh said that Wentworth had left his proxy with Lord Boston, who, with Denbigh, would 'endeavour to supply his office of Chairman till Lord Wentworth returns home . . .'. This arrangement had been discussed with the King, who told him that Wentworth would not be replaced.

On 30th December, 1771, Wentworth wrote to Denbigh to thank him for making this arrangement and went on to say that he had told the King that his health obliged him to spend the winter in a warmer climate and that the King was content with the substitutes. However, Wentworth was evidently uneasy about his frequent absences. On 15th December, 1773, Rochford told Denbigh that Wentworth wished to resign as he was obliged to go to Bath for his health, but had been prevailed upon to continue on the understanding that the Lords who had previously undertaken business on his behalf would do so again. It is plain that, despite his poor health and uneven record of attendance, Wentworth remained in office until his death on 31st October, 1774.

© *The Parliamentary History Yearbook Trust 2015*

Writing to Rochford on that day to inform him of the fact, Denbigh said 'I thought it right to give you this early information that you may have time before the Parliament meets to think of a proper person to set upon his stool'.

Some evidence relating to the appointment of Wentworth's successor, Lord Scarsdale, has come to light since 1974. A letter from Scarsdale to Lord Gower, Lord President of the Council in North's administration, dated 26th November, 1774, is to be found in the latter's papers at the National Archives (TNA 30/29/12114, f. 695). It is evident that Gower was the instrument chosen to convey the offer of the post of Chairman to Scarsdale. In his reply, the latter accepted the offer while stating that he was 'little versed in the Rules and Orders of Parliament, and perhaps may find the attendance severe'. He asked to be excused from immediate attendance on account of his wife's state of health, which explains why he did not enter actively on his duties until the following February. That the Chairmanship was not Scarsdale's first choice of office is evident from his postscript in which he says that 'As Lord North spoke in such obliging and amicable terms in respect of me, I flatter myself that if the Constable of the Tower (which is my favourite) or the Jewel Office, or the Hounds, or Cofferer, or Lord Justice in Eyre, or Dutchy of Lancaster, or anything of that sort should become vacant, that I may be permitted to exchange my present employment for it'. Scarsdale's acceptance of the post is recorded in a note in a booklet at Kedleston. A copy of the relevant page has been deposited in the Parliamentary Archives. The note states 'December 1774: Accepted the Office of Chairman of the Committees in the House of Lords'.